The Contradiction in Disability Law

The Contradiction in Disability Law

Selective Abortions and Rights

Smitha Nizar

OXFORD
UNIVERSITY PRESS

OXFORD
UNIVERSITY PRESS

Oxford University Press is a department of the University of Oxford.
It furthers the University's objective of excellence in research, scholarship,
and education by publishing worldwide. Oxford is a registered trademark of
Oxford University Press in the UK and in certain other countries.

Published in India by
Oxford University Press
YMCA Library Building, 1 Jai Singh Road, New Delhi 110 001, India

ISBN-13: 978-0-19-946665-8
ISBN-10: 0-19-946665-3

Typeset in Minion Pro 10.5/13
by Tranistics Data Technologies, Kolkata 700 091
Printed in India at Rakmo Press, New Delhi 110 020

CONTENTS

. . . .

PREFACE

· ·

When I conceived my first baby, I was, like any other woman, all excited and enjoyed the emotional feelings absolutely exclusive to a woman. Even though I was eager to know the sex of my first baby, just to purchase gifts, it was legally prohibited in India. However, I felt proud of the powerful law that has banned scientific tests, to disable sex-selective abortions. But the very same law *generously* allowed tests that could tell if my baby would fall under the *normal* category, to make me eligible to give birth. Every test verified that the baby was perfectly alright and would not cause any harm or risk to my life. It was a pleasure to know that my baby was *normal*. I was grateful to science and the law for letting me know about my babies in advance.

I was happy to have two girls and I challenged the Indian law that prohibits prenatal tests to know the sex of the baby. Had the Pre-natal Diagnostic Techniques (Regulation and Prevention of Misuse) Act (PNDT), 1994 permitted me to know the sex of my children in advance, I would have been happier to welcome them with many cute gifts. However, as a law student, I saluted the PNDT Act, a powerful and passionate law, that supports the birth of girl children by regulating and restraining science and it inspired me to pursue a research. The absolute legal ban on sex-selective abortions made the society acknowledge the wrongfulness of such practices that deny the right of existence, in effect denying right to equality and non-discrimination to one kind of humans, that is, the females. Thus, I started discussing the PNDT Act on all legal podiums, and won a gold medal for my post-graduation in law.

However, the decision of an American woman of Indian origin to give birth to her first baby who had congenital disabilities prompted me to examine the murky side of my favourite PNDT law. I was not even aware of the exact conditions of congenital disabilities, but as a first-time mother I thought that women were not supposed to give birth to such babies. The law that prohibits prenatal diagnoses to know the sex permits it to know the disability. And it treats providing information about disabilities as unproblematic, even though that information facilitates selective abortion. The woman was determined to give birth to her first baby, ignoring the strong advice given by doctors to abort the foetus. In contrast to the medical assessment of *abnormality*, the child thus born is now a popular public speaker, of course still with all those *abnormalities*.

This prompted me to review the PNDT Act, which prohibits the use of technology for sex selection but permits selecting out foetuses for many other conditions referred as *abnormal*. I curiously studied each of those conditions as stipulated under the act. The first condition was Down syndrome. I quickly connected it to Ikru, one of my childhood friends. He used to run out of his house, exactly at the time of my school bus, to give me a lovely smile. He would accept all the gifts from me, but he was a genius not to accept it from my other friends who used to befriend him to compete with me!

This realization of individuality of persons with disabilities has inspired me to question the law in prohibiting sex identification but permitting identification of any other condition. The legal order on disability-selective abortion provided under the domestic laws—the PNDT Act, 1994 and the Medical Termination of Pregnancy Act, 1971—thus present a paradox. It provides a sophisticated medico-legal strategy to abort foetuses with disabilities. Thus, five years of my life have been passionately spent on writing this book to demonstrate and address how the unproblematic disability-selective abortions are actually problematic.

In the beginning, this legal research was to find out the fault in the law to challenge it. But, as if destined, during my research, I met with an accident resulting in severe head injury and short-term loss of memory (amnesia). Also, my friendship with persons with disabilities, especially my best friend Anna Clements, Michigan, USA, kept me on track with individuality and rights of persons with disabilities. How could I justify this book without experiencing disability in some form was the most inspired and whole-hearted consolation that I had during my short-term memory loss.

The extant literature on disability rights and selective abortion does not intertwine the rights and persons with disabilities while this book entwines both. This work also identifies the power of legal discourse to construct and to normalize or legitimize world views, which is of crucial importance for persons with disabilities. That is why this book analyses two main themes: the medical view of disability and the role of law that is gaining social acceptance for this prejudiced view of disability.

The law plays an unjust and unethical role when it simply prohibits and allows abortions based on the grounds of sex and disability respectively. This book analyses the legal developments on domestic and international levels. It examines whether the availability of disability-selective abortion negates the rights of persons with disabilities. Can the scientific and technological advances in the area of prenatal testing be carried forward without breaching disability rights?

ACKNOWLEDGEMENTS

. . . .

'All praise is due to God Almighty alone, the Sustainer of all the worlds.' It was my first expression of acknowledgement when I completed this work. This book has been a work in progress for the last few years.

Human life is so uncertain in this fast-moving new era. At the beginning of this work, this was just one of my philosophical tasks. However, I was destined to experience it myself, when I met with an accident. A severe head injury and the consequent memory loss made me realize the reality of this life. Anyone may lose the proud feeling of completeness at any point of their life. This realization is the spirit of this work.

Let me remember all the personalities I met during this journey. I remember, with gratitude, the intellectual and emotional debts I have incurred in the completion of this work. In this connection, I would like to pay my tributes to Adrienne Asch, who offered me inspiration through her philosophical arguments and writings. Though we never met in person, I felt her absence when I got to know about her demise. Her writings are the most inspiring and encouraging part of my research.

I have incurred uncountable and invaluable intellectual support from many. I would like to express my gratitude to my mentor and supervisor, Amita Dhanda, for the intellectual and emotional debts. She made me believe that all of us are end in ourselves, not the means of others. Her continuous counter-arguments and criticisms sharpened and shaped this work.

I thank Anna Clements, the nicest person I have met in this life. Her continuous criticism and suggestions from her own experiences of disability helped me gain a new insight on disability perspective. I also thank Pat Ingoldsby for surprising me with the gift of a signed copy of his own wonderful book of poetry, 'How was it for you Doctor?' I cannot forget the support and inspiration I have gathered from Nilesh Singit, a true disability rights activist.

I thank Arlene Kanter for her appreciation and acknowledgement of the difficulty to pursue this work. She continued her support when she invited me to Syracuse University to share my ideas. I also thank Tom Shakespeare, for sending me his personal copies of research articles and research papers. I am indebted to Renu Addlakha for her intellectual support and sharing her individual research papers and many other research works relevant to my work.

I thank everyone in the working group of drafting Disability Rights Bill. It was a privilege to know how difficult, but meaningful, it is to draft a law and ensure the participation of its stakeholders. But, the present Disability Bill, diluted by the executive, demonstrates how hard it is for persons with disabilities to avail their rights without negotiating.

I also acknowledge my students, friends, and well-wishers who shared my passion for this work, and also registered their criticism that forced me to move on.

I owe a particular debt of gratitude to the multitude of scholars who have travelled before me in investigating the various contexts related to my research. I have acknowledged them in the footnotes and bibliography in this volume.

I thank *Indian Journal of Medical Ethics* and *Christ University Law Journal* for granting permission to print the revised versions of my articles in this volume.

I would also like to acknowledge the value of presence and emotional support of some persons in my life. To them, 'thank you' as the formal words will just be meaningless.

K.P. Mansur is the one who never let me give up on this philosophical task. Many times, his demanding support made me to emulate high values. This work would not have been possible without his complete emotional support.

Thanks to my brother Jaffar for beng with me (as if he had a choice!). Finalization of this work would not have been possible without his technical efforts and emotional support. His comfort level with computers made sure no draft of this work was ever lost. He was the sole bearer of my eternal research troubles.

My thanks to Khalid C.H. for his complete support. I also acknowledge all my teachers who will always be my inspiration to see life as a learning process.

I appreciate all the great personalities who accept persons with disabilities as complete human beings and fight to protect their rights.

I remember with gratitude all persons with disabilities. My friends, I conclude my lines of gratitude by taking a line of Pat Ingoldsby from his poem 'Lovely Lost and Lonely': 'The world is a poorer place while you remain outside it!'

ABBREVIATIONS AND ACRONYMS

. . . .

AIR   All India Reporter
ALR   Australian Law Reports
CEDAW   Convention on the Elimination of All Forms of Discrimination against Women
CEHAT   Centre for Enquiry into Health and Allied Themes
CRC   Convention on the Rights of the Child
DSPD   Declaration on Social Progress and Development
EFM   Electronic Foetal Monitoring
ICCPR   International Covenant on Civil and Political Rights
ICESCR   International Covenant on Economic, Social and Cultural Rights
IDC   International Disability Caucus
ILO   International Labour Organization
IOR   India Office Records
MASUM   Mahila Sarvangeen Utkarsh Mandal
MTP   Medical Termination of Pregnancy
NAI   National Archives of India
NSWSC   New South Wales Supreme Court Reporter
NWP   North Western Provinces
PIL   Public Interest Litigation
PNDT   Pre-natal Diagnosis Techniques (Regulation and Prevention of Misuse)

QB	Queen's Bench
SC	Supreme Court
SCALE	Supreme Court Almanac
UDHR	Universal Declaration of Human Rights
UN	United Nations
UNCRPD	United Nations Convention on the Rights of Persons with Disabilities
WFD	World Federation of the Deaf
WHO	World Health Organization
WNUSP	World Network of Users and Survivors of Psychiatry

LIST OF STATUTES

. . . .

Indian Penal Code, 1860

Act for the Prevention of the Murder of Female Infants (Female Infanticide Act), 1870

Act for the Suppression of Trade in, and Circulation of, Obscene Literature and Articles of Immoral Use, 1873

Constitution of India, 1950

Medical Termination of Pregnancy Act, 1971

National Genetic Diseases Act, 1976

Pre-Natal Diagnostic Techniques (Regulation and Prevention of Misuse) Act, 1994

Sexual and Reproductive Health Act of Spain, 2010

TABLE OF TREATIES

. . . .

Convention on the Elimination of All Forms of Discrimination against Women, 1979

Convention on the Rights of the Child, 1989

International Covenant on Civil and Political Rights, 1966

International Covenant on Economic, Social and Cultural Rights, 1966

United Nations Convention on Rights of Persons with Disabilities, 2006

Universal Declaration of Human Rights, 1948

TABLE OF CASES

. . . .

INTRODUCTION

. . . .

MYSTERY OF HUMAN BIRTH

Women have always been part of the birthing experience, either as the birthing woman, or the supporting woman or midwife. Women bonded over the birthing process, as part of their day-to-day life and within the social remit of their environment. This entrustment of nature is still the significant difference between males and females. Even though men were not allowed to be part of this natural part of reproduction, women have always had problems in making midwifery professionally accepted in the modern society.[1]

Midwives generally promote a non-medicalized approach to pregnancy and birth. For instance, they avoid the use of electronic foetal monitoring (EFM) and prefer stethoscope auscultation instead.[2] They tend to discourage women from the need for pain relief, emphasizing the valuable function of pain for a more instinctive connection with the child, and thus for a satisfying experience of childbirth.[3] They also defend their professional interest by not promoting such interventions, as only specialists can administer these interventions.

---

[1] Jónsdóttir (2012: 15).
[2] De Vries (2005).
[3] De Vries (2005: 158).

However, even though midwives incline to the natural process of birth, as soon as there is a complication, the higher-ranking, most often male, obstetrician is called upon to assist.[4] In contrast to the midwife, a medical professional treats a pregnant woman as someone who requires care and assistance. Thus, the pregnant body does not belong to the woman;[5] the health professional objectifies it as the container of an unborn baby, which needs to be taken care of. Women's bodies are seen as being in production when going through childbirth. According to Foucault, this kind of objectification of the body can be done with the idea of normalization through the modern medical gaze.[6] According to Martin, if birthing is seen only as production, then health professionals should manage it with the assistance of technology.[7] The pregnant woman takes part in a medicalized system that is considered normal. As such, childbirth has moved from the social remit of the woman's environment, where women bonded over the birthing process, into a sterile medical environment.

MEDICALIZATION OF REPRODUCTION

The concept of medicalization was first defined in the 1970s in the social sciences. It indicates the process through which the medical institution extended its domain over daily life, transforming certain categories of people into 'patients' and certain attitudes or behaviours into 'illnesses'.[8] This approach to human birth casts an obstetrician in the role of a lead decision-maker about the birthing process and places the birth in a hospital setting with intensive use of high technology. Medical science views pregnancy and the reproduction process as a deviant condition that could be dangerous and is in need of medical surveillance. Consequent to this view, medical intervention involves special assistance to monitor the mother's health, her obstetric history, and antenatal conditions of the foetus. Thus, the medical professionals progressively took over

---

[4] Turner (2005: 89–90).
[5] Young (2005: 46).
[6] Eckermann (1997: 163).
[7] Martin (1992: 145).
[8] Zola (1972).

the responsibility of the birth of a 'normal child', in addition to supervising the natural process of childbirth. Medical science makes available a number of prenatal monitoring machines for EFM or cardiotocography, and so on.

The plethora of information can be overwhelming and frightening. Yet, the imperialistic perception of medicalized childbirth claims it to be uplifting, empowering, and wonderful. The rise of antenatal care, however, is noticeable for being more than an extension of medical service to the mother. The interest in the foetus marks a significant shift in the medicalization of birth. Screening tests such as amniocentesis and EFM that detect foetal conditions that are medically termed 'abnormal' have become more common. This process of screening foetal conditions ensures the monopoly of medicine over the entire process of childbirth.

According to Oakley, childbirth stands between nature and nurture, as it has been considered both a biological and a cultural process.[9] It is biological because of the way babies are born; it is cultural because of the interference and impact that technology, science, and politics can have on the process. A woman decides to go through technocratic birth because only when she submits herself to the norms of medicalization of childbirth is she deemed responsible. Society has deemed childbirth to be dangerous and therefore it is safe only in the hands of health professionals.[10] This is the reason why babies are no longer born at homes, but in hospitals. Many feminist accounts of the relocation of childbirth from the home to the hospital emphasize the political machinations of the emerging medical community and the impact of its propaganda on women's beliefs and preferences.[11] According to these accounts, doctors used their growing political and cultural authority to redefine childbirth as a dangerous, pathological event, to denigrate and eliminate midwives, and to fuel the perception that middle- and upper-class women are less capable of withstanding the challenges of childbirth.[12] This is despite all the possible complications

[9] Oakley (1980).
[10] Apatow (2007); Crossley (2007); Nolan (2011).
[11] Beckett (2005).
[12] Beckett (2005: 253–5).

that can be caused by technological interventions during childbirth in a hospital.[13]

The natural discourse in the reproduction process has thus changed to a medical discourse. According to Foucault, it is possible to create socially accepted individuals who are acceptable to the medical system, by using power through discipline.[14] The disciplinary process is done through the regulation of the smallest part of their lives. In the case of a pregnant woman, it would be by regulating the baby that would make the mother do as she is medically prescribed. Technology will let her know the minute details of the foetus growing in her body. Medical experts would examine the present and future 'medical problems' associated with the baby. They claim that this will empower a woman to take an informed decision about her unborn baby. For a woman, it is wonderful to know the *details* of her baby before birth.

The medicalization of human birth has thus resulted in scrutiny of the qualities of the foetus, deviating from its original objective of safety of the child and mother. The mother then does not seem to fit into the medical picture of childbirth, as she is objectified as merely the carrier of the baby. Childbirth, a natural everyday act, thus proceeded to become a medical act, where the qualities of the new human life are scrutinized to decide what kind of baby should be born. So, an unborn baby is not deemed to be a legal subject that could have rights over the mother's reproductive rights. Consequently, even the 'technological fix' hovers around a spectrum of issues such as: Who is a human? When does human life begin? Does the foetus possess the characteristic of a person to claim the right to life?

IS THE FOETUS A PERSON AT ANY DEVELOPMENTAL STAGE IN THE WOMB?

Traditionally, birth was synonymous with viability, the point at which the *human entity growing in the womb* becomes an independent

---

[13] O'Dwyer et al. (2012); Ronsmans and Graham (2006). It has been found that women who experienced a highly technological childbirth were more likely to experience post-partum depression.

[14] Gastaldo (1997: 125).

entity. However, improved medical understanding has changed this concept. It attributes the distinct creation of human life to different stages of foetal development. Science specifies that the meeting of sperm and ovum results in the creation of a zygote possessing a totally independent genetic package. Within a week of fertilization, the zygote implants itself in the uterine wall, which enables technology to diagnose pregnancy. 'Twinning', and occasionally recombination, takes place[15] during the first 14 days after fertilization.

This suggests that conception occurs over an extended time period. Science is not sure when 'existence' begins. However, early foetal development continues through the 8th week of pregnancy, after which all organs of the foetus exist in rudimentary form. At this stage, technology can detect readable, but not understandable, brain activity. Subsequent development consists of growth and maturation of structures formed during the embryonic period.[16] Somewhere between the 12th and 16th weeks, 'quickening'—foetal movement perceptible to the mother—occurs. Given the current medical knowledge and technology, the foetus is viable somewhere between the 20th and 28th weeks.

Science has developed sophisticated methods to discontinue pregnancy. The medical term given to this method is 'abortion' or 'termination'. Thus, technological sophistication has institutionalized reproduction as a medical phenomenon. The development of reproductive technology compels a woman to forget the living entity inside her womb as part of her body. Childbearing and childbirth has thus been accompanied by apprehensions and expectations.

However, even after legalizing abortion, it continues to evoke passionate feelings and disagreements. Some people believe that human life begins from the conception of an embryo; hence, a foetus has the same value as a human being. Therefore, they disagree with destruction of a foetus. At the same time, some people do not ascribe life to the foetus and contend that it is the right of a pregnant woman to decide whether to continue the pregnancy or not. These arguments are termed pro-life and pro-choice, respectively. The pro-choice argument is linked to the woman's right to take a decision about whether

---

[15] Hellegers (1970: 3).
[16] Hellegers (1970: 8–9).

she wants the baby, after considering several factors. Hard as these questions are, they are not the concern of this book. This book is concerned with automatic or thoughtless selection in making decisions about abortion.

Reproductive technology developed further when it created sophisticated prenatal tests to diagnose the distinctive conditions of a foetus. These sophisticated tests are prescribed to know about foetal development, but they are also used to select out certain foetuses, if they fall into the 'not-so-liked' category of human beings. Thus, the growth of medical science enables humanity to eliminate undesired human life, before they enter the world, through selective abortions.

SELECTIVE ABORTIONS

Selective abortion refers to terminating a pregnancy on the grounds of some distinctive condition of the foetus that is presumably undesired by society. These 'foetal conditions' vary in different cultural and social contexts. With the aid of technology, parents decide to abort based on criteria prejudicially prescribed by society. Selective abortions can be termed social abortions. They have nothing to do with the medical strategies of prevention, healing, or palliation of diseases. They also do not support a woman's individual decision about her body, as the decision is automatic and not based on informed choice.

What we see here is that selective abortions have little in common with medicine or surgery. In selective abortions, medical technology is used as a means to achieve socially desirable goals. The original principle of medicine, 'healing', has been manipulated for selective elimination. It raises enormous ethical implications. It generates the question of what value we place on such selectively eliminated human life. Sex-selective abortion is a prominent form of selective elimination of one kind of humans. Let us examine sex-selective abortions prevalent in India.

Sex-selective Abortions

In the Indian cultural and social context, being female is an undesired social identity. Consequently, when technology to eliminate such lives before their birth had not developed, female infanticide was widely prevalent in India. Many parents in India prefer boys to girls, as a girl is considered a financial burden. The undesirability of a condition in this context can mean undesirability from the viewpoint of the foetus (future child), its parents, or society. The undesirability of a condition from the foetus' or future child's perspective would mean that the condition in question would reduce that child's chances of living a satisfactory life, a life worth living. Her life would imply limited opportunities to achieve things that are seen as important for people's well-being. The viewpoint of the parents or the family stresses the possible social, emotional, or economic burden that the child may impose on others because of her undesirable condition. At the societal level, the undesirability of the child's condition usually means that the child would become an economic burden instead of an economically contributing citizen of society. In a patriarchal Indian society, the life of a female child is not worth living, from either her own perspective or from that of her family or the society. In many Indian families, the birth of a girl child is not welcomed.

Since the life of a female child was considered a burden on herself and her family and society, female infanticide was a customary practice, prevailing in India from the early nineteenth century. The societal ramification of female infanticide is well-recorded in the archives on female infanticide during the colonial rule.[17] Until 1931, the census records related caste to female infanticide. The post-Independence record however shows region-wise statistics. Accordingly, female infanticide had changed to female foeticide, wherever sex-determination facilities were available.[18] A large amount of literature available depicts the diminishing social perception of females, which justified female infanticide.[19]

Since sex-selective abortions were conducted by medical professionals, they remained family affairs for a long time. Medical professionals also provided it as a service on high demand, as society had internalized it. However, women's rights activists and social

---

[17] Viswanath (2007: 269).

[18] Viswanath (2007: 283).

[19] Caldwell (1978) cited in Greenhalgh (1995); Little (2008); Nandi (1980: 30).

scientists were quick to question the easy access to this foetus-selection technology, as it influenced equality and often resulted in devaluation of females. They started questioning the technology that enabled identification of sex of the foetus and subsequent selective abortion. Consequently, the new technology began to be analysed as more than a mere application of benevolent neutral technology in the aid of biology.[20] It would be worthwhile to understand the reasons for this change from the unproblematic perspective to the problematic perspective of female infanticide or female foeticide.

Why Sex-selective Abortions are Problematic

The consistent deficit of girls revealed by national statistics on the sex ratio was the alarm bell that triggered checks on new reproductive technology and sex-selective abortions. Nevertheless, the declined sex ratio was not the only reason for this change. In fact, the sex ratio was not really an issue of number; rather, it reflected social behaviour towards the females. Many studies revealed the truth that neither education nor affluence had brought any significant change to prejudice against women.[21] Scientific development had only transferred the stage of the elimination of the girl child, from after-birth to pre-birth.

The undesirability of, or non-preference towards, a female child forced many women to try new selective reproductive technology to have the desired baby. Both the eugenic and birth-control movements have had a certain relationship in affecting the life of women.[22] Thus, the need for theoretical interrogation and exploration of the issues and dimensions involved in sex-selective abortions has been addressed in various literature.[23]

---

[20] Patel (2007a: 27).

[21] Patel (2007a: 28).

[22] Patel (2007a: 36).

[23] For instance, the ethnographic interest in gender and reproduction, largely seen as a women's issue, as a study of related domains of production and reproduction together with undervaluing women's contribution, in Patel (1982) and Basu (1992).

For instance, while white, middle-class women in the West gained through contraception and abortion rights, they soon realized that they had lost control over their bodies to the medical establishment as a marker of scientific practice and modernity.[24] The woman's body was not only seen as dispensable, but was also seen as deficient, requiring modern medicine's intervention.[25] Thus, women soon realized that they were losing their recognition to obstetric domination in the medical system.[26]

Civil-society movements, through their organizations, representations in mass media, and 'public interest litigations', have been publicly enunciating multiplex adversity in the wake of new reproductive technology. The recognition of persistent discrimination against women was the major reason that prompted activists to demand a national legislation to ban such selective technology.[27] It is important to note that this demand was made without compromising on the women's right to abortion.

However, a complete ban on these tests was mainly opposed by members of the medical profession. The medical professionals convinced others that such tests were intended to detect genetic defects and foetal 'abnormalities'. In spite of that, in 1986, at a conference of medical experts, administrators, voluntary organizations, and legal experts, it was recommended that prenatal tests for the prediction of sex of the foetus be banned.[28] The parliamentary debates on the subsequent Pre-Natal Diagnostic Techniques (Regulation and Prevention of Misuse) Bill, 1991 show that the joint select committee[29] had conceded to the medical professionals' arguments. Many legislative members argued for banning clinics with sophisticated genetic technology and conducting genetic tests. However, they were defended based on the medical professionals' argument that prenatal tests have

[24] Foucault (1977).
[25] Martin (1992).
[26] Patel (2007a: 37).
[27] Joint Select Committee (1991).
[28] Parliament of India (1994: 550).
[29] The bill was first introduced in the Lok Sabha on 12 September 1991. However, it was referred back to the joint select committee on 16 December 1992.

the creative purpose of diagnosing mental and physical disabilities.[30] It was argued that:

> The clean and healthy atmosphere of our society demand [sic] that not only the present generations but also the future generations should enjoy the benefits of the advancement made in the field of science and technology so that the coming generations are protected from physical and mental deformities. That is why the existence of clinics equipped with most sophisticated genetic technology is essential.[31]

Malini Bhattacharya, one of the members of the joint select committee, submitted:

> Banning of these tests is not possible because these tests are only incidentally to be used for sex determination. Their real use is for something different. They are used for detecting genetic defects and abnormalities in foetuses and for other reasons and, therefore, it is not possible to have these tests banned altogether. Therefore, it is necessary not to ban these tests but to regulate and to prevent their misuse.[32]

Thus, the demand for an absolute ban on prenatal tests was defeated based on the medical professionals' motive to prevent genetic diseases, as well as to detect hereditary or metabolic deformities, sex deformities, or characteristic dissimilarity of a few unborn.[33] Consequently, defying the original demand for a blanket prohibition, prenatal tests were regulated, permitting use of the technology for other reasons. This shows that sex selection alone was seen as problematic, while other reasons for selection were viewed in unproblematic terms, as members of the medical profession had presented them as medical conditions. Consequently, even though prenatal tests were recognized as problematic from the beginning, the society has now internalized it.

---

[30] Statement of Girija Devi, Parliament of India (1994: 586–7).
[31] Statement of Girija Devi, Parliament of India (1994: 588).
[32] Statement of Malini Bhattacharya, Parliament of India (1994: 567).
[33] Statement of Malini Bhattacharya, Parliament of India (1994: 586).

PROHIBITION AND PERMISSION: DIFFERENT DISCOURSE OF TECHNOLOGY ON SELECTION

Sex selection has turned problematic, as it includes the possibility of selecting out a particular group of humans, that is, females. Selection of the foetus with the aid of technology may prevent a female child from entering this world. The practice of prenatal diagnosis with the intent to abort if the foetus appears to be female articulates the 'undesirability' of, and consequent discrimination against, women. The arguments for equality and value for women, and the simultaneous urging of selective technology, were contradictory. Since the selective technology targeted women, it was seen as problematic. Until then, it was viewed as an unproblematic medical intervention. However, medical professionals' argument about the benefit of science to detect disabilities, or 'deformities' in medical language, and the legislature's agreement, has resulted in viewing any other reason for selection as unproblematic.

The medical community considers the physical, cognitive, or emotional characteristics of individuals as deformities, not human characteristics. For instance, medical professionals characterize nearly all persons with prenatally detectable conditions, whether Down syndrome, spina bifida, fragile X syndrome, Duchenne muscular dystrophy, sickle-cell anaemia, retinitis pigmentosa, or achondroplasia, as 'deformed'.[34] Many in the field of bioethics argue that it is better to not have a disability than to have one, and that it is preferable to select out a foetus with a disabling trait.[35] Selective technology is thus promoted with a view that 'disabilities are not generally advantageous, not something to be hoped for; indeed, they are to be avoided, if possible. They are not merely neutral forms of variation'.[36] Thus, the medical perception of disability as an undesirable medical condition and the urge to not accept persons with such conditions has resulted in regulating the use of prenatal tests to detect those conditions, but not the sex of the foetus, unarguably a human condition. Selection on the basis of sex discriminates against women.

[34] Asch (2003: 315).
[35] Asch (2003: 321).
[36] Steinbock (2000: 108).

In contrast, the characteristic of disability is perceived as a medical condition and not a human condition. Hence, disability-selective abortion is perceived as selecting out the condition, not the human.

The Pre-Natal Diagnostic Techniques (Regulation and Prevention of Misuse) (PNDT) Act, 1994 was enacted to regulate the use of new reproductive technology.[37] Accordingly, prenatal technology cannot be used for sex selection but can be used for other reasons. It can be used to screen certain human conditions, which medicine considers as abnormalities. It articulates the 'undesirability' of and the consequent discrimination against persons who possess this human condition. Sex-selective abortions are viewed as problematic, as they target a particular category of humans, namely women. Similarly, in disability-selective abortions, the category of persons with disabilities are targeted.

As disability activist and lawyer Lisa Blumberg put it, 'the social purpose of these tests is to reduce the incidence of live births of people with disabilities.'[38] What impact is it going to have on persons with disabilities who are being selected out? It also raises the question of legitimacy of disability-selective abortions. In order to determine whether a case is made out to undertake a work on this topic, I have surveyed the extant literature on the issue. While surveying the literature, I encountered different arguments—in the area of eugenics, on the value of human life, prenatal tests, and rights of persons with disabilities and social justice.

ARGUMENTS FOR EUGENICS AND SELECTIVE KILLING
OF IMPERFECTS

Traditionally, persons with disabilities are categorized as lesser or incapable human beings who do not deserve to be born. This social prejudice against persons with disabilities caused the adoption of various methods to prevent their existence. Earlier methods of

---

[37] The PNDT Act, 1994 was amended in 2002, and renamed the Pre-Conception and Pre-Natal Diagnostic Techniques (Prohibition of Sex Selection) Act.

[38] Blumberg (1994b: 224).

preventing the existence of people with disabilities demonstrate the disparaging attitude prevalent against them. In 1883, Galton proposed 'eugenics' as a science to improve the human race, by selective killing. He argued that, from the viewpoint of eugenics, 'superior mental and behavioral capacities, as well as physical health, are advantageous, not only to an individual but for the well-being of society as a whole.'[39]

Daniel Jo Kevles argued that there exists an interplay between the social assertions made by eugenics and the advances in pertinent science, particularly genetics.[40] The eugenic incidents of the Nazi

[39] Galton (1907) [1883] proposed 'eugenics' as a science to improve the human race. His book begins with an essay on 'Variety of Human Nature', about features, bodily qualities, energy, sensitivity, special senses, etc. In the course of this chapter, the leading results of the author's well-known investigations on composite portraiture are brought in. In the next chapter, he describes the desirability of keeping family records of the anthropometry of children. The author argues that without such systematic observations, one may continue his life without knowing that he presents a hereditary peculiarity. Thus, this suggestion reflects the foundation of Galton's proposed science of 'eugenics'. In a following chapter, he discusses the type of characters that leads to criminality. Using statistics, he argues that it is strongly inherited. Moving on to intellectual differences, he gives an elaborate account of 'mental imagery'. The concluding chapter argues that 'eugenics' yields the idea of promoting evolution, the most important field of human activity. Thus, this book submits that eugenics would obviously improve the race by selection.

[40] Kevles (1985) takes a comparative approach to the history of eugenics in the US and the UK from the nineteenth century to the last century in the book. The research also gives attention to similar practices that occurred in other countries such as Germany. It is a comprehensive account of the history of eugenic 'science' of improving the human stock by giving 'the more suitable races or strains of blood a better chance of prevailing speedily over the less suitable' (pp. 24–5). Then the research embarks on the establishment of brave new biology, human genetics, and the challenges it poses. The analysis reveals that eugenics involved not only scientific rationalizations of class and race prejudice, but also disputes regarding how men and especially women of the modern era were to accommodate the changing standards of sexual and reproductive behaviour. It explores the interplay between the social assertions made by eugenicists and advances in genetics.

Holocaust and racial hygiene prompted scholars to seek knowledge of the consequences of the arguments for biological determinism. It was when physicians and politicians gathered support for eugenic science as an answer to inherited 'disorders' and racial discrimination that disagreeing arguments also emerged against them. In connection with this, many scholars examined the reach and power of science to make the state concede to it. One major argument is regarding the role of the scientific community as an architect of selectively killing 'imperfect beings' in Nazi eugenic programmes.[41] The morality and

---

It sketches the remarkable progress in genetics and topics that are indicative of emerging problems. The author explores eugenic enactments such as the Mental Deficiency Act and Sterilization Act of the twentieth century, which provide powers to the state to detain and segregate persons with mental disabilities. These eugenic laws also prohibited their marriage and mandated compulsory sterilization. The author analyses human genetic research as a form of new eugenics. Genetic engineering appears defensible in principle, as it reveals the complexity of heredity in human beings, scientifically within reach.

[41] Proctor (1988) gave an account of the consequences of biological determinism when scientists, physicians, and politicians felt they had the answer to the problem of inherited 'disorders' and racial discrimination. The author examines the pervasion of science and the power of a state that gave birth to modern medical science in Germany. The book analyses the morality of physicians and medical scientists and their relationship with human life. The author also provides a broad overview of racial hygiene within the context of prevailing scientific or political values and beliefs. He examines the Nazi racial policy against the backdrop of the social history of German medical science during Hitler's period. The author describes how the scientific community served as a willing architect of Nazi racial policies and programmes. The author destroys the argument that the German scientific community was coerced into participating in the Nazi programme. On the contrary, the author submits, with reasons, that the Nazi party fulfilled the philosophical and social expectations of German science. The author documents how the German medical profession profited from Nazi eugenic and racial policies. The Nazi eugenic realm promoted intrinsic measures by interfering with the reproductive potential of people whom the state defined as genetically undesirable. Sterilization of such 'undesirable' was promoted to free future generations from the risk of inherited 'disorders',

social justice issues pertaining to genetic programmes and screening was the most thriving research theme for decades.[42] By this time, bioethics had developed, and the life of an individual could be medically ended on the reason of illness. If any person or his/her relatives did not wish to continue a life because of an illness, medical aid could

---

which included epilepsy, feeble-mindedness, schizophrenia, manic-depressive disorder, and chronic alcoholism. This process of intrinsic purification involved the sterilization of approximately 500,000 German citizens. While the sterilization programme was supposedly confined to 'medical' diagnosis, in fact, it was extended to include racial grounds.

Intrinsic purification extended to the medical murder of inmates of mental hospitals, who were considered unfit for life. This programme of medical homicide was also justified on economic grounds that the state was freed from financial obligation to sustain the lives of these people. Proctor provides examples of how the euthanasia programme was justified on economic grounds with calculations (to the decimal point) of how much food was saved by the elimination of over 70,000 'useless eaters' occupying the wards of the mental hospitals. In Nazi Germany, the terms 'eugenics' and 'race hygiene' were used synonymously, often with the term 'genetics'. The eugenic programmes of compulsory sterilization used for intrinsic purification among the German people were extended to the extrinsic programme of racial hygiene. What began as legislated discrimination in the public service in 1933 was extended to legislated discrimination with the goal of racial purification as enacted in the infamous 1935 Nuremberg race laws, which made race a medical diagnosis. The author explores the power and values of medical science, in the context of eugenic policies.

[42] Wikler (1999) has provided a brief history of the eugenics movement and a moral analysis of some of its tenets. After a brief historical summary of eugenics, the essay attempts to locate any wrongs inherent in eugenic doctrines. The author argues that the label 'eugenic' does apply in some instances, but that when this is the case the 'eugenic' effect or intent of the practices ought not always to engender alarm or opposition. The paper shows that the modern eugenics movement took its cue from biology: first, Darwin's theory of natural selection, with a boost later on from Mendelian genetics. Eventually, the author examines the question, 'Is eugenic doctrine inherently evil?' However, the author does not see a comprehensive answer to the above question; he states that we can draw the important lesson that progress in genetics must pay attention to these questions of distributive justice.

be opted for to end such a life. Science introduced it as 'euthanasia'. This new development has been analysed in the light of previous Nazi eugenic practices.[43] The growth of bioethics and its advances to prevent the existence of 'imperfects' is reflected in judicial decisions as well. Carrie Buck was listed by the State of Virginia in the United States (US) to undergo salpingectomy, a sexual sterilization surgery. She challenged[44] the Virginia State Involuntary Sterilization Law, which categorized Buck and her mother as 'mentally deficient'—a reason being given to sterilize her. She gave an argument that the operation of salpingectomy is illegal according to the sterilization law, violating her constitutional right of bodily integrity and is therefore repugnant to the 'due process' affirmed under the Fourteenth Amendment. Buck's defense against violation of her fundamental right to bodily

---

This very general, yet morally crucial, requirement ought to guide us now, as we decide which programmes of genetic testing and screening to undertake. It ought to also guide us in the future, as we contemplate the possibility of refashioning the human genome to engineer a new, perhaps improved version of 'homo sapiens'. Thus, the paper concludes that the question of moral importance is not whether this constitutes eugenics; it is whether it can be done fairly and justly. The moral challenge posed by eugenics for genetics in this time is to achieve social justice.

[43] Macklin (2001) is considered as one of the founders of the field of bioethics. In this paper, she analyses euthanasia in the light of the Nazi medical killings. The paper is based on a case that came before a hospital ethics committee. The physicians of a 70-year-old patient, who was in ICU, suggested to her family that they write a 'Do Not Resuscitate' order. However, the family was reluctant to do it and hoped that she would recover. But, for the hospital the financial consideration was the overriding factor, as the patient was absorbing a disproportionate share of the hospital's resources. The physicians informed the ethics committee that the patient and her husband were Holocaust survivors, and that it underscored their family's unwillingness to forgo life-prolonging treatment. The author asks whether the patient's family was mistaken in thinking that withdrawal of care bears any resemblance to what happens in Nazi Germany. 'Were there any aspects of the euthanasia programme under the Nazis that could legitimately be described as "euthanasia" in our sense of term?' The paper analyses the similarities between 'medical killing' during the Holocaust and recent biomedical practices.

[44] *Buck v. Bell*, 274 U.S. 200 (1927).

integrity was answered in a notorious judicial statement, 'Three Generations, No Imbeciles': 'Though Buck set the stage for more than sixty thousand involuntary sterilizations in the US and was cited at the Nuremberg trials in defense of Nazi sterilization experiments, it has never been overturned'.[45] Thus, condemning legal action against persons with disabilities, not treating them as persons before law, laid the base from Buck's judgement.

Further growth of science has facilitated killing of imperfect babies even before their birth. The growth of bioethics in genetic engineering, organ transplantation, termination of life-sustaining treatment, and new reproductive technology inaugurated research in the area of medical killing of neonates with 'severe defects'.[46] This has challenged the reproductive choice of women. It has been argued that medical technology limits the choice of women to choose only perfect or model babies, but not babies with 'defects'.[47] The prospect

---

[45] Lombardo (2008); the title of this book is based on the judgement by Oliver Wendell Holmes, Jr, J.

[46] Jonsen (1998) presents a historical analysis of bioethics in the book. The author examines the growth of bioethics from 1947 onwards. It examines the origin and evolution of the debates over human experimentation, genetic engineering, organ transplantation, termination of life-sustaining treatment, and new reproductive technology. It assesses the contributions of philosophy, theology, law, and the social sciences to the expanding discourse of bioethics. The author describes the pioneers in bioethics, who the author knew and worked with. The book also touches on different perceptions of abortion and contraception. The author pays particular attention to the influence of Catholic religious doctrines and the theologians Joseph Fletcher, Richard McCormick, and Paul Ramsay. With regard to choosing whether to allow neonates to die, the author states, 'The hope seems so great and the loss so devastating to parents that the decision to give up is particularly agonizing' (p. 252). And with respect to the new forms of technology, he says that the difficulty of unravelling its ethics 'may be due to our impoverished ability to recognize and appreciate what is normal about being human' (p. 313).

[47] Bailey (1996). This essay reports the results of a qualitative study of parents whose children are clients of a state-wide rural genetic outreach programme in the US. The analysis seeks to connect the lived experience of parents of children with genetic conditions or impairments to choices with

that science could prevent the existence of one kind of humans was challenged for its contradicting arguments—welfare of everyone but selective killing of certain kind of humans. The eugenic potential of prenatal tests has been analysed in certain studies. Since prenatal tests are performed to select out undesired people, it was argued that this resembles eugenic ideas.[48]

The extant literature relating to eugenics contains arguments about social and scientific ideas that treat certain kinds of humans as inferior and justifies their elimination. The literature in this area has addressed the similarity between eugenic practices and the subsequent development of science to prenatally select out undesired humans. However, these works do not address the issue of whether prenatal testing and selective abortions are sophisticated methods of preventing the existence of people with disabilities.

---

which women are confronted as prenatal testing technologies continue to proliferate. It reports the finding that a majority of parents in the study chose not to choose: avoiding future pregnancies, declining prenatal testing for subsequent pregnancies, or limiting testing to 'for information only'. These decisions do not reflect simple rejection of medical intervention, opposition to abortion, or affirmation of a positive parenting experience with an affected child. Rather, choosing to avoid the condition of choice appears to be a strategy of responsible parenting that emerges from ambivalence towards the options presented by reproductive technology.

[48] Wolbring (2001) has disputed the claims that science and technology are value neutral and that the problems caused by technology are either unintended side effects or abuses. The author argues that the advances in science and technology do not benefit all segments of society equally. However, to minimize opposition, technology proponents rarely acknowledge the distributional inequalities and ramifications of scientific advances. This has the potential to divide human beings into desirables and undesirables. The essay analyses this intolerance with the increase in eugenic practices. The author submits that human conditions of disability and disease are the main targets of today's eugenic practices. Both disability and disease are viewed as 'a medical problem in need of medical eugenic solution' (p. 38). The essay analyses the eugenic potential of predictive tests such as prenatal screening. It carries with it the possibility of personal eugenic practices. The paper concludes that prenatal selective tests introduce a shift in societal eugenics.

Prenatal testing is mainly performed to identify foetuses with conditions considered undesirable by parents, medical practitioners, or society. When science promotes selecting out one kind of humans, does it feed prejudice against such lives? I will analyse this with the aid of existing arguments in eugenics.

The available literature in the area of eugenics and the disagreeing arguments therein has assisted me in exploring the literature on the value of human life. In contrast to the eugenic arguments for selective killing, the literature on the 'value of human life' argues for using theological, ethical, and legal principles that inherently value any form of human life.

VALUE OF HUMAN LIFE

The argument for the inherent value of human beings was initiated by examining the moral issues involved in abortion. Ronald Dworkin, a renowned philosopher, argued that there is a common thread that runs through the traditional battle over abortion and the recent controversy over euthanasia. This argument maintained that the fundamental moral principle at stake in both cases is the principle of the 'sanctity of life'. The crucial jurisprudential question, then, is whether the principle of the sanctity of life should be given effect in law and, if so, in what form.[49] In this light, the philosopher raised the argument that law demands moral judgements to enhance the principle of the sanctity of life.[50] Thus, issues such as

---

[49] Dworkin (1993) contended that the principle of the sanctity of life should not become a legal principle, because it admits different 'quasi-religious' interpretations. If the principle were to be given effect in law, the courts or legislature would have to take sides in what are essentially religious disputes and adopt an 'official' (state) view of the sanctity of life. This, however, would be contrary to the democratic ideal of freedom of religion. On this basis, Dworkin seeks to show that the appropriate jurisprudential stance over abortion and euthanasia is one that accommodates both the conservative and the liberal positions.

[50] Dworkin's (1996) collection of essays discusses the constitutional issues of the abortion, euthanasia, capital punishment, and free speech. The author offers a consistently liberal view of the American Constitution and argues that law demands that judges make moral judgements.

abortion,[51] euthanasia,[52] and capital punishment were debated under the canopy of the sanctity of life. However, these issues were also debated as theological issues, as the doctrine of the sanctity of life is of theological origin.

For instance, Christianity and Islam accord divine value to the creation of humans. This entails no harm to human life at any stage.

The author proposes that the abstract language of the Constitution should be interpreted by reference to moral principles.

[51] Keown (1998) illustrates the ongoing legal revolution on 'medical killing'. The author argues that the courts and legislatures across the Western world have seriously compromised the principle of the 'sanctity of life'. This compromise promotes the notion that only some human lives, those that pass a certain 'quality' threshold, alone merit protection. According to the author, this revolution is being promoted gradually, without violence, through the pillars of the legal establishment. Keown puts forward the example of abortion law that overturned the historic prohibition on abortion. Thus, law has transformed abortion from a very serious criminal offence to a minor medical procedure. It is commonly performed for reasons of social convenience rather than medical necessity. This article suggests that the doctrine of the sanctity of life was misrepresented, misunderstood, and mistakenly rejected by legislatures and judges. The law on abortion shows non-understanding and non-respect for the ethics of value of life. The author argues that the courts should restore moral and intellectual consistency, coherence, and clarity to the law by reinstating the law's consistent application of the 'sanctity of life' doctrine.

[52] Cohen (2006) examines the judiciary's treatment of the principle of the sanctity of life and its effect on the right to physician-assisted suicide. After supplying two traditional derivations of the principle of the sanctity of life—one religious and one humanistic—she argues that the proper approach in right-to-die cases is the humanistic approach. Cohen argues that in order for meaningful adjudication of right-to-die issues to occur, it is imperative that religiously informed decisions do not control the debate.

Lavi (2003) traces the changes that occurred during the nineteenth century in 'deathbed' ethics. It outlines a three-stage transformation of deathbed ethics—from the realm of religion, to the jurisdiction of medical ethics, to positive law regulation. This three-stage transformation reflects the entire normative system governing the experience of dying. The paper concludes with a proposal for regulating dying legally through euthanasia.

Hence, abortion in particular has been entangled in theological prohibition. Christian theological principles condemn abortion.[53] Islamic principles explicitly accord inherent value to human life in any form. The very first stanza of the Holy Qur'an revealed the 'secret' of a new human life, declaring that humans are created by Almighty God from a mere drop of liquid.[54] Consequent to this explicit information about the dignified creation of humans, and the value ascribed to human life, abortion and infanticide are squarely condemned and prohibited practices in Islamic theology.[55]

[53] Maguire (2006); Cunningham (2009). A Christian motto says man is made in the image of God. Hence, in Christian theology, human life has inherent value. Therefore, contraception was banned by the church during the nineteenth century. Later, the ban was removed, permitting its use for time space between progeny. In Christian theology, abortion is considered an inhuman offence against human beings. These works describe the Christian principles on the value of human life.

[54] Qur'an (96: 1–2).

[55] Asad (1980). In this work, the author gives the English translation of verses in the Holy Qur'an and explains the divine value accorded to human life. Fifteen hundred years ago, the Qur'an was revealed to Prophet Muhammad, commanding, 'Read in the name of thy Sustainer Almighty, who has created, created man out of a germ-cell' (96: 1–2). The holy text explicitly asked man, 'O MAN! What is it that lures you away from thy bountiful Sustainer, who has created you, and formed you in accordance with what thou art meant to be, and shaped thy nature in just proportions, having put thee together in whatever form He willed [thee to have]?'(82: 6) The Qur'an also prohibits female infanticide, revealing:

> Whenever any of them is given the glad tiding of [the birth of] a girl, his face darkens, and he is filled with suppressed anger, avoiding all people because of the [alleged] evil of the glad tiding which he has received, [and debating within himself:] Shall he keep this [child] despite the contempt [which he feels for it]—or shall he bury it in the dust? Old, evil indeed is whatever they decide! [Thus it is that] the attribute of evil applies to all who do not believe in the life to come—whereas unto God applies the attribute of all that is most sublime (16: 57–60) ... you shall most certainly be called to account for all your false imagery! (16: 56)

Consequent to this authority of the Almighty over human life, and the inherent dignity accorded to human life, abortion and infanticide are considered condemned practices in Islam.

Later years have witnessed certain compromises to the principle of the sanctity of life, surprisingly, by the judiciary—for instance, wrongful birth and wrongful life claims seeking compensation against medical professionals for not detecting or neglecting the disability of the child in the womb. That negligence denies the mother the choice of abortion is the rationale. Many works have generally examined the impact of screening tests in view of wrongful life and birth claims,[56] and some have examined the implications of such actions in tort and the value of lives of persons with disabilities.[57]

The research available on the value of human life focuses on the general application of the doctrine of the sanctity of life to humanity. However, when it comes to wrongful life and wrongful birth tort actions, it seems that it was applied very rarely. Courts have applied

---

[56] Perry (2008) has analysed the contradictory arguments relating to wrongful life actions in tort. A wrongful life action is a tort action of a child with disability against medical practitioners, whose negligence enabled the child's birth. This paper, with the title of a classic movie from 1946, examines whether it is possible to say that a severely 'disabled' child has been harmed by the mere fact of being born. The author argues that without a satisfactory solution from conventional wisdom, the life-as-injury debate may be the Gordian knot of tort law. The author attempts to untie this knot to allow such children to live without challenge or validate the deep-seated perception of life.

[57] Hensel (2005) examines the problematic aspects of wrongful birth and wrongful life actions in tort. The author argues that wrongful life and wrongful birth suits may exact a heavy price not only on the psychological well-being of individuals with disabilities, but also on the public image and acceptance of disability in society. In contrast to a traditional tort action that focuses on the defendant's conduct, both wrongful birth and wrongful life suits ultimately focus on the plaintiff's disability, a status that is partially a societal construction. The author argues that when individuals with disabilities have made significant strides towards integration and acceptance, societal attitude towards disability has been challenged by prenatal genetic testing and corresponding tort actions of wrongful life and wrongful birth. The author submits that although much has been written about the impact of genetic testing as a general matter, little legal scholarship has focused on the impact that these tort actions might have on the community of people with disabilities. Thus, ultimately, this paper argues that the cost of recognizing wrongful life and wrongful birth actions is too high.

the doctrine to wrongful life claims alone, presumably not to diminish life with disabilities. However, there is a vacuum of knowledge in addressing the contradiction between the legal principle involved in wrongful life and birth actions and the sanctity of life. In this book, I will examine the inherent value of human life and its contradiction to selective abortions. In the following paragraphs, I have surveyed the arguments surrounding selective abortions, and sex-selective abortion is an area to which many scholars have contributed ethical and legal arguments.

Sex-selective abortions reflect the social prejudice against women. A vast body of writing examines the reasons for sex-selective abortions and their impact.[58] A crucial and consistent argument

---

[58] Patel's (2007c) volume, a collection of 11 essays, unravels sex-selective abortion as a civilizational collapse. The contributors, all distinguished demographers and social scientists, describe the political economy of sentiments and sexual mores that lead parents to kill unborn daughters. The contributors examine ways in which reproductive technology, such as the ultrasound, are 'misused' at the family, community, and state levels. The book highlights both the participation and defiance of various authorities dealing with reproduction, health services, and the problem of female foeticide. Engagement with the state is analysed in the light of colonial policies, the law of adoption, health policies, family planning programmes, and the PNDT Act, 1994 and its amendment in 2002. The editor, in a comprehensive introduction, examines the political economy of emotions that govern the preference for a son and the selective elimination of female foetuses with the help of new reproductive technology such as amniocentesis, chorionic villi biopsy, foetoscopy, ultrasound, and in-vitro fertilization. This volume establishes the argument that sex-selective abortion or female foeticide reflects the secondary status granted to the female gender through the following essays:

1. Visaria (2007) estimates the magnitude of deficit of girls in India as a whole and in some female-disadvantaged states. The author compares the situation in such states with that in Kerala, considerably a female-advantaged state. The author analyses related legislations: the Medical Termination of Pregnancy (MTP) Act, 1971 and the PNDT Act, 1994. She argues that the manifestation of preference for son and non-preference for daughter needs to be understood in the context of these legislations that permit abortions and prohibit sex-selective abortions. This chapter submits

that challenges sex-selective abortion is that it diminishes and discriminates against women,[59] for being a woman is a 'not-so-desired' category of individuals. Feminists and activists strongly challenged the advanced reproductive technology that detects the sex of the baby in the womb itself.[60] It is significant that this 'selectiveness'

---

indirect evidence of female-selective abortion based on primary data collected from two states in India. It also documents the voices of women to understand what compels them or their families to abort female foetuses. It shows a collusion of culture and social norms that is all-pervasive and promotes pre-birth elimination of girls.

2. Bose (2007) examines the complexity of attitudes of women, families, and medical doctors that construct female foeticide as an immoral practice. The doctors prescribe prenatal tests as a routine health test, and women are interested in knowing the sex of the unborn child. Sex-selective abortions emerge from the inherent 'son complex' of the patriarchal Indian society. Sex-selective abortions are justified as part of family planning. The author argues that sex-selective abortion is a symptom of increasing crime against women. Accordingly, it would be wrong to consider sex selection as a problem of medical technology alone. This chapter points to the need to look at gender issues in all their ramifications in this increasingly dysfunctional society.

3. Patel (2007b) provides a context to the use of new reproductive technology in India. The author narrates how in everyday life daughters come to be considered a 'burden' on parents and their families. The essay discusses the mindset of people that enables and perpetrates elimination of female foetuses. The author argues that this 'mindset' is postulated not simply as an abstract entity of the conscious mind. It is to be seen both as a conscious and reflexive activity as well as influenced by shared and embedded predispositions. She asks, since female foeticide is a socially adaptive act, how does the mindset relay the patriarchal structuring of the family with the aid of science.

[59] Patel (2007c).
[60] Muthulakshmi (1997) attempts to study the problem of female infanticide from historical and futuristic perspectives. As female infanticide was rampant in Tamil Nadu, an area from the state was selected for analysis. Muthulakshmi's book presents a number of case studies to identify the various dimensions of the problem. The study also includes analysing the views of women on female foeticide. The author creates a theoretical framework for the issue of female foeticide.

was challenged while retaining the right of the woman to choose, because the process of 'selectiveness' was driven by prejudiced social choices and not by women's choices. Consequently, the legislature had to concede to the above arguments and prohibit the use of such technology for sex selection.

However, this body of writing focuses only on sex-selective abortions, and does not analyse selective abortions for any other reason. No research has analysed the common thread between sex-selective abortions and disability-linked abortions.[61] This book examines the contradictory perspectives on sex- and disability-selective abortions and the need to join the common thread between them. Within this framework, this book will find various arguments that challenge prenatal tests and disability-selective abortions. In the beginning, disability-selective abortions were analysed by comparing them with assisted suicide.[62] However, there has been little discussion of prenatal testing

---

[61] Ghai and Johri (2008) question the ideology that regards abortion as the only option when prenatal testing reveals a 'birth abnormality', an option sanctioned by the PNDT Act, 1994. The authors contend that disability is, to a great extent, socially constructed: its conceptualization reflects societal attitudes that view the lives of persons with disabilities as tragic, worthless, and a burden. The paper recognizes the tension between feminist and disability activists around the issue of women's choice. These issues are discussed through the voices of mothers of both children with disabilities and non-disabilities. The article establishes the argument that the concept of individual choice, which is reified through the PNDT Act, 1994, is socially constructed and contextually located. The authors also contend that while the pro-choice perspective is important to feminists, the thoughtless use of prenatal testing could reduce rather than expand women's choices.

[62] Bagenstos (2006) introduces the criticisms asserted by many disability-rights activists against non-treating of infants with disabilities, legalization of assisted suicide, and the practice of prenatal tests followed by selective abortion. In each of the three areas, disability-rights activists have developed an argument that identifies powerful social forces that intrude on 'free' choices, and accordingly may justify regulation in the name of choice. The author argues that this laissez-faire position on disability-selective abortion may simply represent a compromise between the potentially conflicting goals of disability equality and gender equality. According to the author, this compromise undermines disability-rights advocates' insistence that assisted

outside the disability-rights movement, and the discussion that did occur was within the context of abortion.[63] But the flourishing of universal rights that accorded full value to persons with disabilities necessitated research in the area of prenatal tests and disability rights.[64] Disability-selective abortions have been compared to Nazi

---

suicide must be banned and not merely regulated. The disability-rights case against selective abortion is virtually identical to the case against assisted suicide. The paper establishes that any compromise to permit disability-selective abortion, without even regulating them to counteract the social pressure to abort, makes it hard to argue for a ban on assisted suicide.

[63] Masden (1992) compares the reconciliatory approaches made by feminists and disability-rights activists to the issue of prenatal testing. First, it considers current mainstream thought regarding the issue of prenatal testing. The aim of prenatal testing is to facilitate selective abortion for the prospective parents, when the tests diagnose any disease or 'defect' in utero. The author refers to this choice as somewhat arbitrary. These abortions are also termed as 'genetic' or 'therapeutic'. The paper examines the possible difficulties with these positions and how they might be resolved. The author argues that a re-examination of prenatal testing is desirable, because of the way that it has furthered the medicalization of pregnancy and childbirth and its potential to remove decision-making control from the hands of women.

[64] Saxton (2000), a disability-rights scholar and activist, discusses why many members of the disability-rights movement believe that prenatal testing and selective abortion sends a negative message to and about people with disabilities. She examines the views of people with disabilities and disability activists on prenatal diagnosis and selective abortions. She views disability-selective abortions as an upshot of the medical view of disability. She considers the impact of prenatal technology on the general attitude of the society to disability. The chapter analyses the social perception of disability-selective abortions that treat a child with disability as a burden on the family and society. Therefore, 'it would be better off not being born' is the message sent by disability-selective abortions. The author introduces many disability-rights activists and their views on prenatal diagnosis and selective abortion. Some of the authors and views are:

1. Lisa Blumberg is a disability activist and lawyer. In her view, 'The social purpose of these tests is to reduce the incidence of live births of people with disabilities.' According to her, 'if suffering does indeed

eugenic practices, where the state decided who should not inhabit the world, and lawyers, physicians, and scientists provided the justification and means to implement those decisions. However, in today's liberal democracies, eugenic principles are part of our largely unexamined and unspoken preconceptions, as scientists and physicians provide the ways to put them into practice.[65] Women are supposed

---

attend life with disability, then the place to begin ameliorating that suffering is with the eradication of social discrimination and not with the eradication of people with disabilities' (1994b: 224).
2. Deborah Kaplan is also a disability activist and lawyer. In her view, if persons with disabilities are regarded as a definable social group, who have faced great oppression and stigmatization, then prenatal screening may be regarded as yet another form of social abuse. These tests essentially reinforce the stereotyped attitudes towards people with disabilities.
3. Adrienne Asch was a renowned disability activist and professor of philosophy. According to her, the core of medical view is that 'disability must be prevented, because persons with disabilities cannot function within the existing society' (1996: 98). She says that the medical system tends to underestimate the functional abilities and overestimate the 'burden' of persons with disabilities.
4. Laura Hershey, a journalist and a disability rights activist, says that the medical language reinforces negativity regarding disability. Terms such as 'foetal abnormality' and 'defective foetus' are deeply stigmatizing and carry connotations of inadequacy and shame.

The author concludes by examining the disability paradigm—the view of disability developed by people with disabilities—which regards disability as a socially constructed phenomenon. It totally differs from the medical model and arose from the experiences of persons with disabilities. This was made prominent in the late 1970s. The analysis of the author shows that oppressive social conditions have distorted public perceptions, as well as how persons with disabilities themselves internalize the perceptions of disability.

[65] Hubbard (2006) explains how a woman's right to abortion fits into selective abortion and the connections between what the Nazis did and what is happening now. The author argues that a woman must have the right to abort a foetus, whatever her reasons, precisely because it is a decision about her body and about how she will live her life. But decisions about what kind of baby to bear are inevitably bedevilled by overt and unspoken

to execute these principles, by choosing screening tests and selective abortions. The 'medical ability' to screen and end a life, which may be born with a disability, is lauded as good for the individual and the society.[66] Opposing this, Adrienne Asch, professor of philosophy and disability-rights activist, and a person with disability herself, said that, in fact, life with disability is not the unremitting tragedy as generally portrayed by medical and bioethics literature. Even on 'quality of life' measures, a life with disability can be rewarding.[67] This argument, however, does not undermine the need for accommodation. Though life is inherently valued, the quality-of-life argument is important to the lives of persons with disabilities. The quality of life for persons with disabilities becomes an issue because ensuring quality requires more resource allocation in a world that has been constructed without acknowledging the presence of disability.

The prominent social justice theories are transcendental and find excuse for this omission by citing equality in distribution. Social justice is a public chart, instructing how basic rights and liberties,

---

judgements about which lives are 'worth living'. To a considerable extent, not initiating or terminating these pregnancies may indeed be what women want to do. However, people with disabilities need opportunities to act in the world, and sometimes that means that they need special provisions and consideration. Thus, this paper proposes that a woman must have the right to terminate a pregnancy, whatever her reasons, but she must also feel empowered not to terminate it, confident that the society will do what it can to enable her and her child to live fulfilling lives. To the extent that prenatal interventions implement social prejudices against people with disabilities, they do not expand reproductive rights. It also obscures questions about a humane society's responsibilities to satisfy the requirements of people with special needs and to offer them the opportunity to participate as full-fledged members in the culture. Until mechanisms exist that give people a decisive voice in setting the relevant scientific and technical agendas and until scientists and physicians are made accountable to the people whose lives they change, technical innovations do not constitute new choices. The author argues that prenatal tests and disability-selective abortions replace previous social constraints with new ones.

[66] Singer (1993); Harris (1985, 1992).
[67] Asch (2001: 299–300).

along with the benefits and burdens of social life, are to be distributed among its members. John Rawls called it the original position in social contract theory, where members coexist on a hypothetical agreement among free and rational persons in an initial situation of equality. In Rawls' perception of social justice, members of the ideal society initially chosen must be 'normal and fully cooperating members of society over a complete life'.[68] Rawls does not count people with disabilities as subjects of justice. The reason for this exclusion is that people with disabilities sometimes require additional distribution of resources to cooperate.

Amartya Sen, a profound social philosopher and economist, refers to disability to demonstrate the limitation of the income-based approach to measure poverty. He stated that 'disabled's' need for income is greater than that of able-bodied people.[69] According to Sen, persons with disabilities require more money and assistance to

---

[68] John Rawls (1971: xiii). Rawls claims that the principles of justice derive from the original position, as he describes it, only if there is some sort of superiority to the circumstances he attributes to that condition over various other possible descriptions of the original position. The original position is defined as, 'it is a status quo in which any agreements reached are fair' (p. 11). His 'two principles of justice' are in fact a more specified version of his 'general conception' of justice. Rawls' account on 'Social Justice' opens with social primary goods and natural primary goods and its equal distribution (p. 54). Liberty and opportunity, income and wealth, and the bases of self-respect are social primary goods. Rights and liberties, opportunities and powers, income and wealth are the primary goods at the disposition of society (p. 54). According to Rawls, other primary goods such as health and vigour, intelligence and imagination are natural goods. However, natural goods and their distribution are influenced by 'basic structure', and other depend on the rational plan of life (p. 54). Hence, Rawls' theory of justice takes primary goods as more solid. At the same time, the general conception clearly shows the great presumption favouring equality. Rawls favours consistent equality, unless there is good reason for inequality. Accordingly, inequality is a position that a wide variety of theories of justice could accept, but the presumption for equality can be overridden only on the egalitarian ground that in doing so the least well-off are thereby advantaged. In this last condition, Rawls' theory parts company with all the other doctrines of justice.

[69] Sen (2009: 258).

try to live 'normal lives'.[70] In his *Idea of Justice*, he called the inability
to earn income 'the earning handicap', which tends to reinforce the
difficulty in converting incomes and resources into good living.[71] This
conversion cost, which he referred as 'the conversion handicap', is
precisely because of disability.[72] Sen made an argument that conversion cost is an inflexible perennial truth, and he set up a case for
rights of persons with disabilities within the prevention paradigm. He
stated: 'It is extremely important to understand that many disabilities
are preventable, and much can be done not only to diminish the penalty of disability but also to reduce its incidence. Indeed, only a fairly
moderate proportion of the 600 million people living with disabilities
were doomed to these conditions at conception, or even at birth.'[73]

However, Amita Dhanda challenged this, as it reinforces the
diminishing of value of persons with disabilities. She said, 'It undermines the fact that a large part of the higher conversion costs emerges,
because the world has not been constructed taking into account the
existence of persons with disabilities.'[74]

---

[70] Sen (2009: 258).
[71] Sen (2009: 258).
[72] Sen (2009: 258).
[73] Sen (2009: 259).
[74] Dhanda (2010a: 132). In this book review, the author brings out what
she terms as a 'sin of omission', the failure of Amartya Sen's idea of justice.
Sen, the Nobel laureate, questions thinking of justice in transcendental terms.
Sen holds that the inadequacies of one set of lives can be demonstrated by
comparing them with other lives. Dhanda raises a point that Sen has posited
his idea of justice in contradiction to Rawls' theory, on the reasoning that to
address manifest injustice, you do not need a theory, just an idea of justice
suffices. Because, according to Sen, Rawls has put forth a transcendental
theory of justice that provides a vision of a just society without engaging
with existing manifest injustice. According to the author, Sen flounders when
he applies his idea of justice to persons with disabilities. Sen first refers to
disability when he uses disability as an example to demonstrate the limitation
of the income-based approach to measure poverty. Sen fails to examine the
question of disability rights from the standpoint of persons with disabilities.
When Sen makes arguments of higher conversion costs, he fails to make the
argument that the adoption of universal design would bring down the rates of
conversion. Sen goes on to contend that 'social intervention against disability

Social justice theories propound justice and equality to all. Equality, as part of social justice, does not mean that everything is divided and distributed in identical shares, but that distributions are geared thoughtfully to individual differences, and different needs of everyone are acknowledged equally. However, disability has remained an excusable argument to deny social justice to persons with disabilities. In the early 1980s, Amartya Sen introduced the concept of 'capabilities' in welfare economics and advocated it as the most appropriate criterion to measure human well-being.[75] Nussbaum, however, put forward the 'capability approach' as a more persuasive model for social justice.[76]

---

has to include prevention as well as management and alleviation.' Sen thus sets up his argument for disability rights on the triad of prevention–management–alleviation. According to Dhanda, a natural consequence of this linkage is that:

> It in no way challenges the devalued existence of a disabled life rather it reinforces the diminished value. It perceives disability as deficit, contends that this deficit has been caused by social inaction and asks society to compensate for the harm it failed to prevent. Disability rights arising from such an outlook fail to respect the dignity of persons with disabilities as persons who need to be valued for themselves. Disability Human Rights on the other hand perceives disability as an integral part of human diversity. The difference of disability should not result in persons with disabilities being denied the development of human capabilities. And persons with disabilities have a right to develop their capabilities on an equal basis with others.

[75] Sen (1982, 1985).

[76] Nussbaum (2006) offers a trenchant critique of theories that invoke the idea of social contract to derive principles of justice. In the book, the author identifies three areas of justice in which the social contract theories turn out to be inadequate. Focusing mostly on the issue of disability, it makes a concrete case for moving beyond the contractarian way of thinking about social justice. It provides the rationale that the social contract theories are unhelpful for developing a satisfactory account of social justice. It points out that the idealized contractarian view of human beings, with its emphasis on independence and rationality, eschews the pervasive fact of human dependency and disability. Thus, the author not only argues that the boundaries of justice should be restructured to construct a social world where people with disabilities will be treated with dignity, she also illustrates that this goal can be achieved by adopting high moral sentiments.

She developed the capability approach as a political theory based on a list of basic capabilities, intended to serve as a benchmark for social justice.[77] It is a non-contractarian idea of justice centred on human dignity. A life of dignity requires opportunities to realize a threshold level of basic capabilities for everyone, including people with disabilities.[78] Even though people with disabilities may not be as free and independent as others, and others in society may gain nothing or comparatively little in cooperating with them, they are full citizens and entitled to dignified lives. This should be the agenda of social justice rather than an act of pity or charity.[79]

Thus, disability-selective abortions question the concept of social justice. Even though there is literature available on social justice and disability, this body of writing does not make a connection with disability-selective abortions and address their legitimacy. In this book I will address the diminishing implication of disability-selective abortions, connecting it to social justice theories. The deepening of prejudice as well as the consequent discrimination created by science is part of this work. As prenatal tests proliferate, the medical and broader communities perceive that such testing is a logical extension of good prenatal care and that it helps parents have healthy babies. This is because the medical model looks at the human body in a mechanistic manner. Medical professionals do not consider the individual as a whole and their connection to the environment. When so viewed, any of the problems that survive the non-conducive environment is viewed as not the structural problem of the environment, but as the problem of the individual. Consequently, disability-selective abortions have not been identified with the kind of people who are selected out; they remain part of medicine. Drawing on a critical realistic perspective, Tom Shakespeare submitted that we need to re-engage with the fundamental question of what disability is and the significance of social relationships.[80] It involves intimacy, care, protection, and

---

[77] Nussbaum (2006).
[78] Nussbaum (2006).
[79] Nussbaum (2006).
[80] Shakespeare (2006). Drawing on a critical realist perspective, the author promotes a pluralist, engaged, and nuanced approach to disability. Rather than rejecting research in medical sociology, bioethics, and social

emotional relationships, which every human requires in order to live in this world.

The disability-rights community criticizes disability-selective abortion as it reinforces discrimination against and misconceptions about people with disabilities.[81] The disability-rights critique of prenatal testing has been formulated as:

> Firstly, prenatal diagnosis reinforces the medical model that disability itself, not societal discrimination against people with disabilities, is the

---

care, disability studies need to re-engage with the fundamental questions of what disability is, and how the lives of persons with disabilities can be improved. The author discusses the dichotomies in the dangerous polarizations of medical model versus social model, impairment versus disability, and persons with disabilities versus persons without disabilities. He analyses the drawbacks of the disability movement's emphasis on identity politics. The book examines the role of bioethics in disability, exploring the issues of choices at the beginning and end of life and in the field of genetic and stem-cell therapies. The author also discusses the significance of care and social relationships, which involves questions of intimacy, friendship, and the role of persons without disabilities. The book promotes a fresh research agenda in disability studies.

[81] Parens and Asch (2000a) debate the implications of prenatal testing for people with disabilities and for parent–child relationship generally. Part 1 of this volume introduces the practice of prenatal diagnosis and the arguments that form the disability-rights critique. The essay entitled 'The Disability Rights Critique of Prenatal Genetic Testing: Reflections and Recommendations', written by the editors, lays out the claims made by those with a disability-rights critique of prenatal testing. It proposes practice and policy recommendations flowing from those claims and evaluations. The second chapter, written by medical geneticist Cynthia M. Powell, offers a brief history of prenatal diagnosis. She describes the current state of prenatal testing in the US, and speculates about the future of such testing.

Part 2 of the book presents several perspectives on the implications of prenatal testing for the experience of parenthood generally. The chapters in this part grapple with what prenatal testing suggests for how prospective parents do and should think about disability and parenthood. In this part, the chapter authored by social scientists and educators Philip M. Ferguson, Alan Gartner, and Dorothy K. Lipsy suggests that the existing literature reveals that a child's disability does not cause the stress and family

problem to be solved. Secondly, it suggests that parents are unwilling to accept any significant departure from the parental dreams that a child's characteristics might occasion. Finally, when prospective parents select against a foetus because of predicted disability, they are making an unfortunate, often misinformed decision.[82]

The growth of rights, especially universal rights that have accorded full value to persons with disabilities, necessitates examining the

---

disruption so often portrayed by many bioethicists and physicians. This chapter represents the claim that the desire for prenatal testing and selective abortion rests on misinformation about what a child's disability means for families.

Philosopher Bonnie Steinbock in her essay 'Disability, Prenatal Testing and Selective Abortion' explores the claim that disability traits are neutral forms of variation that should no more be the basis for selective abortion than should traits like sex or eye colour.

Bruce Jennings, a political scientist, in his chapter 'Technology and the Genetic Imaginary: Prenatal Testing and the Construction of Disability' places prenatal decision-making in a social context. The author invites us to step back from examining the 'free' choices of individuals and urges us to consider how genetic science increasingly frames and thus determines how people understand their experience of pregnancy and parenthood.

Chapters in part 3 of this volume probe the contention that the creation and use of prenatal testing for disabling traits express negative views about people who live with those traits. The fourth and final part of the book addresses practical questions about how policymakers, courts, and professionals do and should determine appropriate prenatal testing practice. In this concluding part, Pilar N. Ossario, a law professor, bioethicist, and biologist, explores how the courts have dealt with cases where plaintiffs argue that they have been wronged by not receiving prenatal information. This chapter shows that, though in the past there have been legal incentives for physicians to over-utilize testing, the courts have been attentive to 'negative message' send by such claims about life with disabilities. The essay offers a strategy for how legal incentives might be created to avoid such over-utilization of prenatal tests.

Thus, this extensive volume, assessing the moral and policy ramifications of prenatal testing, contains the views of parenthood, views of disability, and views about the role of medicine and science in family life. The book illustrates a variety of perspectives about disability and parenthood.

[82] *Buck v. Bell*, 274 U.S. 200 (1927).

problem within the purview of these rights. The United Nations Convention on the Rights of Persons with Disabilities (UNCRPD), 2006 has caused a paradigm shift in international human rights law.[83] The UNCRPD represented a historic break from a state-centric model of treaty negotiation, in which instruments are negotiated behind closed doors, away from the very people they are intended to benefit. It moved instead towards a participatory approach that considered the views and lived experiences of the affected. It also shifted paradigms in the manner in which disability is conceived. The UNCRPD embraced a social human rights model that focused on 'capability' and 'inclusion', and lifted the environmental and attitudinal barriers that prevent persons with disabilities from complete inclusion and equal participation in all aspects of life. It introduced the equality idiom to grant both same and different opportunities to persons with disabilities. It also recognized autonomy with support for persons with disabilities and, most importantly, made disability a part of the human experience.[84] These are fundamental to the UNCRPD and the dynamic process that brought it to life. It reminds us of the thrusting question raised by Adrienne Asch, 'Is it possible for the same society to espouse the goals of including persons with disabilities as fully equal and participating members and simultaneously promoting the

---

[83] Melish (2007).

[84] Dhanda (2008: 45) examines the UNCRPD in order to highlight and analytically describe what it does for disability rights and how it contributes to human rights jurisprudence. Though the explicit provisions of the UNCRPD enunciate the rights of persons with disabilities, the philosophy informing these rights, as also the procedure followed for arriving at the text of the UNCRPD cannot be limited to disability alone. Thus, this paper examines the significance of the UNCRPD for persons with disabilities and its contribution to human rights jurisprudence in general. According to the author, the UNCRPD has signalled the change from 'welfare' to rights. Second, it provides a fresh perspective on the basic dilemmas of human rights advocacy. Indivisibility of human rights, recognition of human interdependence, double discrimination, and the right to participate have been analysed as the contribution of UNCRPD to human rights jurisprudence. The author submits that the UNCRPD reconstructs both the 'human' and 'rights' in human rights.

use of embryo selection and selective abortion to prevent the births of those who would live with disabilities?'[85]

The UNCRPD requires special attention because it has 'the wisdom of a straggler'.[86] The rights-based approach to disability essentially means viewing persons with disabilities as subjects of law. It entails recognizing them for their intrinsic value as people and not as means towards the ends of others. Its final aim is to empower persons with disabilities, and to ensure their active participation in political, economic, social, and cultural life in a way that is respectful and accommodating of their difference. The UNCRPD is a landmark step towards affirming equal rights and dignity to persons with disabilities.

The literature available on disability rights and disability-selective abortions does not connect both. The available works treat both areas as independent. This book weaves the common link present in both—in the case of rights and selective abortion, the target group is persons with disabilities. While universal law accords equal rights to persons with disabilities, disability-selective abortions unproblematically permit their selective elimination, preventing them from coming into this world. The present society has new powers of prediction and intervention about people yet to be born.[87] Disability-selective abortion targets persons who may be born with disability. But, such scientific tests are not permitted for selective elimination of another kind of people.

The existing literature makes a case that while sex-selective or other selective abortions are not promoted, not even as part of

---

[85] Asch (2003: 315).

[86] Dhanda (2008: 48).

[87] Glover (1992). With the development of more advanced reproductive technology, the author examines whether we should we aim for the birth of 'normal' babies rather than those with disabilities. He argues that the positive answer to this question raises some of the most abstract issues in ethics. According to him, what is controversial is to eliminate or prevent disability by eliminating or preventing the existence of the person who has the disability. This essay put forward the point that screening programmes and disability-linked selective abortions undermine respect for persons with disabilities, violating the principle of 'equality' to all. Glover concludes his paper saying, 'individual differences of ability are quite irrelevant' (p. 444).

technological growth, disability-selective abortions are unproblematically permitted. Prenatal tests and disability-selective abortion, as a sophisticated means of preventing the existence of one kind of humans, completely contradicts their rights, dignity, and equal value as human beings. The extant literature in the areas of eugenics, value of life, prenatal tests, and disability rights and social justice for persons with disabilities commonly miss 'persons with disabilities'. Studies have been conducted independently in all these areas, without concerning themselves with 'persons with disabilities'. Both disability-selective abortion and disability rights target people with disabilities. While the former is to prevent their existence in this world, the latter is to accord complete and equal value and dignity to them. This paradox needs to be studied. Therefore, the present book connects persons with disabilities, the stakeholders, to the extant arguments. It analyses the legitimacy of disability-selective abortions from the perspective of its stakeholders.

This book is an effort to demonstrate why disability-selective abortions are problematic. I would like to state that this book is not about the controversies surrounding pro-life and pro-choice issues relating to abortion. It attempts to demonstrate the wrongness of 'selective' abortions, but without entering the realm of a woman's right to take decisions about her body. It questions the automatic decision taken to abort the foetus, once diagnosed with disability. It is an attempt to explicate the unproblematic perception towards disability-selective abortions.

While the Indian legislation on prenatal tests, the PNDT Act, 1994 prohibits the use of prenatal tests for sex selection, it permits the use of very same tests to select out foetuses with disabilities. The selection is not to promote the health of the baby or the mother. It entails eliminating life with disabilities. The MTP Act, 1971 permits termination of such lives. Does this legal position on disability-selective abortion mean that persons with disabilities do not deserve to be born, as their lives are not worth living?

Does disability-selective abortion in some manner negate the rights of persons with disabilities? Can this technology be carried forward without breaching disability rights? This book intend to analyse the legality of disability-selective abortions permitted under the PNDT Act, 1994 and the MTP Act, 1971 in the context of the UNCRPD.

STRUCTURE OF THE BOOK

Prenatal testing is mainly performed to identify foetuses with conditions considered undesirable by parents, practitioners, or society in general. Therefore, selective abortions in practice prevent the existence of such humans. The PNDT Act and the MTP Act, while prohibiting prenatal tests and sex-selective abortions, permit disability-selective abortions. This paradoxical legal position implies that scientific technology is permitted to systematically eliminate one kind of humans. Chapter 1 appraises the ideas and events that have resulted in the life-threatening prejudice against persons with disabilities. This is to assess the appropriateness of disability-selective abortions.

Chapter 2 studies the theological, ethical, and legal philosophies that value the inherent worth of human life, which contradict selection and elimination of human beings. Chapter 3 analyses this contradictory position in India's selective-abortion laws. This chapter studies the discrimination generated by a legal order that assumes contradictory stances with regard to gender- and disability-selective abortions.

Chapter 4 examines the wider implications of prenatal tests and disability-selective abortion. The impact of UNCRPD and rights of persons with disabilities have been assessed in Chapter 5 in order to examine whether disability-selective abortions diminish the value of persons with disabilities and whether this legal stance contradicts the universal law. Chapter 6 assesses the justifiability or legality of disability-selective abortion law.

While specific findings and suggestions in relation to each context have been recorded in the same chapter, the general findings of the study have been presented in the concluding Chapter 7.

CHAPTER ONE

The Interplay between Natural and Social Selection

. . . .

Science has revolutionized many aspects of our lives, changing it in ways that would not have been possible to imagine a few decades ago. However, scientific understanding is not immune from its own fallibilities and biases. Science decides the standard of human perfection and whenever it is unable to defend its arguments or perceptions, it cites 'prevention'. Sometimes, the medical strategy of prevention extends to preventing the existence of persons with medically undesirable conditions. Thus, the medical understanding of 'human perfection' produces norms and ideas regarding which entities should be allowed to live and which should not.

New reproductive technology, prenatal tests, and selective abortions not only enable women to decide about the time, number of babies, and mode of giving birth, but also the kind of babies they should be giving birth to. Science provides the 'standards' for a viable baby and if the baby is not up to that standard, then it can be aborted on 'therapeutic' grounds. Society selects humans who deserve to live within this medical framework. Selective abortions are life-threatening for the group that is targeted. Disability-selective abortion targets persons with disabilities. It shows that a life-threatening prejudice exists against persons with disabilities. However, prevailing ideology contends that science and technology are value-neutral, and any problems caused by technology are unintended side effects.[1] The prejudicing impact of such unintended side effects or abuses remains unattended. This chapter shows how, consequent to this neglect, science can both produce and feed prejudice.

IS DISABILITY-SELECTIVE ABORTION A SCIENCE OF HUMAN SELECTION?

Prenatal tests and disability-selective abortions unfold the 'prejudicing' aspect of science. Prenatal tests were celebrated as an achievement in science, used to detect 'sex' and other genetic conditions of the foetus in the womb. However, sex screening had resulted in selecting out of female foetuses by way of foeticide. This was particularly so in certain cultures that treated women as less valuable human beings, or not on a par with men. When questions of equality and non-discrimination were raised about the devaluation of women, the science that enabled people to act on their prejudice was challenged. Consequently, the use of technology for sex selection became subject to scrutiny and was banned. However, the use of technology for other reasons still endures. This paradox necessitates an examination of the scientific understanding of disability selection. The question is, when foetuses against which social prejudice exists are selected out, is not medical technology at the service of this prejudice? When prenatal tests are applied to select out persons with disabilities without examining their impact, is complete justification possible?

To dwell on this question, it would be worthwhile to recount certain theories, ideas, and incidents that reflect the understanding that one kind of people is inferior to others and hence dispensable for the benefit of others. Early-twentieth-century eugenic ideologies and policies linked with the Malthusian population and

---

[1] Wolbring (2001: 38).

Darwinian theories demonstrate the pre-scientific ideas of human selection. Eugenic beliefs that emerged from social Darwinism and evolution theories point towards the social and scientific ideas that treat certain kinds of humans as so inferior as to justify their elimination.

EUGENICS AND THE SPECTRUM OF HUMAN SELECTION

Although the literature of eugenics extends back to Plato, the modern movement took its cue from biological theories such as the Malthusian theory on food production and population, Darwin's theory of natural selection, and Mendelian genetics. The early scientific theories of population and natural selection explained nature's role in dispensing human beings with 'inferior' or 'undesired traits'. These theories caused an understanding to develop that the existence of a certain kind of humans is not favourable for the rest of humanity. The Malthusian population theory explained the impossibility of increasing subsistence without impeding population growth.[2] This theory introduced the need for human intervention to check population, as nature's intervention might harm the entire population.

Malthusian Theory and Preventive Checks: A Scientific Reason to Check Reproduction

The Malthusian population theory begins with the proposition that the means of subsistence cannot increase as fast as population, and population always expands to the limit imposed by the means of subsistence.[3] Since population always expands when it can, the means of subsistence can never be abundant for long.[4] The necessities of life are thus chronically in short supply, and their scarcity affects human society adversely. This theory was used to make evident the rapidity with which the population can increase, if unimpeded, and how impossible it would be for subsistence to increase as fast. To show that population does, in fact, grow faster when the means of subsistence

---

[2] Malthus (1798).
[3] Malthus (1798).
[4] Malthus (1798).

are plentiful, Malthus presented empirical evidence of the American colonies.[5] Wherever the means of subsistence were abundant, population had grown with startling rapidity, and in long-settled parts of Europe, population growth had surged in the wake of devastating epidemics.[6] Prevention, then, became inevitable, either by nature or by humans themselves.

The factors that hold population down to the limit established by the means of subsistence were called 'checks'. Malthus' population theory classified them as 'positive checks',[7] over which humans have no control, and 'preventive checks',[8] which involved voluntary activities that affect birth rates. The principal positive checks are war, pestilence, and famine; while infanticide, abortion, and sexual practices that defeat conception exemplify preventive checks.[9] Since Malthus viewed these voluntary expedients as vicious, he referred to the human outcome of the 'principle of population' as 'misery and vice'.[10]

This theory proposed that if population were not controlled by preventive checks, social inequality would be re-established. This would divide society into a relatively impervious elite and an underclass perennially afflicted by misery and vice. This division would violate the law of nature, and the elite and the miserable could not coexist. Thus, the population theory in essence inaugurated the need for human intervention through preventive checks for the survival of elite humans. The work of Malthus, who considered himself a political economist, had a profound impact on the biological sciences. It influenced Darwin to develop his theory of natural selection and survival of the fittest in the nineteenth century.

Natural Selection of Inferior Human Stock

Darwin proposed his theory of natural selection to state how the struggle for existence could weed out the less fit members of a

---

[5] Malthus (1798: 32).
[6] Malthus (1798: 36).
[7] Malthus (1798: 39).
[8] Malthus (1798: 39).
[9] Malthus (1798: 31).
[10] Malthus (1798: 31).

population, leaving those who were fit to pass on their character to future generations.[11] Darwin attributed the struggle for survival and the consequent victory to 'competent' categories. Thus, in Darwin's theory, nature preserves limited means of subsistence, and the competition between the weak and the strong provides a natural means of selection, struggle for survival, and the consequent victory to 'competent' categories.[12] The natural selection theory also accepted Alfred Wallace's explanation to speciation that 'the inferior would inevitably be killed off and the superior would remain.'[13] Darwin also condemned the halting of natural selection by modern medical advances and state welfare policies. 'We civilized men,' he bemoaned, 'do our utmost to check the process of elimination [of the unfit]; we build asylums for the imbecile, the maimed and the sick; we institute poor laws; and our medical men exert their utmost skill to save the life of everyone to the last moment.... Thus the weak members of civilized societies propagate their kind.'[14]

The aforesaid assertion towards a public policy checked the propagation of the weak. The process of human selection began with the application of these ideas and theories. Framed as a simple and necessary natural process, these theories played a significant role in producing the norm of a perfect society consisting of healthy and better humans. This inevitably produced the norm of elimination of the unhealthy or undesired among the human stock for the betterment of the rest. Thus, the theory of survival of the fittest served to construct the idea of superior and inferior human beings in society. Consequently, this division created a social hierarchy among human beings, which ultimately resulted in the use of social power by the dominant. The dominant social power was further used to selectively eliminate the inferior stock.

Darwinian thought caused many social theories to emerge which connected man and society and the subsequent use of social power. Merging evolutionary thought with social theory is therefore connected both with people's genetically inherited capacities and the

---

[11] Darwin (1969: 120).
[12] Price (1998).
[13] Wallace (1905: 361–2).
[14] Darwin (1922: 136), cited in Haller (1963: 4).

many and varied attempts of the powerful to control them. Herbert Spencer, the creator of grand evolutionary schemes, was not content to let natural selection play a part in the origin of biological species; he saw the same process at work in human society. Accordingly, if some people were poor, it was because they were less fit than their more prosperous fellows, and if they died in disproportionate numbers and thereby produced fewer progeny, the human race benefited.[15] Social Darwinism and its sloganeering of 'survival of the fittest' fed this public attitude.

SOCIAL INTERVENTION UPON FAILURE OF NATURE

Social Darwinism propounded a vision of society with maximum healthy people, who reproduce their own kind of healthy offspring. It advocated society's role in adopting means and measures to preserve the superior traits of human beings and eliminating the undesired traits for the betterment of society. All such measures were categorized as means for making a new and orderly society. Thus, the Malthusian theory of food production and population growth married with Darwinian theories resulted in a public-policy understanding that the weak people would be dispensed with by nature if public policy would not dispense with them. However, this would cause harm to a number of others. In order to avoid such a situation, it was necessary for public policy to undertake this elimination in a systematic manner. Consequently, twentieth-century Social Darwinism and eugenic theories developed public policies to eliminate many 'inferior' humans. Euthanasia, sterilization, and massive killing programmes were adopted as part of this mission.

EUGENICS: A SOCIAL INTERVENTION TO 'BETTER THE HUMAN STOCK'

Eugenics, the science of 'improving human stock' promoted whatever tends to give the more suitable strains of blood a better chance of prevailing over the less suitable than they would otherwise have

---

[15] Carneiro (1967).

had.[16] Accordingly, society's stock of talent could be greatly enlarged if members of favoured families were to increase their rate of child-bearing, as a strategy of positive eugenics[17]. This balance could be further improved by discouraging reproduction by those who had less to offer, termed negative eugenics by Glad.

Accordingly, 'what nature does blindly, slowly, and ruthlessly, man may do providently, quickly, and kindly'.[18] Eugenicists believed that the possibility of improving the race of a nation depended on the power of increasing the productivity of the best stock.[19] This improvement in best stock was only possible when bad stocks were eliminated. Hence, eugenics promoted the social control that may improve or impair the racial or physical and mental hereditary qualities of future generations.[20] Eugenicists identified human worth with the qualities they presumed themselves to possess.[21] As Henry Goddard contended in 1927, 'perhaps our ideal should be to eventually eliminate all the lower grades of intelligence and have no one who is not above the twelve-year old intelligence level.'[22] Eugenics as a movement for social betterment with the aid of modern science claimed the allegiance of most genetic scientists.[23] By the late 1920s, acceptance of eugenic theory was widespread, and many types of people were deemed 'socially inadequate' or 'socially parasitic' and perceived as target groups.[24]

Practices such as 'Better Baby Contests' and 'fitter families for future firesides' show the prevalence of positive eugenic thought as a means of promoting the multiplication of better traits. Better baby contests

[16] Galton (1907: 17).
[17] Glad (2008: 13).
[18] Kevles (1985: 12).
[19] Galton (1909: 24).
[20] Galton (1908: 321).
[21] Kevles (1985: 76).
[22] Goddard (1927: 45; 1914: 573–4), arguing that people with intelligence should be placed in a special environment separate from the rest of society, also quoted in Lombardo (2008: 57).
[23] Wikler (1999: 183).
[24] Smith (2000: 115). Those considered to be 'feeble-minded', 'insane', 'criminalistics', epileptic, visually impaired or blind, hearing impaired or deaf, diseased, and 'dependents taken as orphans, the homeless, tramps, and paupers' were targeted.

were arranged particularly to identify gifted tots and in some cases to arrange a future marriage between them. Fitter family competitions were mounted at state fairs, with governors and senators handing out awards.[25] Fitter family contests eventually morphed into a vehicle of the official eugenics movement, as they were designed to identify the bearers of the prized 'germ plasm', the eugenicists' term for what is now known as DNA.

Most eugenicists accepted Galton's view, supported by the 'germ plasm' hypothesis of August Weismann of selection rather than environment determined heredity. Indeed, the mainline eugenicists tended to believe that a person's station in life reflected his or her capabilities and could thus be used as an indication of the genes likely to be passed down to subsequent generations.[26] In Germany, eugenics became an integral element of medical thinking, which envisioned a three-way division of healthcare involving medical care for the individual, public health for the community, and eugenics for the race.[27] Thus, 'inferior' stock had been selected out on the basis of colour and health.

SELECTIVE ELIMINATION AND PURIFICATION

The Nazi nationalist eugenic programme recognized no limits in the pursuit of 'racial hygiene'.[28] Eugenics was central to the entire Nazi enterprise, joined with romantic nativist and racist myths of the 'pure-bred Nordic'.[29] The emphasis on 'blood' called for a purifying of the nation's gene pool so that Germans could regain the nobility and greatness of their genetically pure forebears. The subsequent programmes of sterilization, 'euthanasia' of the unfit, and eventually the Holocaust itself were all part of the unfolding of this central idea.[30]

However, the initial mindset towards racial hygiene was quickly extended to a variety of 'unworthy' groups. The 'unworthy' or the

---

[25] Rafter (1988).
[26] Wikler (1999: 185).
[27] Proctor (1988).
[28] Wikler (1999: 185).
[29] Wikler (1999), referred from Wippermann (1991).
[30] Proctor (1988).

life not worthy to be lived included 'mentally ill', 'feeble minded', and people with physical disabilities, alcoholism, criminal behaviour, and epilepsy. The driving force behind the Nazi programme was the perception of 'growing numbers of "hopeless people" who consume so much of the gross national product'.[31] Even after the advancement of Enlightenment ideas of the nineteenth century, Germany had sought to take care of persons with disabilities, the outbreak of war in 1914 precipitated significant changes, adding social and economic repercussions of the existence and survival of people with disabilities. Adolf Hitler suggested 'wartime was the best time for the elimination of the incurably ill'.[32] The argument of killing of those suffering from incurable and painful diseases is evinced in *Mein Kampf* (1923). The next phase of the propaganda involved a campaign with a series of documentaries distorted to show the need to get rid of the 'useless eaters' who were burden on the German workers.[33] In 1920, the concept of 'life worthy of life' became an ominous term, which shifted the burden of human existence from simply being alive to requiring an explicit justification for living.[34] This gained impetus from a tract published as *Permission for the Destruction of Life Unworthy of Life* by two university professors.[35] It articulated key implications of the existence of persons with disabilities. It called persons with disabilities as 'incurable idiots' having no will or sense of willing.[36] Killing them therefore was simply involuntary euthanasia, that is, simply imposing others' will.[37]

Nazism thus propagated sterilization and euthanasia as civic duties, to destroy lives not worth living. Selective elimination through

---

[31] Macklin (2001: 121).

[32] United States Holocaust Memorial Museum (n.d.) and Mostert (2002: 157).

[33] Rieser (2007).

[34] Mostert (2002). The author informs us that persons with mental disabilities and physical disabilities were treated as having 'unworthy lives'. This means that even a slight difference from the majority-perceived 'perfectness' was not tolerated.

[35] Binding and Hoche (1920).

[36] Mostert (2002).

[37] Mostert (2002).

sterilization and euthanasia were legitimized by the Nazi government, professing public health and welfare. The Nazi government made laws for the protection of hereditary health, which stated that anyone who suffered from an inheritable disease may be surgically steril-ized.[38] Resultantly, the academic fields of anthropology, biology, and medicine were reformulated in racial and eugenic terms. The medi-cal profession in Germany was compromised by its participation in government programmes of identification, sterilization, and murder of those deemed unfit.[39] The eugenic ideology towards an 'inferior' class was demonstrated by the speech delivered by Irving Fisher[40] on 24 June 1921. He said:

> If we allow ourselves to be a dumping ground for relieving Europe of its burden of defectives, delinquents and dependents, while such action might be said to be humane for the present generation, it would be quite contrary to the interests of humanity for the future. Not only should we be giving these undesirable citizens far greater opportunity to multiply than they had at home, but we would be taking away the checks on the multiplication of those left at home. It would be a step backward, a step towards populating the earth with defectives, delin-quents and dependents.[41]

Eugenics therefore, he said, should content itself with the all-important function of weeding out those elements of disease,

[38] Hiscock (1999) and Lusane (2004: 83), Law of Protection of the German Race: Hereditary Health, adopted on 14 July 1933, Article 1 provided:

1. Anyone who suffers from an inheritable disease may be surgically sterilized if, in the judgement of medical science, it could be expected that his descendants will suffer from serious inherited mental or physical defects.
2. Anyone who suffers from one of the following is to be regarded as inherit-ably diseased within the meaning of this law: 1. congenital feeble-mindedness; 2. Schizophrenia; 3. manic-depression; 4. congenital epilepsy; 5. inheritable St. Vitus dance (Huntington's Chorea); 6. Hereditary blindness; 7. Hereditary deafness; 8. serious inheritable malformations.
3. In addition, anyone suffering from chronic alcoholism may also be sterilized.

[39] Wikler and Barondess (1993: 39).
[40] He was the president of the Eugenics Research Association, United States in 1921.
[41] Fisher (1921: 227).

feebleness, and degeneracy in the race, which were tainting healthy stocks and impairing their vitality. It ensured that a large class of persons who were really not fit to carry on the struggle for existence would be looked after; it prevented a host of feeble-minded[42] babies coming into the world, and thus prepared the way for further advances towards the eugenic ideal.[43] These eugenic thoughts apprehended an ever-increasing burden imposed by the 'inferior humans' on the rest of the community.[44] Therefore, eugenics was ultimately used as a justification for compulsory sterilization, genocide, and euthanasia of the weaker sections of society, largely persons with disabilities.

Eugenic theories and their different concepts demonstrate how the prestige of science was used to disguise the moral premises and motives of a human selection movement. Eugenics shows how class, racial, and other biases were powerfully employed to exercise influence over the movement. Thus eugenics offers a justification for those practices that use science of heredity to purify the human stock, by eliminating the undesired stock. Thus began a regime of selection and eradication of purportedly inferior traits based on colour, race, health, and disability. According to eugenic ideology prevailing during the earlier part of the twentieth century, the presence of disability in a society was a matter of urgent concern.

Eugenic Human Selection and Disability

Eugenics possessed a social theory and a set of social policies, which claimed a scientific foundation. Social position, it argued, was largely the result of individual qualities such as mental ability, predisposition to sickness or health, and moral tendency. It postulated that these qualities were inherited, and thus a rough equation could be drawn between social standing and the worth of heredity. Insanity, deafness, mutism, serious congenital defects of vision, epilepsy, and haemophilia were considered grave inferior human conditions. 'Defective'

---

[42] The term then commonly applied to people believed to have mental disabilities.

[43] Fisher (1921: 219).

[44] Manson (1912: 123, 129).

was the label for persons with disabilities. 'Defectives' were defined in legislations to mean idiots, imbeciles, feeble-minded persons, moral imbeciles, and mentally infirm persons.[45] The experts raised the spectre of social degeneration, insisting that feeble-minded people were responsible for a wide range of social problems. This resulted in interference with human reproduction and prohibition on inferiors to reproduce. Application of such eugenic ideologies on persons with disabilities is manifested in the laws relating to compulsory sterilization and physician-assisted euthanasia.

STERILIZATION AND BREEDING OUT DISABILITY

Sterilization laws were the inevitable implication of the negative eugenics query of 'was it possible to "breed out" undesirable characteristics by preventing reproduction, either voluntarily or involuntarily?'[46] Thus, involuntary or coercive intrusion into the reproductive choices of selected people was the stated objective of sterilization laws.

Proponents of the sterilization laws advanced arguments that implied that they considered the presence of 'physical defectives' a curse that should be eradicated from society.[47] For example, the 1914 report of the American Breeder's Association[48] included a model statute for eugenic sterilization.[49] This model eugenic sterilization statute would allow sterilization of potential parents of socially inadequate offspring: 'feebleminded, insane, criminalistics, epileptic, inebriate, diseased, blind, deaf, deformed and dependent'.[50]

---

[45] Manson (1912: 129). In London, the Mental Deficiency Bill, which was passed its second reading in the year 1912, 'defectiveness' meant idiots, imbeciles, feeble-minded persons, moral imbeciles, and mentally infirm persons.

[46] Jonsen (1998: 169).

[47] Chamberlain (1923: 429).

[48] 'Report of the Committee to Study and to Report on the best Practical means of Cutting off Defective Germ-Plasm in the American Population' was drafted by Harry Laughlin, assistant director of Eugenics Records Office, United States.

[49] Jonsen (1998: 170).

[50] Laughlin (1922: 446).

Thus, breeding out of disability stuck to the eugenic ideology as a mode of designing a future society devoid of 'physical or mental imperfections'.

It can be ascertained that the sterilization laws were selectively implemented and were primarily intended for people with disabilities, in particular, against people with mental disabilities. Eugenicists found around them a vast population of the feeble-minded, a capacious term that included persons with 'serious mental disorders, the mentally retarded, the slow learners, the ignorant' and the 'degenerate' of all sorts.[51] The eugenic society frequently apprehended the growing number of mental asylums and the veritable burden on taxpayers to support the 'defectives'.

It was strongly asserted that such caregiving, 'afford(s) the opportunity for them to propagate their unfit kind'.[52] The lawmakers were seduced by the power to sort the fit and the unfit and to select citizens who were worthy of having children. Hence, they increasingly turned to sterilization measures. Eugenics propagated sterilization as a medical means to preserve public health.

THE PUBLIC HEALTH JURISPRUDENCE: JUSTIFICATION FOR EUGENIC STERILIZATION

The American eugenicists, such as Charles Davenport and Harry Laughlin, propounded the development of taxonomy of human traits, and to classify individuals as 'healthy' or 'unhealthy' and 'normal' or 'abnormal' in their taxonomic scheme. This segregation of individuals on the criteria of 'health' resulted from lobbying by eugenicists.

It can be seen that eugenicists adopted the rhetorical language of public health law jurisprudence as the solution for eliminating social problems. The public health rationale was invoked as a justification for coercive legislation by eugenicists, insisting that the 'social problem classes' were a public health issue and a medical problem. The specific methods of segregation and sterilization were entirely within the province of medical profession. Sterilization surgeries, which

---

[51] Wallace (1991: 169).
[52] Kevles (1985: 72).

included castration, vasectomy, and salpingectomy,[53] were considered standard medical practices. These were practised through legally approved channels.

STERILIZATION LAWS IN ACTION

The most powerful vehicle of the eugenic ideology was the law.[54] Between 1900 and 1970, proponents of eugenic theory drafted and endorsed nearly a hundred statutes. Between 1900 and 1928 more than 25 states in the United States (US) adopted laws providing for the sterilization of various groups of people with disabilities.[55] In 1907, Indiana passed the first law authorizing compulsory sterilization of any criminal, idiot, rapist, or imbecile in a state institution whose condition was confirmed as 'un-improvable' by a panel of physicians.[56] By 1931, 30 states had such laws. These laws authorized institutional superintendents to order sterilization of inmates with little or no due process. California's law, passed in 1909 and amended in 1913, provided for sterilization of mental patients upon their release from the asylum.[57] The 1937 Georgia sterilization law targeted anyone with a 'physical, mental, or nervous disease or deficiency' who might have children with similar problems, and created a state board of eugenics that directed superintendents of state asylums to name candidates for sterilization surgery.[58]

Between Indiana's 1907 sterilization statute and Georgia's 1937 legislation, 30 other states adopted laws that eventually led to the

---

[53] Sterilization surgery for females.

[54] Lombardo (2000: 105).

[55] Burgdorf and Burgdorf (1977: 1000).

[56] Maurer School of law: Indiana University (1963). This work further provides the information that the statute remained in effect until 1921, when the Indiana Supreme Court in Williams V. Smith held that the law violated 'due process' procedure under fourteenth amendment of the Indiana federal Constitution, as the law failed either to provide an opportunity of hearing to the individual who was selected for sterilization or the right to cross examine the doctors who took the decision for sterilization surgery (p. 276).

[57] Reilly (1991: 48).

[58] Lombardo (2008: 63).

surgery of more than 65,000 people.[59] These large-scale legitimized sterilizations were performed in the US, a nation where rights of citizens were protected under the Bill of Rights. Hence those statutes were often challenged for violation of either the equal protection or due process clauses of the Fifth and Fourteenth Amendments to the United States Constitution. Several state statutes were struck down on these grounds. For example, *Skinner* v. *Oklahoma*[60] struck down a law providing for the forcible sterilization of felons who had offended more than three times. But in 1927, the United States Supreme Court upheld state-forced sterilization in *Buck* v. *Bell*.[61]

BUCK V. *BELL*: THE BIRTH OF JUDICIAL PROPAGATION OF HUMAN SELECTION

Legal authority for the involuntary sterilization of a person with mental disability was addressed by the Supreme Court in 1927 in *Buck*. *Buck* was the first and only instance in which the court allowed a physician, acting as the agent of the state government, to perform an operation that was neither desired nor needed by the 'patient'.

The *Buck* case was instituted as a lawsuit over a doctor's malpractice for the use of 'therapeutic prerogative' to sterilize a woman without her consent. In 1916, Dr Albert Priddy sterilized a woman and her daughter who had been certified as 'feeble-minded'. They were the inmates of the Virginia Colony for the Epileptic and Feebleminded. They were institutionalized over allegations of disreputable habits of sexual lust and being certified as feeble-minded. Carrie Buck, the daughter, was institutionalized when after being raped she gave birth to a child, allegedly not 'normal'. The state claimed that the Buck line suffered from hereditary feeble-mindedness. At that time, the state of Virginia permitted sexual sterilization when it was determined that a 'patient' or 'inmate' was afflicted with hereditary forms of insanity or imbecility.

Assistant director of the Eugenics Record Office, Harry Laughlin, studied Buck's medical records and concluded that she exemplified

---

[59] Lombardo (2008: 104, 116).
[60] 316 U.S. 535 (1942) (hereinafter referred to as *Skinner*).
[61] 274 U.S. 200 (1927) (hereinafter referred to as *Buck*).

the 'shiftless, ignorant, and worthless class of anti-social whites in the South'.[62] Harry Laughlin acted as 'expert' consultant to the state and, although he had never personally examined Carrie, her child, or her mother, testified that Carrie Buck was a 'potential parent of socially inadequate offspring'.[63] Therefore, the state of Virginia alleged that Carrie Buck was a 'feeble-minded' inmate, and that allowing her to reproduce would likely lead to epileptic, insane, or feeble-minded offspring. Thus Buck was ordered to be sterilized against her will by the superintendent of the institution under the Virginia Eugenic Sterilization Act. Buck's guardian originally appealed against the sterilization order, but lost as the order was confirmed by the Court of Appeals of the State of Virginia. Buck challenged the judgement, contending that the operation of salpingectomy, as provided for in the statute, was illegal as it violated her constitutional right of bodily integrity. It was also contended that the law was repugnant to the due process clause of the Fourteenth Amendment.

In 1927, the United States Supreme Court summarily dismissed Buck's claim that the procedure violated her right to 'equal protection' and 'due process' under the Fourteenth Amendment. The court emphasized that Carrie Buck was the daughter of a 'feeble-minded' mother and the mother of an 'illegitimate' feeble-minded daughter. Justice Oliver Wendell Holmes, Jr wrote the following judgement in a widely quoted opinion for the majority:

> We have seen more than once that the public welfare may call upon the best citizens for their lives. It would be strange if it could not call upon those who already sap the strength of the State for these lesser sacrifices, often not felt to be such by those concerned, in order to prevent our being swamped with incompetence. It is better for all the world, if instead of waiting to execute degenerate offspring for crime, or to let them starve for their imbecility, society can prevent those who are manifestly unfit from continuing their kind. The principle that sustains compulsory vaccination is broad enough to cover cutting the Fallopian tubes. *Three generations of imbeciles are enough*.[64] (emphasis added)

---

[62] Gould (1984).
[63] Reilly (1991: 68).
[64] *Buck*, 274 U.S. at 207.

The opinion in *Buck* endorses both an explicit eugenic rationale and the public health underpinning.[65] The comparison of the sterilization statute to the compulsory vaccination laws implies that society has the right to demand sacrifices from its citizens to secure common welfare. The statement that the 'principle that sustains compulsory vaccination is broad enough to cover cutting the Fallopian Tubes' suggests that, wiping out an epidemic with a vaccine was comparable to wiping out mental disease with sterilization.[66] 'The danger to society' rationale was borrowed from *Jacobson* v. *Massachusetts*,[67] a public health case decided in the wake of the small pox epidemic.

In *Jacobson*, the court upheld a Massachusetts statute that compelled citizens to receive smallpox vaccines and imposed fines upon those who refused. *Jacobson* was the only precedent cited in *Buck*. By drawing an analogy between sterilization and vaccination, and by denying the right to bear children to a woman with mental disability, the court seemed to imply that disability was a dangerous human condition. Disability was not only harmful to the individual who possessed it but also to the whole society. Thus *Buck* confirmed many common misconceptions about disability.[68]

From the above, it can be analysed how a one-sided view could be unproblematically articulated. Buck's life story and the humiliating experience demonstrates how 'selecting out' disability works, when not viewed in its entirety. Buck was denied her right to dignity and bodily integrity for allegedly expressing her desire for sex, a natural instinct of humans. This was because the desire was expressed by a woman with mental disability born to another woman with the same condition.

However, after *Buck*, the sterilization programmes, which had slowed down in fear that they were in violation of 'equal protection and due process', continued until the Second World War. As historian Daniel Kevles writes, 'the revelations of the Holocaust had all buried the eugenic ideal. After the Second World War, "eugenics" became a word to be hedged with caveats in Britain and virtually a dirty word

---

[65] Lamabrdo (1996: 11).
[66] White (1993: 405).
[67] 197 U.S. 11 (1905) (hereinafter referred to as *Jacobson*).
[68] Hahn (1994: 97).

in the United States, where it had been identified with racism.'[69] Serious doubts about eugenics also came from within the scientific community. Those who had followed the development of genetics from social Darwinism appreciated the complexity of the eugenic science. Hermann Muller declared: 'Eugenics is a hopelessly perverted movement ... powerless to work any change for the good and doing incalculable harm by lending a false appearance of scientific basis to advocates of race and class prejudice.'[70]

The spectre of Nazi eugenics is thus a reminder of what can go wrong with attempts to improve the health of population.[71] Eugenic policies and programmes could eliminate people only after they were born. However, from the mid-1930s, genetics was converted from a pseudo-scientific prop for eugenics to a tool for medical diagnosis and treatment.[72] By the early 1960s, medical genetic clinics had been established to provide diagnosis for persons who were suspected of having hereditary disease. With the development of genetics, using biochemical and chromosomal tests, it became possible to screen populations for certain genetic conditions.

In the mid-1960s, amniocentesis came into use, which made prenatal testing possible, potentially enabling physicians to detect a wide range of foetal 'defects'. In the early days of the procedure, some physicians refused to perform the tests unless the woman agreed to abort the 'affected' foetus.[73] Consequently, amniocentesis was termed a 'search and destroy mission'.[74] American legislations such as National Genetic Diseases Act, 1976, had added screening for Tay-Sachs disease, cystic fibrosis, Huntington's disease, and muscular dystrophy.

These testing and screening programmes were proposed to prevent genetic deterioration. However, the screening-linked abortions cast a shadow over the initiation of prenatal screening programmes. These programmes were challenged over their discriminatory aspect.

---

[69] Kevles (1985: 251).
[70] Muller (1935) cited in Jonsen (1998: 174).
[71] Bailey (1996: 144).
[72] Jonsen (1998: 177).
[73] Jonsen (1998: 177).
[74] Jonsen (1998: 177).

'Is it laudable to eliminate the disease by eliminating its victim? Or to mark the surviving victim as defective? Or to stigmatize a group as carriers of a defect? Should a diagnosis be offered when there is no treatment for the disease?'[75] These were the questions that challenged the Hippocratic duty to do no harm to humans.

Therefore, many scientists, genetic practitioners, philosophers, and theologians were sensitive to the discriminatory and stigmatizing effects of genetic knowledge. They judged the screening of unborn and newly born to be a species of 'statistical morality', cost effectiveness analysis, and an ethics of the "greatest net benefit", which leads to the vanishing of individual into the mass'.[76] Leading scientists also raised questions surrounding the diagnosis, prevention, and treatment and screening for inherited diseases. Genetic counselling, intrauterine diagnosis, sex selection, population screening, early detection of late-onset genetic diseases, artificial insemination, embryo research, cloning, gene therapy, and so on were also challenged on ethical reasons. Of these various methods, sex-selective abortions were largely condemned.

Thus, it can be inferred that eugenics and genetic theories have had a similar consequences as the population and natural selection theories. Eugenics and genetics resulted in an understanding that one kind of people was dispensable and public policy should be organized to undertake elimination of this dispensable group, in a systematic manner.

These early attempts to achieve a perfect society filled with perfect bodies and minds destroyed many lives. It also resulted in diminishing the value of people who were targeted for their different traits. Due to the similarity of these goals, contemporary genetic practices are being compared with early eugenic measures. Early eugenics and the Nazi Holocaust represent the social control that necessitated perfection as a condition for human existence. Today's genetics, in particular the deployment of Genome Project, has created the notion that perfection is indeed possible using logical positive methods.[77] Ruth Hubbard, a retired professor of biology at

---

[75] Jonsen (1998: 178).

[76] Ramsey (1973: 151).

[77] Ramsey (1973: 145).

Harvard University,[78] stated: '... my problems with amniocentesis stems [sic] mostly from my concern about how it is creating eugenic thinking. We act as if we can look at a gene and say, "Ah-ha, this gene causes this ... disability" when in fact the interactions between the gene and the environment are enormously complex'.[79]

This concern of Hubbard points towards the dangers of relying on the social instinct for human selection. It can be seen that both the early eugenic measures and contemporary reproductive technology aim to eliminate 'imperfects' from humanity. Eugenic measures such as forced sterilization and euthanasia could target them only after birth, but new genetic methods are used before birth. Consequently, genetics promote the very same goal of social control that decides who should and who should not inhabit this world.

It is claimed that contemporary clinical genetics is aimed at preventing and treating genuine illness, rather than 'purifying the population' or eliminating racial and social minorities.[80] It is true that social Darwinism, racial hygiene, and Nazi Holocaust practices are no longer acceptable in any democratic society. But, a spillover effect of eugenic goals and discrimination can be seen from several discriminatory practices against persons with disabilities. Incidents of forced sterilization of women with disabilities exemplify a major form of discrimination against persons with disabilities. For instance, in Japan, between 1948 and 1995, almost 16,520 women with disabilities were sterilized against their will. In Sweden, doctors were allowed to sterilize persons with physical and mental disabilities as well as those who suffered from hereditary diseases.[81]

Similarly on 4 February 1994, India woke up to an arbitrary government decision to surgically remove the wombs of 25 women inmates of a government-certified school of 'mentally deficient girls', at Shirur, Pune, Maharashtra.[82] The government had requested a gynaecologist to perform mass hysterectomies on those women inmates

[78] She fled Austria in her youth after the Nazi takeover. She is decidedly pro-choice.
[79] Quoted in Finger (1990: 32); Blumberg (1992: 137).
[80] Shakespeare (2006: 87).
[81] Brady and Grover (1997).
[82] *Indian Express* (1994: 1).

of the government-run institution, merely for the reason that the women were unable to care for their personal hygiene.[83] The doctor claimed that 'these women often became the victims of sexual assault that resulted in pregnancy and that he had already performed around hundred such surgeries.'[84] While social activists protested against this 'mass hysterectomy plan', the state and the medical profession justified it on the basis that it was to protect those women from sexual abuse! Members of the medical profession projected themselves as do-gooders.[85] Surprisingly, at a time when women's rights were being framed, this discriminatory strategy was carried out against some women with mental disability, ostensibly to protect them from sexual abuse. The fallacy of this 'protection strategy' lies in the medical fact that hysterectomy would ensure that these women did not become pregnant, but there was no protection against sexual abuse. It shows the prejudice subsisting against persons with disabilities.

However, while these were state-compelled sterilization programmes, when it comes to the current medical prescription for pre-natal screening, selecting out is a voluntary option. But these decisions for 'voluntary abortion' resemble state-forced sterilizations. Both target persons with disabilities. The latter target them by preventing their existence as offspring of persons with disabilities. The former target them by medically screening them out, making the society internalize it as a legitimate medical practice that benefits everyone.

This clearly shows that new reproductive technology is used for selecting out particular kind of foetuses using disability as a reason; it represents a 'quality control' measure, as in the 'old' eugenics.

---

[83] 'In the Guise of Human Dignity: A report on the mass hysterectomy performed in February 1994 on mentally handicapped of the Government Certified School of Mentally Deficient Girls, Shirur, Maharashtra', a report brought out by a team of representatives of Stree Kruti, Shramajeevika, Forum for Women's Health, Forum Against Oppression of Women, Lokashashi Hakk Sanghatana, etc. Available online at http://www.unipune. ac.in/snc/cssh/humanrights/07%20STATE%20AND%20GENDER/12.pdf (last accessed on 9 January 2016). (Hereinafter referred to as 'In the Guise of Human Dignity')

[84] 'In the Guise of Human Dignity'.

[85] 'In the Guise of Human Dignity'.

The eugenic nature of current prenatal tests and selective abortions give rise to a wide range of implications in contemporary society, which is constructed on the principles of equality and non-discrimination. State policies in the reproductive realm seem to be in breach of these principles.

However, when the state undertook this task, through eugenics and genetics, questions began to be asked, because the public policy of elimination did not stop with persons with disabilities. It targeted several other kinds of humans. But, at that point of time, scientific knowledge and skills could do no more than eliminate people after they were born. Now, we have technology which can undertake elimination before birth takes place. Within the frame of 'eugenic quality control', using prenatal tests as a means to select out disability raises the problem of prejudiced understanding of one kind of life.

TECHNOLOGY FOR SELECTIVE ABORTIONS

Prenatal testing is mainly performed to identify foetuses with conditions considered undesirable by parents, practitioners, or society in general. Therefore, selective abortions in practice prevent the existence of such humans. Public policy supports testing and abortion for a particular group of characteristics, but not other characteristics. It suggests that the birth of people with a particular set of characteristics should be prevented. It implies that prospective parents select against an otherwise wanted child because of its gender or disability, showing that people with these characteristics might be less desirable to others and less happy than others. Thus, it can be seen that science postulates a prejudice that life with disability is not worthwhile or good for humans. The selective technology and medical strategy of primary prevention through disability-selective abortions thus feed this prejudice produced by science.

DISABILITY-SELECTIVE ABORTIONS AND THE EUGENIC ANALOGY

The unproblematic aspect of disability-linked abortions provides an assumption that persons with disabilities are the kind of humans who can be dispensed with. Public policy promotes this selection as a measure to improve the health of the population. When persons with disabilities, against whom social prejudice subsists, are being selected out, it can be said that medical technology is at the service of this prejudice. Then can science and technology be considered dramatically different from social Darwinism? If not, should we not subject disability-selective abortion to greater scrutiny or at least as much scrutiny as sex-selective abortions?

Disability-selective abortions prevent disability, not in an existing human being or in a foetus likely to come to term, but by preventing the foetus from being born as a person with disability. It implies that if people do not meet a certain health standard, they should not be welcomed into the family of the world. This selective technology divides us into two classes, 'desirables' and 'undesirables'.[86] Persons with disabilities, whose characteristics are considered not up to the desirable standard, are undesirables. The right of the 'undesirables' to exist is put at risk.[87] Consequently, contemporary policies and practices of prenatal tests and disability-selective abortions make for a direct analogy with the twentieth-century eugenic practices. If science or technology does not take the social-Darwinian and eugenic view that one kind of people is dispensable, then disability-selective abortions should be scrutinized the same way as sex-selective abortions.

Disability-selective abortions will inevitably discriminate against, and diminish the value of, people with disabilities and their attendant visibility in the community.[88] Their existence and visibility is crucial to overcoming a legacy of prejudice. Selective abortions to prevent their birth send a strong message that persons with disabilities are one kind of people who are dispensable. Moreover, if it becomes easier to prevent them from being born, the social and political commitment to treatment, social services, and non-discrimination protections for people with those conditions may weaken substantially. Therefore, a scientific bias can also cause the elimination of 'selected kind of humans'. As Adrienne Asch diplomatically puts it: 'Despite the professional commitment to non-directiveness in genetic counselling, it is clear that many professionals do not practice in a way that legitimates

---

86 Wolbring (2008).
87 Wolbring (2008).
88 Begentos (2006: 439).

the choice to maintain a pregnancy of a foetus affected by a disabling trait.[89]

The medical profession will agree that it is not possible to make a completely accurate prediction of the presence of disability. If prevention of disability is the objective of disability-selective abortion, disability being an inherent human condition, we may acquire it after birth as well. Science maintains silence on its own fallibility. Parents wrongfully place trust in the opinions of these professionals, believing that the advice offered is given by individuals with superior scientific knowledge.[90] However, there is no empirical evidence to support the benefits of aborting a foetus in order to avoid a potential disability. Most medical professionals perceive disability as an undesirable medical condition and therefore advise against having a child with disability. This often gives rise to a situation where prospective parents have to take a decision on the basis of biased information provided by genetic counsellors.

From this viewpoint, the danger in selective abortion lies in the prejudice it reflects and perpetuates. The manner in which genetic technology is used against one particular trait raises the question of prejudice played by science. By promoting selective abortions by reason of disability, medical science reinforces the paradigm that 'extreme forms of diversity are undesirable'.[91] And the availability and employment of selective abortions may also entrench discrimination and prejudice against people with disabilities by reinforcing the medical perception that disability is a tragic mistake that could and should have been avoided. People with disabilities are therefore justifiably marginalized.[92]

Consequently, persons with disabilities are viewed as burdensome. In this manner, prenatal testing and disability-selective abortions represent a significant step towards the ultimate achievement of 'the eugenicist's dream of eliminating disabilities' by eliminating people with disabilities.

---

[89] Asch (2003: 334). Also see Parens and Asch (2000: 6).
[90] Sutherland (2007).
[91] La Sontaine (2003).
[92] Saxton (2000).

***

As prenatal tests proliferate, the medical and broader communities perceive that such testing is a logical extension of good prenatal care. But these tests are primarily used to decide to abort a foetus with undesired characteristics or conditions. However, when such tests were used to detect the sex of the foetus, and eliminate it on that basis, it was questioned as it discriminated and prevented existence of women. Thus, unarguably prenatal tests and selective abortions reinforce discrimination against humans who are selected out. In this context, prenatal tests and disability-selective abortions arguably reinforce discrimination against and misconceptions about people with disabilities. Prenatal diagnosis and selective termination communicate that disability is so terrible that it warrants not being alive. It sends the message to all persons with disabilities that 'there should be no more of your kind in the future.'[93] When this is done within the narrow confines of the 'perfect human' model, it avoids viewing the selected-out humans as 'full beings'.

The state-sanctioned practice of disability-selective abortions resembles the eugenic practices of selection and elimination. It is true that modern democracies do not have 'eugenic' ideologies. Ideas about 'racial hygiene' and social Darwinism are no longer acceptable in the mainstream. Prenatal tests and disability-selective abortion laws claim immunity from the 'eugenic shadow' as they do not mandate eugenic practices. But it is pertinent to note that such practices have not been permitted for sex selection. This necessitates a challenge to disability-selective abortions as they reinforce the biological ideas of elimination of 'inferior' stocks for the benefit of 'superior' humans. Contemporary genetic practices are accepted as they are aimed at preventing and treating genuine illness, rather than 'purifying the population' or eliminating racial and social minorities. The common belief is that genetic technology generated by scientific investigations is always accurate, highly predictive, and capable of identifying an inevitable predetermination of future disability. The facts are diametrically opposed to this belief.

Disability-selective abortions express the idea, abetted by science, that all persons with disabilities must be eliminated. For many years, access to prenatal diagnosis and selective abortions has been driven

---

[93] Asch (1999: 319).

by the goal of getting rid of certain groups of humans. And persons with disabilities as a 'medically undesired' group are specifically targeted before they are born. When such tests targeted the female foetus, the law intervened to not permit it. This warrants greater scrutiny or least equivalent scrutiny for disability-selective abortions. The absence of such scrutiny and the consequent unproblematic practice of using prenatal diagnostic laws could justify the analogy between the earlier biological and eugenic practices and contemporary genetics that facilitates disability selection. Such selective elimination also contradicts the inherent value of human life. In the following chapter, I will examine the fundamental value of human life.

CHAPTER TWO

Competing Discourses on Value and Quality of Human Life

All societies and their institutions exist to protect and preserve the lives of their member human beings. This predominant concern for human life exists because of the value attached to human life. The fundamental value of human life is the underlying principle of any social institution and its endeavour towards ensuring human dignity. Ethical and legal doctrines of equality and equal human protection are grounded in the inherent value of human life. We may wonder many times how or why such value has been attributed to us. There are theories of theology, ethics, science, and law that explain the reason of giving so much importance to human life. The principle of the sanctity of life is the fundamental principle acknowledged by all these faculties and accords an absolute value to human life. Derived from theological ideology, it provides the moral code for all disciplines and their dealing with human life. Hence, 'sanctity of life' has been acknowledged in all ethical, legal, and scientific principles. Before dwelling on the theological, ethical, and legal aspects of the sanctity of life, it would be appropriate to begin with its meaning.

SANCTITY OF HUMAN LIFE

Sanctity of life refers to the intrinsic worth of human life. Philosophers have extensively explored the 'sanctity of life'. Philosophical writings introduce two approaches to this concept. The first approach views the sanctity of life as a God-given value, one that is external to humans.[1] The other derives it from experiential or psychological foundations internal to humans.[2] According to the renowned philosopher John Keown, each human life is sacred or inviolable, and so has an intrinsic worth.[3] He also proposes 'vitalism' as an integral doctrine of the sanctity of life. 'Vitalism' holds that human life has an absolute moral value and considers it wrong to shorten the life of a human being or failure to preserve it. It also holds that life should be preserved no matter what the cost and how much suffering it may cause.

Ronald Dworkin, another philosopher, contends that the value of life is multidimensional. According to him, the value of human life has instrumental, personal, and intrinsic values. A life has instrumental value as far as it contributes to the interest or well-being of others. It has personal value to the extent that it is good for the person herself. The intrinsic or impersonal value refers to the value that is independent of the aforementioned two values—the value of a human life beyond being valued irrespective of its goodness to others or to the person herself. A human life has intrinsic value just because it is a human life.[4] The intrinsic value of being a human being is the underlying principle of the sanctity of life.

Dworkin cites examples of work of art, biological species, and human cultures to explain intrinsic value.[5] The destruction of valuable art or extinction of species may be instrumentally bad for the people

---

[1] Dworkin (1996: 138).
[2] Cohen (2006).
[3] Keown (1997).
[4] Dworkin (1993: 70).
[5] Dworkin (1993: 76).

who may benefit from it.[6] At the same time, this is bad imperson-
ally or intrinsically because something wonderful has been destroyed
forever. As per the absolute value proposed by Dworkin, the life of a
human organism has intrinsic value in any form it takes.[7] Intrinsic
value differentiates the value of human life from personal value. This
would mean that human life has value, whether that life is worth it for
others or to the person herself. The absolute value of human life is the
foundation of the birth of many ethical and legal doctrines aimed at
protecting and preventing the destruction of human life. However, it can
be seen that the notion of protection and prevention of destruction of
human life underlying the sanctity of life has originated from theology.

SANCTITY OF HUMAN LIFE IN THEOLOGY

Islamic Theology

In Western thought, the development of the sanctity principle owes
much to the Judaeo-Christian tradition. That tradition's doctrine of
the sanctity of life holds that human life is created in the image of God
and, therefore, possesses an intrinsic dignity. Many religions profess
that 'Men are creations of God'. The Christian motto says humans are
made in the image of God. However, Islam does not support 'image
of God' theory.[8] According to the Qur'an, Almighty God created the
original man and woman—a pair—from a single soul, breathing into
them God's spirit.[9] This text conveys the creation of humans as an
absolute discretion of God. Let us examine the value of human life in
Islamic theology.

---

[6] Dworkin (1993: 71).

[7] Dworkin (1993: 69).

[8] Both religions profess the divine creation of original man and woman,
who were named Adam and Eve respectively.

[9] 'Lord who created you from a single soul and from it created its mate
and from them twain hath spread abroad a multitude of men and women'
(Qur'an 4: 1); 'So when I have made him and have breathed into him of my
spirit, do ye fall down, prostrating yourselves unto him. So the angels fell
prostrate, all of them together' (Qur'an 15: 29, 30).

All translations of the Qur'an in this chapter are quoted from the work
titled *The Message of the Quran* by Muhammad Asad (2003).

Humans, the Most Dignified Creation of God

Fifteen hundred years ago, the Qur'an was revealed to Muhammad, the last prophet, commanding, 'READ in the name of thy Sustainer Almighty, who has created, created[10] man out of a germ-cell.'[11] It informs that humans are the most dignified creation of the Almighty God. Significantly, the honour bestowed to humans has been repeatedly stated in this text. For instance, it states: 'It is Almighty who creates you out of dust,[12] and then out of a drop of sperm, and then out of a germ-cell; and then the Almighty brings you forth as children.'[13] When it repeatedly confirms the endowment of human life by Almighty God, it informs of the biological origin and creation of life in the womb in the following words: 'Almighty has created you [all] out of one living entity, and out of it fashioned its mate ... creates you in your mothers' wombs, one act of creation after another, in threefold depths of darkness.'[14] Is man, then, not aware that it is We[15] who create him out of a [mere] drop of sperm.'[16]

Besides recognizing the sanctity of human life as a dignified creation, it also accords this sanctity to a foetus. The reason is that the

[10] This word has been repeated to stress the authority or ownership of creation.

[11] Qur'an 96: 1, 2.

'READ in the name of thy Sustainer, who has created, created man out of a germ-cell! Read—for thy Sustainer is the Most Bountiful One who has taught [man] the use of the pen—taught man what he did not know.' With these opening verses of the 96th chapter—with an allusion to man's humble biological origin as well as to his consciousness and intellect—began, early in the seventh century of the Christian era, the revelation of the Qur'an to Prophet Muhammad.

[12] The divine creation of the first human being, who was named Adam.

[13] Qur'an 40: 67.

[14] Qur'an 39: 6.

[15] In the Qur'an, references to God—often in one and the same phrase—as 'He', 'God', 'We', or 'I', with the corresponding changes in the pronoun from 'His' to 'Ours' or 'My', or from 'Him' to 'Us' or 'Me' are found. It is a linguistic device meant to stress the idea that God is not a 'person' and cannot, therefore, be really circumscribed by the pronouns applicable to finite beings. See Asad (2003: 3).

[16] Qur'an 36: 77.

beginning of a new life has been stated to be a safe deposit in the womb. In essence, in Islamic theology 'no female ever conceives, nor ever gives birth, save with Almighty's knowledge.[17] The bountiful Sustainer, who has created them, and formed ... whatever form He willed.'[18] The holy text explicitly asks man, 'O MAN! What is it that lures you away from thy bountiful Sustainer, who has created you, and formed you in accordance with what thou art meant to be, and shaped thy nature in just proportions, having put thee together in whatever form He willed [thee to have]?'[19]

It can be seen that when this text declares the ownership and design of humans by the Supreme Almighty, it commends high responsibility to man to provide respect and care for the pregnant woman. The period of pregnancy is highly valued by this text and commands humans to be grateful to their parents, especially the mother. The text commands:

> We have enjoined upon man goodness towards his parents: his mother bore him by *bearing strain upon strain*,[20] and his utter dependence on her lasted two years:[21] [hence, O man,] be grateful towards Me and towards thy parents, [and remember that] with Me is all journeys' end. Do good unto [thy] parents. Should one of them, or both, attain to old age in thy care, never say 'Ugh' to them or scold them, but [always] speak unto them with reverent speech, and spread over them humbly the wings of thy tenderness, and say: 'O my Sustainer! Bestow Thy grace upon them, even as they cherished and reared me when I was a child!'[22]

Thus, gratitude towards parents, who were instrumental in one's coming to life, is here stipulated as a concomitant to one's gratitude towards God, who is the ultimate cause and source of one's existence. This also links to the mandatory two-year feeding time prescribed

---

[17] Qur'an 41: 47.

[18] Qur'an 82: 7, 8.

[19] Qur'an 82: 6.

[20] Emphasis added because it shows the concern of the Creator to inform the humanity about the struggle of women to give birth to a new life.

[21] Qur'an 31: 14. It refers to the two-year period of compulsory breastfeeding for the baby, by the mother or by a foster feeding mother paid by the father.

[22] Qur'an 17: 23–25.

by this text. Either the mother or a foster mother paid by the father should feed the baby for two years.[23] It specifically endorses the human nature of 'dependence'. That is why, while the individual freedom of separation of spouses is permitted, the text prescribes greater caution before divorcing a pregnant wife.[24]

This text also mandates that a pregnant woman should not get remarried until she gives birth to her baby and the divorced husband should provide for her till the end of the two-year feeding period.[25] Thus, the mandatory waiting period for remarriage for a divorced woman is until she delivers her baby.[26] If she has not conceived out of the marriage, the waiting period to remarry is four months and ten days.[27] This waiting period has been prescribed to know whether the woman has conceived a new life in her womb. This evinces the value ascribed to a new human life. This holy text also banned female infanticide, which was a heinous practice among the Arabs. It was condemned as an evil deed of humans.[28] It specifically states: '[D]o not kill your children for fear of poverty—[for] it is Almighty who shall provide sustenance for all; and do not commit any shameful deeds, be they open or secret; and do not take any human being's life—[the life] which God has declared to be sacred.'[29]

Islam, thus, being a way of life, considers childbearing, giving birth, mandatory two-year feeding, and care giving as a human responsibility to the 'Creator'. It envisages the idea that, if humans do not take it as a responsibility to the Creator Almighty, but as inherent part of individual life, it would still be beneficial to humans. Many of us look upon the contributing factors of sound childbirth, such as personal care during pregnancy, medical assistance, 'eugenics', and

---

[23] 'And the [divorced] mothers may nurse their children for two whole years, if they wish to complete the period of nursing; and it is incumbent upon him who has begotten the child to provide in a fair manner for their sustenance and clothing.' (Qur'an 2: 233).

[24] Qur'an 65: 4.

[25] Qur'an 65: 6.

[26] Qur'an 65: 4.

[27] Qur'an 2: 234.

[28] Qur'an 16: 57–60.

[29] Qur'an 6: 151.

so on as being independent of God. But, all these contributing factors are, like the birth of the child itself, postulated as an outcome of
God's will and grace: a manifestation of what the Qur'an calls 'the way
of God'. Thus, in Islamic theology, the birth of a human being, from
the point of conception in the womb and its gestation, is designed
by the unique authority of the Almighty. Hence, any interference in
this natural process is prohibited. Consequently, abortion is a squarely
condemned and prohibited practice. Islam treats any practice leading
to termination or restricting human birth as against the basic tenets
of the Qur'an.[30] We can also find this text itself as a strong law in
favour of dignity of every human life, bestowing equality and non-
discrimination. For instance, 1,500 years ago, this holy text banned
female infanticide.

The Original Law and Female Infanticide

The pre-Islamic Arabs believed that goddesses as well as angels, whom
they conceived as females, were 'God's daughters'.[31] As against this,
they desired only male issue, because pre-Islamic Arabs regarded
daughters as no more than a necessary evil. Consequently, the birth of
a baby girl was not a tiding that should have been regarded as a happy
one. A female baby's birth was an occasion to decide whether to keep
the child as an object of perpetual contempt, or to bury it alive, as was
frequently done by the pagan Arabs.

Gender discrimination in its original form is explicitly condemned,
revealing the aggregate nature of gender discrimination, in the Qur'an
(16: 57–60).

> And [thus, too,] they ascribe daughters unto God, who is limitless in His
> glory—whereas for themselves [they would choose, if they could, only]
> what they desire: for, whenever any of them is given the glad tiding of
> [the birth of] a girl, his face darkens, and he is filled with suppressed
> anger, avoiding all people because of the [alleged] evil of the glad tiding
> which he has received, [and debating within himself:] Shall he keep this

---

[30] Islamic Fiqh Academy (2005: 171).

[31] 'Never did God take unto Himself any offspring, nor has there ever
been any deity side by side with Him.' (Qur'an 23: 91).

[child] despite the contempt [which he feels for it]—or shall he bury it
in the dust? Old, evil indeed is whatever they decide! [Thus it is that] the
attribute of evil applies to all who do not believe in the life to come—
whereas unto God applies the attribute of all that is most sublime: for He
alone is almighty, truly wise!

The above passage declares both alternatives as evil. It utterly con-
demns men's attitude towards women in pre-Islamic Arabia, and
has—as is always the case with the Qur'anic references to historical
events or customs—a meaning that goes far beyond this specific social
phenomenon and the resulting infanticide. It would seem that the
pivotal point of the whole passage is to establish the inherent dignity
of female progeny, which pre-Arabians despise. It imposed an ultimate moral responsibility against their own hedonistic inclinations
to perceive women as diminished beings. This explicit condemnation
of female infanticide brought about far-reaching changes towards the
socially prejudiced attitude against women. Consequently, while the
holy text completed its framework, it also developed a society that
equally respects women. As a result, dowry (*mahr*) became the right
of women. Thus, Islamic theology explicitly declares the 'sacredness'
or 'sanctity' of human life in any form, as the most dignified and passionate creature of Almighty God.

Similarly, Hinduism believes that men are created by *parabrahma*
(*Parameshwar* or Supreme God). This is the basis of *sanatana* vedic
dharma. The oldest divine book of the world, the *Rig Veda*, also
declares divine authority for human creation.[32] Likewise, most other
religions profess human being as God's divine masterpiece. The
cumulative appreciation of the divine creation accorded respect, dignity, and value to human life. It produced the fundamental doctrine
of the sanctity of life, a doctrine that bestows inherent value to human
life and hence vehemently opposes its destruction.

The religious belief of divine creation prohibits destruction of
human life and it is treated as equal to destruction of the divine order

---

[32] The Rig Veda (10: 121), (Griffith 1896). 'Prajapati! thou only compre-
hendest all these created things, and none beside thee'. Prajapathi means the
Lord of the People in the Bhagavad Gita, it is said, 'I Brahma am! The One
Eternal GOD' which revealed the truth, 'there is no god but Parameshwar',
Parameshwar refers to the Almighty God (Arnold 1885).

and Almighty God. That is why intentional killing, including foeticide, taking one's own life, and euthanasia are morally prohibited by most religions, espousing their high respect for human life. Hence, it can be understood that the tenet of respect for human life originated from the religious doctrine of the sanctity of life. The religious instruction of Roman Catholics on contraception and abortion can be viewed as the most explicit practices that reflect the inviolability of human life.

Christian Theology

Prohibition of Contraception

Contraception was considered taboo throughout the nineteenth century, owing to the ban by the Roman Catholic Church on contraception. The consistent stand of Roman Catholics on contraception describes the importance of human value in theology. The great value given to human life is reflected in this stand. The use of contraception is banned under Catholic religious doctrines because it is believed to interrupt God's order of transmission of life. Any interference with the origin of human life is not tolerated and considered a violation of the law of nature or the law of God. Affirming procreative value, the sexual union is viewed only as a means of producing another life, not as a means of pleasure.

Postulating procreation as the primary end of human sexuality, Roman Catholics prescribe unitive and procreative aspects in a human being's married life. Since sex is the means of procreation, no artificial interference is permitted to prevent the origin of a human life. Therefore, the catechism of the Catholic Church labels prevention of procreation through any means of contraception as 'intrinsic evil'.[33] It is clear that the church has taken this stand on contraception to espouse its position on the sanctity of life. Based on the underlying principle of the sanctity of life the church wants to prevent man's control over the life of fellow beings. Hence, it prohibits usage of any means that deprive the power of procreating life. The wilful prevention of conception is thus considered as opposed to the moral of the religion.

---

[33] Stable (2005: 174).

The unambiguous catechism of Roman Catholic Church on banning contraception has been reiterated and reaffirmed by the periodic statements issued by the popes. Pope Gregory IX in the decretal[34] of 1230 treated both contraception and abortion as 'homicide'.[35] In 1930, the encyclical Casti Connubii of Pope Pius XI reaffirmed earlier church statements that procreation was the primary end of human sexuality and that the use of means to deprive the sexual act of its power of procreating life violates 'the law of God and of nature, and those who indulge in such practices are branded with the guilt of a grave sin'.[36] The church maintained its strong position despite extensive opposition to its teachings on contraception. Pope Paul VI firmly reiterated the position in Humanae Vitae, his 1968 encyclical on the regulation of birth. It declared: 'It is a serious error to think that a whole married life of otherwise normal relation can justify sexual intercourse which is deliberately contraceptive and so intrinsically wrong.'

The aforementioned position, based on the belief in the value of life, has not been restricted to papal letters. Instead, the church has tried to spread the message about the immorality of using artificial contraception. For example, consistent with these teachings, the Ethical and Religious Directives for Catholic Health Care Services, developed by the National Conference of Catholic Bishops[37] to provide authoritative guidance on moral issues facing Catholic healthcare, include a provision that Catholic hospitals may not promote or condone contraceptive practices.[38] Later the church compromised a

---

[34] A papal letter giving an authoritative decision on a point of canon law.

[35] Maguire (2007).

[36] Pius XI (1930); Stable (2005: 174). Also available online at http://w2.vatican.va/content/pius-xi/en/encyclicals/documents/hf_p-xi_enc_31121930_casti-connubii.html (last acessed on 22 January 2016).

[37] Statement issued by National Conference of Catholic Bishops, 2009, available online at http://www.usccb.org/issues-and-action/human-life-and-dignity/health-care/upload/Ethical-Religious-Directives-Catholic-Health-Care-Services-fifth-edition-2009.pdf (last accessed on 22 January 2016).

[38] Stable (2005: 174). The directives have a twofold purpose: '[f]irst, to reaffirm the ethical standards of behavior in health care that flow from the Church's teaching about the dignity of the human person; second, to provide authoritative guidance on certain moral issues that face Catholic health care today.'

bit on its stringent prohibition of contraception to the extent of natu-ral family planning.

While artificial birth control is considered a mortal sin or intrinsic evil, the church permits natural family planning in certain circum-stances. Rhythm method is the only natural form of contraception permitted by the church. Rhythm method refers to the sexual union of couples during the least fertile period of the woman. This was permitted on the moral ground that no artificial interference with the natural course of conception of life is involved in this method. In 1994, Pope John Paul II clarified the church's position on natural birth control.[39] He declared its respect for the unitive and procreative dimension of the marital act as wisely regulated by nature itself in its biological rhythm. It can be ascertained that the religious teachings of the Roman Catholic Church strongly condemn the use of any means of artificial birth control. The general condemnation of the church towards contraception was mirrored in the public policy and the laws of the nineteenth century.

For instance, the nineteenth-century federal Comstock laws in the US prohibited rendering any information or advice regarding contraception and abortion. A feminist physician, Alice Stockholm, was arrested under one of such statutes for preaching forms of birth control to the public. She was arrested under the 1873 Comstock law, called the 'Act of Suppression of Trade in, and Circulation of, Obscene Literature and Articles of Immoral Use'.[40] Another 1879 Connecticut State law prohibited the use of 'any drug or instrument for the pur-pose of preventing conception'.[41] The law provided that 'any person who uses any drug, medicinal article or instrument for the purpose of preventing conception shall be fined not less than 50 dollars or imprisoned not less than 60 days nor more than one year or be both fined and imprisoned'.[42] In 1961, this law was challenged by

[39] Catholics for Choice (2008).

[40] An Act for the Suppression of Trade in, and Circulation of, Obscene Literature and Articles of Immoral Use of 1873, c. 258, §2, 17 Stat. 598, 599 (1873). The federal obscenity law has been amended many times; it is now codified at 18 U.S.C. § 1461.

[41] Goldstein (1994: 8).

[42] General Statutes of Connecticut § 53–32 (1958), quoted in *Griswold* v. *Connecticut* 381 U.S. 479 (1965) (hereinafter referred to as '*Griswold*') at 480.

Wilder Tileston, a physician claiming that the statute posed a danger to the lives of some of his patients, in *Poe v. Ullman*.[43] However, the United States Supreme Court declined to decide the matter on merits, as the petitioner's own constitutional rights were not involved in the case. The refusal of the court to allow the claim indicated that courts were not inclined to declare an unwritten constitutional right to contraception. Consequently, these laws prevailed in the US until the Supreme Court invalidated the Connecticut law in *Griswold*[44] in 1965, affirming 'sexual freedom' to its citizens.

The above analysis shows that the Roman Catholic Church's long-standing position of anti-contraception is an extension of the sanctity of life, which pays high respect to human life. It entails the church's belief in the dignity of human life, its sacredness, and the general Catholic insistence that all human life must be protected from conception to death. The church has mitigated its traditional doctrine only for 'natural family planning', through the 'rhythm method'. Despite strong criticism within the church itself, it has stood firm on this point, in both its papal teaching and catechism and it shows the value of human life in theology. Under this broad rubric of the sanctity of life, Catholic teaching includes prohibition of contraception, abortion, and direct euthanasia.[45] The religious doctrine of prohibition of contraception is the foundation for many other principles derived from the sanctity of life. The religious prohibition of abortion is another practice that grounded its reasons in intrinsic value of human life under the doctrine of the sanctity of life.

Doctrine of Anti-abortion

Abortion is an 'abominable crime'[46] according to Roman Catholic principles. Abortion is considered an inhuman offence against human beings and an unlawful method of birth control.[47] Since abortion involves the intentional taking of human life, the theological doctrine

---

[43] 367 U.S. 497 (1961) (hereinafter referred to as '*Poe*').
[44] 381 U.S. 479 (1965).
[45] Cunningham (2009).
[46] CNN (2011).
[47] Paul VI (1968).

of anti-abortion considers it as an offence against God. Pope Paul II described abortion as 'a senseless impoverishment of the person and of society itself'.[48] The catechism characterizes every 'procured abortion' as a 'moral evil'.[49] The said anti-abortionist position of the church was derived from its moral principle, grounded on the sanctity of life, which forbids intentional killing. Roman Catholics view human life as sacred from the moment of conception until the moment of death. It considers a foetus as a human being and thereby affirms its right to life. Hence, destruction of the foetus is considered destruction of human life, which is prohibited according to the principle of the sanctity of life. Therefore, the foetus is given the same respect as a human being and any effort to destroy the foetus is treated as an offence.

The high value accorded to human life can be seen in the church's position on therapeutic abortion. The church was adamantly opposed even to therapeutic abortion. According to this view, abortion is not morally permitted to save the life of the mother also.[50] In the Humanae Vitae of 1968, Paul VI reasserted the Church's opposition to abortion, including therapeutic abortion. He declared that 'the direct interruption of the generative process already begun and, above all, direct abortion, even for therapeutic reasons, are to be absolutely excluded

---

[48] Pope John Paul II made this comment while referring to Cuba (*The Wall Street Journal* 1998).

[49] Catechism of the Catholic Church, Article 5, the Fifth Commandment (2271), available online at http://www.vatican.va/archive/ccc_css/archive/catechism/p3s2c2a5.htm (last accessed on 22 January 2016).

[50] Pope Pius XII, 'Address to Midwives on the Nature of Their Profession', 29 October 1951, available online at http://www.papalencyclicals.net/Pius12/P12midwives.htm (last accessed on 22 January 2016). He said in this speech that 'to save the life of the mother is a very noble act; but the direct killing of the child as a means to such an end is illicit'. The prohibition of therapeutic foeticide was reaffirmed in an encyclical of 29 October 1951, and occasioned many adverse comments. Hence, the Pope issued a further statement on 28 November 1951, which explained that the prohibition was confined to a direct killing. For example, he said, if the saving of the future mother's life, independently of her pregnant state, should urgently require a surgical act or other therapeutic treatment which would have as an accessory consequence, in no way desired or intended, but inevitable, the death of the foetus, 'such an act could no longer be called a direct attempt on an innocent life'.

as lawful means of regulating the number of children.'[51] A strict adherence to the moral against killing prevented the church from not only permitting therapeutic abortion but also permitting abortion at the early stages of foetal development. This is at a time when the foetus is considered less developed and hence not qualified to be a person. However, the church seemed to consider the foetus as a full human being from the time of conception.

Consequently, the battle surrounding the question of 'when life begins' made the issue of abortion more controversial. Public opinion tended to justify abortions before 'quickening' of the foetus, the point of time that was considered as the beginning of human life. But the church differed on this point and held that human life begins very early, as soon as the time of conception. It accorded the full status of an individual to the foetus. Hence, for several decades the Christian tradition condemned foetal destruction at any stage. Here, it can be ascertained that, apart from prohibition of 'intentional killing', the 'right to life' of a foetus is also very much embedded in the doctrine of anti-abortion. Ascribing right to life to the human foetus based on the assumption that human life begins from the conception of an embryo is the essential argument of the pro-life theory. This pro-life doctrine serves as a fundamental principle that argues for the ban of abortion for the reason of value of life. Any moral or legal opposition to abortion begins from the pro-life notion of human life.

PRO-LIFE AND HUMAN VALUE

The principle of the sanctity of life accords an intrinsic value to human life from the time of its conception in the mother's womb. Catholics and other pro-life religious groups propound the view that the foetus is a human being. They argue that the foetus has a right to life from the moment of its conception. The theory that acknowledges the right to life of the foetus is known as the pro-life theory. Pro-life advocates argue that right to life begins from the conception of an embryo. They argue that a foetus has the same value as a human being and possesses the fundamental right to life. They take the support of

[51] Paul VI (1968). See http://www.papalencyclicals.net/Poul06/p6humana. htm (last accessed on 22 January 2016).

biological facts that evidence the genetic identity and individuality of the unborn child from the moment of conception. The right to life for the foetus derives from the principle of the sanctity of life, which holds that the life of any human organism, including a foetus, has intrinsic value, whether or not it also has instrumental or personal value. For instance, in the words of Ronald Dworkin: 'If we treat any form of human life as something we should respect and honour and protect as marvellous in itself the abortion remains morally problematic.'[52]

Dworkin further strengthens this morality argument stating that: 'The great majority of people who have strong views about abortion—liberal as well as conservative—believe, at least intuitively, that the life of a human organism has intrinsic value in any form it takes, even in the extremely undeveloped form of a very early, just-implanted embryo.'[53]

Since pro-life movement advocates for the right to life of the foetus, it considers abortion as murder as it takes away the life of a human being. Consequently, people advocating pro-life seek a total ban on abortion. On the other hand, the pro-choice theorists do not ascribe life to the foetus and contend that it is the right of pregnant women to decide whether to continue the pregnancy or not. Though the battle surrounding abortion continues endlessly, it was considered as an offence until its legalization through national laws. For instance, in India until enacting the Medical Termination of Pregnancy Act, 1971, abortion was punishable under section 312 of the penal code.[54] Accordingly, Indian women were not given right to abortion on any ground until 1971. The abortion law has thus been enacted to categorize abortion a non-offence in India, if it is within 20 weeks of pregnancy on specified grounds. However, in 1973, the anti-abortion

---

[52] Dworkin (1993: 72).

[53] Dworkin (1993: 68–9).

[54] Section 312. 'Causing miscarriage—whoever causes a woman with child to miscarry, shall, if such miscarriage be not caused in good faith for the purpose of saving the life of the women, be punished with imprisonment of either description for a term which may be extend to three years, or with fine, or with both; and if the woman quick with child, shall be punished with imprisonment of either description for a term which may extend to seven years, and shall also be liable to fine.' Explanation: A woman who causes herself to miscarry is within the meaning of this section.

regime was globally shaken by the decision of US Supreme Court in *Roe* v. *Wade*[55] that declared the right to abortion as a personal choice of a woman. Consequently, when it comes to a woman's right to abortion, her choice preside over the foetus, as it is exclusively a part of her body.

Here, the noteworthy point is that despite the laws that permit abortion, it is still debated on moral grounds. An endless conflict still surrounds abortion, on pro-life and pro-choice theories. Independent of religious grounds, abortion is viewed as something not morally permissible, owing the argument for right to life of the foetus. The accusation that abortion is destructive of human life, derived from the theory of the sanctity of life, is still unbeatable despite its legitimization. This is evident from abortion laws that provide a time limit for abortion. The restrictions on abortion give the meaning that right to abortion is not an absolute right and certain moral and legal objections restrict the said right, based on the ethics of killing. Thus, it can be ascertained that the theological standing that prohibited contraception and abortion, valuing the life of human being is the foundation of principles of inherent value of human life.

LAW AND THE SANCTITY OF LIFE

For centuries, the law in both common-law and civil-law jurisdictions has stoutly upheld the principle of the 'sanctity of life'.[56] The sanctity of life is one of the most fundamental principles of the legal system that prohibits unjustified termination of human life in any form.[57] Human life is regarded by the law to be both sacred and precious, and every nation has an interest in the preservation of life, which prevails over all the other interests.[58]

The universal recognition of the right to life, right to equality, and prohibition of intentional killing or taking away of one's life,

---

[55] 410 U.S. 113 (1973) (hereinafter referred to as '*Roe*').

[56] Keown (1998).

[57] Lavi (2003).

[58] Convention for the Protection of Human Rights and Fundamental Freedoms, 1950. came into force in 1953, available at www.european-convention. eu.int (last accessed on 4 September 2010).

etc. in law are induced by the principle of the sanctity of life. The duty-of-care principle for medical professionals towards their patients is a manifest recognition of the value of human life. It can be stated that the principles that aim to protect the life of human beings are derived from the doctrine of sanctity of human life. It postulates the notion that 'every human life is valuable without regard to its quality'. The sanctity of life is non-discriminatory in the sense that every human life is valuable, uninfluenced by any social categories. Thus, the principle of the sanctity of life is equally applicable to all persons regardless of their ability or disability, since each person's life is of equal value in law. The sanctity principle has long been accepted throughout the modern world, as is evidenced by its recognition in international conventions on human rights. Article 2(1) of the European Convention for the Protection of Human Rights and Fundamental Freedoms, 1950, for example, provides that: 'Everyone's right to life shall be protected by law. No one shall be deprived of his life intentionally save in the execution of a sentence of a court following his conviction of a crime for which this penalty is provided by law'.[59]

The sanctity of life, the doctrine that postulates an intrinsic dignity of human life, grounds the principle that every human life is valuable and it must be protected. The principles of law that endeavour to protect the life of a human being are the reflection of the sanctity of life. It is this principle that operates as the determinative factor in prenatal legal actions such as wrongful life and wrongful birth.

WRONGFUL LIFE CLAIMS

The principle of the sanctity of life has been bestowed abundant legal recognition in wrongful life claim cases.[60] A wrongful life claim is a tort action by a child with disability against a medical professional, on the reason of failure to warn the mother that she would give birth to a child with disability. The medical doctor's failure to provide the information denied the mother the choice of abortion. Wrongful life cases fall within the ordinary medical malpractice paradigm, when a doctor

---

[59] Article 2(1), Convention for the Protection of Human Rights and Fundamental Freedoms, 1950.

[60] Nizar (2011).

fails to comply with a professional standard of care, resulting in pain, suffering, and unplanned costs.[61] In such claims, a child with disability asserts that but for the negligent behaviour of the doctor, he or she would not be in existence, and hence would not be suffering pain and impairment associated with his or her disability. The cause of action in such claims is the failure of the doctor to diagnose the presence of foetal disability. The operable injury would be the life with disability. The plaintiff, the child with disability, would argue that non-existence would be preferable to his or her life with disability. Thus, denying the dignity of life, wrongful life claims mean that 'it would be better off for him/her not to have been born'.

However, courts and legislations are reluctant to accept this life-diminishing contention. The Kansas Supreme Court, in *Bruggeman* v. *Schimke*,[62] rejected wrongful life as a cause of action on the grounds that a child does not suffer an injury simply from being born. The claim was rejected on the basis that:

> It has long been a fundamental principle of our law that human life is precious. Whether the person is in perfect health, in ill health, or has or does not have impairments or disabilities, the person's life is valuable, precious and worthy of protection. A legal right not to be born, to be dead, rather than to be alive with deformities—is a theory completely contradictory to our law.[63]

Nations have enacted legislations prohibiting 'wrongful life'[64] actions in recognition of the value of human life. Consequently,

---

[61] *Gleitman* v. *Cosgrove*, 227 A.2d 689 (N.J. 1967).

[62] 239 Kan. 295 (1986) (hereinafter referred to as '*Bruggeman*').

[63] *Bruggeman*, 239 Kan. at 254.

[64] In the US, nine states—Idaho, Indiana, Michigan, Minnesota, Missouri, North Dakota, Pennsylvania, South Dakota, Utah—have passed such legislations (Idaho Code §5-334, Ind. Code Ann. §34-12-1-1, Mich. Comp. Laws Ann. 600.2971. Minn. Stat. Ann. §145.424, Mo. Stat. 188.130, N.D. Century Code 32-03-43, 42 Pa. Cons. Stat. Ann. §8305, S.D. Cod. Laws §21-55-1, Utah Code Ann. §78-11-24). The Congenital Disabilities (Civil Liability) Act, 1976 (UK) prohibits wrongful life claims in UK. The Patients' Rights and Quality of Care Act (passed on 4 March 2002) prohibited the award of compensation to a child 'wrongful life' claims in France.

nearly all Western jurisdictions have categorically denied wrongful life claims. The courts, in many jurisdictions, have rejected wrongful life actions on three grounds. The first and most significant reason is the precious value of human life. Second, the actions depend on acceptance of the proposition that some people would be better-off dead. Third, judges reject wrongful life actions because it requires them to compare the existence of a life with disability to its non-existence. The concerns of the sanctity of life have been voiced by courts in various jurisdictions whilst rejecting claims of wrongful life actions. The universal hostility to wrongful life claims in recognition of sanctity of human life can be ascertained from the rationale for rejecting wrongful life claims across jurisdictions.

PRECIOUSNESS OF HUMAN LIFE

The United States judiciary holds that a child born with congenital disabilities cannot claim damages from the medical professional whose negligence resulted in his or her birth. Preciousness of human life was the ratio decidendi, laid down by the Supreme Court of New Jersey in the leading case of *Gleitman* v. *Cosgrove*[65] in 1967. In this case, a pregnant woman informed her obstetrician that she had suffered from rubella during the first month of her pregnancy. The doctor assured her that this would not affect her foetus although he knew that 20 per cent of foetuses exposed to the virus during the first trimester would be born with disability.[66] The woman gave birth to a child who suffered from vision, hearing, and speech disabilities.[67] The child alleged that the 'injury' caused by the physician's negligence was 'be[ing] born to suffer with an impaired body', since his mother would have aborted him had she been fully apprised of his impairments.[68] Concluding that it was 'logically impossible' to 'measure the difference between lives with disability against the utter void of nonexistence', the court rejected the claim as not cognizable under law.[69] Ultimately,

---

[65] 227 A.2d 689 (N.J. 1967) (hereinafter referred to as '*Gleitman*').
[66] *Gleitman*, 227 A.2d at 690.
[67] *Gleitman*, 227 A.2d at 691.
[68] *Gleitman*, 227 A.2d at 693–4.
[69] *Gleitman*, 227 A.2d at 692.

in *Gleitman*, the court refused to recognize a claim for wrongful birth or wrongful life because of the 'countervailing public policy supporting the preciousness of human life'.[70] In *Becker* v. *Swartz*,[71] a similar case, the court concluded that the action was fundamentally flawed, primarily because the infant plaintiff could not be shown to have suffered a legally cognizable injury in the absence of a corresponding right to be born as a whole, functional human being.

Many states in the US have denied wrongful life claims following *Gleitman*. The legislatures of several other states have explicitly barred wrongful life claims.[72] Some statutes provide that there shall be no cause of action based on the claim that, but for the conduct of another, the claimant 'would not have been conceived or once conceived, would not have been permitted to have been born alive'. Many courts have reasoned that a life burdened with 'defects' is better than no life at all and thus that the plaintiff child suffered no legally cognizable injury in being born. Except three states,[73] courts in the US have consistently rejected wrongful life claims based on the value-of-life principle and policy concerns of diminishing the value of life with disabilities.

'BETTER OFF NOT TO BE BORN':[74] DIMINISHING THE VALUE OF LIFE WITH DISABILITY

If the physician presumes to take into consideration in his or her work whether a life has value or not, the consequences are boundless and the physician becomes the most dangerous man in the state. The

---

[70] *Gleitman*, 227 A.2d at 693.

[71] 46 N.E.2d 401 (N.Y. 1978) (hereinafter referred to as '*Becker*').

[72] See, for example, Idaho Code Ann. § 5-334(1) (2004); Ind. Code Ann. § 34-12-1-1 (LexisNexis 1998); Mich. Comp. Laws Ann. § 600.2971(2) (West Supp. 2007).

[73] Only the Supreme Courts of California, New Jersey, and Washington recognized a cause of action for wrongful life. See, for example, *Curlender* v. *Bio-Science Labs*, 165 Cal. Rptr. 477, 489–90 (Cal. Ct. App. 1980); *Procanik* v. *Cillo*, 478 A.2d 755, 764 (N.J. 1984); *Harbeson* v. *Parke-Davis, Inc.*, 656 P.2d 483, 496 (Wash. 1983) 985 (N.J. Super. Ct. App. Div. 1988).

[74] Kennedy and Grubb (2000: 1586).

seminal English decision of *McKay* v. *Essex Area Health Authority*[75] in 1982 laid the foundation for rejection of wrongful life claims on the reason that they would diminish the value of life with disability. In *McKay*, a pregnant woman infected with rubella was unaware of the risk because the defendant's laboratory failed to diagnose her illness through blood tests.[76] She gave birth to a girl with disability. The girl filed a wrongful life action against her mother's doctor. The Court of Appeal unanimously rejected the child's action for wrongful life,[77] as human life possesses an inherent value irrespective of its quality that prevents the claim of 'it would have been better off than to be born'.

In 1996, the Supreme Court for civil and criminal matters in France (Cour de cassation) quite surprisingly allowed for recovery under a wrongful life claim. In the *Perruche*[78] case, the court allowed the wrongful life claim of a boy born with both mental and physical disabilities. The contention was the negligence of medical personnel who incorrectly informed the boy's mother that she did not have rubella during pregnancy. The error resulted from the combined negligence of her physician and the laboratory that examined her blood. The court held: 'Since the faults of the doctor and the laboratory committed in the performance of their contracts with the mother had prevented her from exercising her choice to abort a severely handicapped child, the latter could claim compensation for the loss resulting from the handicap and caused by the faults.'[79]

In this case, the court looked into contractual aspects rather than the value of life. The court had taken into consideration of the failure of the doctor's duty to inform the mother as to the 'foetal defect'. Had the court looked through the prism of value of human life, the decision would have been a different one. However, this French revolution

---

[75] [1982] QB 1166 (hereinafter referred to as '*McKay*').

[76] *McKay*, at 1172–4.

[77] Also see *Harriton* v. *Stephens* [2006] 226 ALR 391 (hereinafter referred to as '*Harriton*').

[78] *Perruche* judgement, Cass.Ass.Plén., 17.11.00, J.C.P. G2000 11-10438, 2309 (Cour de Cassation).

[79] Cass.Ass.Plén., 17.11.00, J.C.P. G2000, 11-10438, 2309 (Cour de Cassation).

was short-lived. The intense criticism resulted in a legislative response and on 10 January 2002, the Assemblee Nationale adopted a bill whereby no person might claim that he or she was damaged by being born.[80] This legislation placed France in line with the vast majority of Western jurisdictions.

LOGIC OF COMPARISON BETWEEN 'EXISTENCE' AND 'NON-EXISTENCE'

The reason for the impossibility of comparing existence and non-existence was taken up by an Australian court for the first time in *Harriton*[81] and *Waller* v. *James*[82] in 2002. In *Harriton*, the plaintiff's disabilities resulted from her mother's exposure to rubella during pregnancy. In *Waller*, the plaintiff's disabilities resulted from a genetic blood-clotting disorder. In both cases, the plaintiffs owed their very existence to the doctors' conduct. The cause of action was the negligence of the doctors in informing the risk of congenital disability. In both cases, the plaintiffs contended that the defendant owed a duty of care to diagnose their mother's illnesses and to advise their mothers that the only way to prevent the serious congenital disabilities was to terminate the pregnancy. The court held that it does not owe duty of care, first, because establishing damage in wrongful life cases would require an impossible comparison between existence and non-existence, and second, because the recognition of wrongful life actions would be contrary to sound legal policy.[83] The sound legal policy mentioned by the court entails the value of human being and his or her right to be protected. The sanctity of life requires the law to treat everyone equally and to protect them

---

[80] Assemblee Nationale, 11eme Legislature, adopted on 10 January 2002, available online at http://www.assembleenationale.fr/ta/ta0757.asp (last accessed on 30 August 2011).

[81] [2006] HCA 15.

[82] [2002] NSWSC 461, [2015] NSWCA 232, the appeal had been dismissed. Copy of the judgement is available online at https://www.caselaw.nsw.gov.au/decision/55ca8eafe4b0a51fc30ef029 (last accessed on 30 January 2016) (hereinafter referred to as '*Waller*').

[83] Stretton (2006: 1).

equally. Thus, the law cannot be biased on the reason of qualities of human life.

These case laws encapsulate the absolute preference for life in wrongful life claims, which has been derived from the general principle of the sanctity of life. Further rejection of wrongful life claims on the ground that they diminish the value of lives with disability points towards recognition of the equal value of all human beings. The fact that many courts and legislatures persistently refused to recognize these actions suggests that there are lingering concerns about the impact and inequality that may emerge from these actions on the community of people with disabilities.[84] If the plea of wrongful life claims were considered by the courts as legally sustainable, it would have been counterproductive. Jurisprudential non-recognition of wrongful life claims developed a precedent for recognition of the value of human life.

Thus, courts have considered wrongful life claims to be against the spirit of the sanctity of life. The sanctity of life propounds that human life has an intrinsic value, that value a person just for being a human being. The sanctity theory does not bother about the personal value of an individual. It does not take into consideration the welfare a human life gives to others and to the person himself. Since the law has adopted principles based on the sanctity of life, it is under an obligation not to discriminate against any form of life. When it comes to wrongful life claims, courts are confronted with the legal obligation to recognize and affirm the value of human life under the sanctity principle. If courts are inclined to treat a life with disability as lesser than any other human life and not worth living, it would mean that courts have discriminated against a human being. However, the above analysis shows that no court has adopted the view that a life with disability is not worthwhile to live. Instead, all the wrongful life cases failed in the court because courts have declined to give up the principle of the sanctity of life. The persistent refusal to recognize wrongful life actions suggests that there are lingering concerns about the impact of these torts on persons with disabilities. However, it would be worthwhile to examine the other set of claims, known as wrongful birth claims, which exist along with wrongful life claims.

---

[84] Hensel (2005: 163).

WRONGFUL BIRTH CLAIMS

Wrongful birth claims are claims brought by the parents of a child with disability for the negligence of the medical professional who denied the choice of abortion to parents by not informing the presence of disabilities of the foetus. In wrongful birth claims, the injury identified is the lost choice of the parents over the future of the pregnancy. The case laws discussed earlier, for wrongful life actions, were brought along with wrongful birth claims by the parents. Here, contrary to wrongful life claims, courts have accepted claims for wrongful birth. But the courts have allowed such claims on grounds such as deterring negligence in genetic testing, preserving parental autonomy, and compensating parents for the medical expenses associated with disability. Thus, it can be analysed that when the medical profession creates a 'single model' of perfect humans, it creates a pressure of adherence. If any human deviates from this model, the only solution afforded by the medical profession is to select out that human. If the medical profession instead prepares to deal with different models of human beings, it would widen the scope of medical science and its service to humanity.

It is important to appreciate that the cause of action for wrongful birth was not recognized by courts until *Roe* was decided. In *Roe*, the US Supreme Court recognized the reproductive choice of women to decide whether to continue a pregnancy or not. Consequently, many courts have recognized wrongful birth claims whilst rejecting wrongful life claims. The lost choice of parents to abort is the label in wrongful birth cases. A critical analysis of judgements and their ratio decidendi shows that, in wrongful birth claims, courts have never rendered their judgement based on the child's life with disability. Instead, the courts have considered the parents' plea of the violation of their parental autonomy. Therefore, courts have limited their rationale to parental autonomy and related matters. Though wrongful birth claims are considered as diminishing the value of life with disability, a scrutiny of the judgements shows that the sanctity of life is not taken into consideration in such claims. At this juncture, we can see the dichotomy between wrongful life claims and wrongful birth claims. Wrongful life claims are not entertained by the courts in recognition of the sanctity of human life. Wrongful birth claims have been entertained by the courts, not by denying the sanctity of life, but by recognizing the right to abortion or parental autonomy.

However, the above interpretation may be correct only for the lone purpose of judicial analogy. An analysis in terms of the sanctity of life may give another picture of diminishing human value, deviating from the sanctity of life. Wrongful birth claims are brought by parents citing the lost choice of abortion that they are unfortunate to give birth to a child with disability. Though the courts have based their reason on parental autonomy to allow wrongful birth claims, the very reason for bringing such a claim is the disability of the child. Then we must say that disability is considered something not worth living with or that disability diminishes the value of human life. However, this would warrant an analysis of knowing the reason for judiciary to take differing stands on wrongful life and birth claims. Have the courts based their reason on the idea of equality and its original enlightenment notion of equal worth of every human being?

A prominent ethical value of this 'equality' propounded in Enlightenment ideas of the eighteenth century, is *human dignity*, the fundamental worth of human beings, and of every individual human being. Immanuel Kant, an enlightenment moralist, goes even further to 'assess' human dignity. Kant values human dignity in a very precise sense, stating that human dignity is a 'value' that cannot be measured against other values, because it can never rationally be sacrificed or traded away for anything at all, not even for anything having an equal or more value.[85] This Enlightenment idea of human dignity has a further extension, which requires that all people be treated as alike in dignity; however, they might differ in other properties. The moral philosopher, Allen Wood analyses this Kantian idea and says:

> Equality based on human dignity is also not like the equality of two bills or coins you might find in your pocket. For these are equal only in what Kant would call 'price'.... Human dignity is equal only in the sense that as a value that is absolute, it is a value that cannot be compared or exchanged, hence a value that cannot be unequal.... This conception of human dignity goes far beyond the mere repudiation of inegalitarian aristocratic conceptions of the worth of human beings.

[85] Wood (2008: 3).

It is a direct challenge to every conception of human self-worth based on anything at all beyond humanity itself—not only on conceptions based on birth, wealth, power or social status, but even those based on intelligence, talent, achievement, or even moral character. Kantian ethics does not, of course, deny that these have value. But it holds that neither the skills or graces or virtues of human beings, nor their hateful or contemptible contraries, can add to or subtract from the worth of a human being.[86]

Thus, we can see here that the idea of equality has been imported to human dignity to affirm the equal worth of every human being. This fundamental egalitarianism built into the idea of human dignity can be understood as the most direct basis of many modern political and legal conceptions and principles. But, in wrongful birth claims, we can see the domination of 'quality of life' over 'human dignity' and the 'sanctity of life'. Then the question is whether a quality-of-life judgement is appropriate or suffices to value human life. If human life has to be valued in terms of its quality, how many would qualify for the test of worthiness to live? However, despite moral and legal worthiness of human life, there are policy ramifications that formulated laws that it is the basis of individual quality.

THE SANCTITY OF LIFE VERSUS THE QUALITY OF LIFE

Contrasting the intrinsic value of human life, the quality-of-life judgement dominates in medical decisions to withhold treatment for newborns with disabilities, physician-assisted suicide and the 'right to die,' and prenatal testing for foetal disability. In such decisions, the life of an individual is valued based on his worthiness to fellow beings and to the individual himself but not on the basis of intrinsic worth of human life. The legality of withholding treatment to newborns with disabilities arose in a set of cases known as the 'Baby Doe'[87] cases in the year 1982 in the US. The *Infant Doe* case,

---

[86] Wood (2008: 2–5).

[87] *Infant Doe* v. *Bloomington Hospital*, 464 U.S.961.(1983) (hereinafter referred to as 'Infant Doe'); *United States* v. *University Hospital*, 729 F.2d 144 (1984) (hereinafter referred to as 'University Hospital'); *Bowen* v. *Am. Hosp. Ass'n*, 476 U.S. 610 (1986) (hereinafter referred to as 'Bowen').

which commenced in 1982, was the first to draw significant political and legal attention to the issue,[88] and its facts are representative.

The case involved a child who was born with Down syndrome, as well as a tracheoesophageal fistula. In this condition, the upper part of oesophagus is not connected to the lower part. Though surgery to connect the oesophagus had a high prospect of success, the obstetrician pointed out to the parents that 'if the surgery were performed and if it were successful and the child survived, that this still would not be a normal child'.[89] Based on the obstetrician's advice, the baby's parents agreed not to authorize surgery, food, or water for the child. Nurses at the hospital initiated legal proceedings to override the parents' decision, but the Indiana courts ruled that the parents had the right to follow the obstetrician's recommendation. The baby died when he was six days old.

The right-to-life and disability-rights activists saw the case as proof that society was now falling down the slippery slope of disrespect for life. The court justified the decision of the parents as being in tune with the doctor's advice, which made a quality-of life judgement about the life of their baby with disability. The message given by the above judgement in support of the medical decision based on quality of life is a clear deviation from the principle of the sanctity of life. It also violated the principle of 'equality', a derivation of the sanctity of life. By justifying the denial of treatment to an infant with disability, the court ignored the constitutional right of equality. In addition, the court rendered a precedent to discriminate against infants with disabilities. It has radiant implications, as the judiciary does not adequately deal with the moral issue of right to life in awarding damages to remedy tortious actions. Consequently, the court also promoted the medical judgement that the life of an infant with disability is of significantly less value than that of a non-disabled infant.

Assisted suicide and its legalization is the other instance that contravenes the sanctity-of-human life understanding. American cases have uniformly allowed competent patients to make quality-of-life

---

[88] Bagenstos (2006: 429).

[89] Minow (1990: 328–33); Haddon (1985). Where science fails to improve the quality of life, in tune with medical criteria, the very same argument is postulated to eradicate those lives.

judgements in determining whether to accept further life-sustaining medical intervention. This was the case, for example, when gangrene-stricken patients declined surgical amputation, which could have pre-served their lives for years.[90] Similarly, quality-of-life decisions have been made by persons with disabilities—usually quadriplegics—who decided upon discontinuance of respirator support or artificial nutrition and hydration necessitated by their debilitating medical conditions.[91]

In 2005, the case of *Terri Schiavo*[92] aroused the longstanding claim that any judgement that death is preferable to life violates the important concept of the sanctity of life. In this case, the court allowed the plea of the husband to let Ms Schiavo die, as her impoverished quality of life in a permanently unconscious state had 'no value'. The Florida court's acceptance of such a determina-tion contravened society's supposed respect for the intrinsic value of all human life. *Shanbaug's* case[93] highlights the voyage taken by

---

[90] *Lane* v. *Candura*, 376 N.E.2d 1232 (Mass. App. Ct. 1978); *In re Quackenbush*, 383 A.2d 785 (Morris County, N.J. 1978).

[91] See *Bouvia* v. *County of L.A.*, 195 Cal. App. 3d 1075, 241 Cal. Rptr. 239 (Cal. App. 1987); *Georgia* v. *McAfee*, 385 S.E.2d 651 (Ga. 1989); *Mackay* v. *Bergstedt*, 801 P.2d 617 (Nev. 1990).

[92] *Schindler* v. *Schiavo* (*In re Schiavo*), 780 So. 2d 176, 180 (Fla. Dist. Ct. App. 2001) (hereinafter referred to as '*Schiavo*'), which affirmed the trial court's decision to withdraw feeding and hydration to Ms Schiavo. The opinion of the trial judge in the Circuit Court of Pinellas County, Florida is unpublished, but its findings regarding the clear and convincing evidence of Ms Schiavo's wishes were summarized in Florida District Court of Appeals Judge Altenbernd's third appellate opinion as follows: (i) Ms Schiavo's medi-cal condition was the type of end-stage condition that permits the withdrawal of life-prolonging procedures; (ii) she did not have a reasonable medical probability of recovering capacity so that she could make her own decision to maintain or withdraw life-prolonging procedures; (iii) the trial court had the authority to make such a decision when a conflict within the family pre-vented a qualified person from effectively exercising the responsibilities of a proxy; and (iv) clear and convincing evidence at the time of trial supported a determination that Ms Schiavo would have chosen in February 2000 to withdraw the life-prolonging procedures.

[93] *Aruna Ramchandra Shanbaug* v. *Union of India and Others* 2011 (1) SCALE 673 (hereinafter referred to as '*Shanbaug*').

the Indian judiciary to sanction passive euthanasia, thereby legally withholding any medical treatment, and to let the person die. Even though the apex court rejected[94] the plea, made by a journalist, of euthanasia for Shanbaug, the court opened the window of opportunity to legalize euthanasia within the existing legal framework.[95] These incidents narrate the dominance of 'quality of life' overriding 'equal worth and dignity' of every human being.

[94] Aruna Shanbaug was a nurse at King Edward Memorial (KEM) Hospital, Mumbai, India. On the evening of November 1973, she was brutally assaulted and suffered acute brain damage, which relegated her to a 'vegetative' status. Since her relatives abandoned Aruna Shanbaug, her colleagues at the hospital took care of her for three decades. In 2009, a dramatic twist occurred in Aruna's life, as Pinki Virani, a journalist, who wrote a book on her, called *Aruna's Story*, approached the Supreme Court of India (SC), seeking a direction for KEM hospital to stop feeding Aruna, to let her die 'peacefully'. However, the court endorsed the recommendation of the team of doctors not to allow euthanasia for Aruna. Since the dean of the hospital filed an affidavit and unequivocally dismissed the possibility of euthanasia for Aruna, the court could have wrapped up the case there. However, while the SC rejected euthanasia for Aruna, it chose to go beyond its call of duty, by deciding on the larger question of whether euthanasia should be permitted in India. The judgement provided the guidelines or procedure to seek permission for passive euthanasia. (Aruna passed away on 19 May 2015.) However, the plea for euthanasia for Aruna clearly shows the lack of 'dignity and equal worth' to value human life.

[95] Mody (2013: 213). The 10th case in the book, narrated in the chapter titled 'Killing Me Softly: The Euthanasia Debate in India', which according to the author changed India, is *Shanbaug*.

Interestingly, the Indian legal system does not recognize the right to die as part of right to life. Both attempt and abetment to suicide are punishable offences under penal law. In *Gian Kaur* v. *State of Punjab* AIR 1996 SC 1257, the very same Supreme Court had taken a stand that right to life did not include right to die. It was by overruling its own decision, in *Rathinam* v. *Union of India* AIR 1994 SC 1844, that it struck down Section 309 (punishment for attempt to suicide) of the Indian Penal Code. The reasoning was that the right to die fell within the ambit of the 'right to life' accorded under Article 21 of Indian Constitution. Within this legal framework, where the right to 'die' is not permitted, the fresh euthanasia sanction ignites the question of what is a 'life-worthy life'.

The right-to-life advocates contend that a quality-of-life ethic undermines the sanctity of life. This disposal lives on quality-of-life account conveys an alarming message. These negative judgements communicate that life with disability is not worth living. This message devalues the life of persons with disabilities and contradicts the notion of the sanctity of life that every human life is valuable without regard to its quality.

Legalization of prenatal testing for foetal disability and selective abortion is the other legal implication of deviation from the sanctity-of-life principle. Since *Roe*, pro-choice activists and politicians have frequently and successfully invoked 'foetal deformity' as a circumstance in which abortions should clearly be permitted. Consequently, prenatal testing was made routine to diagnose foetal deformities and abortion laws have been liberalized to abort such foetuses. These laws give a negative message about the lack of value of persons with disabilities. Any legalized practice that suggests that a certain kind of human life is not worthwhile violates the principle of the sanctity of life. In addition, disability-selective abortions are unproblematically carried out by relying on quality-of-life arguments. Such arguments perceive a disabled life to have less quality, hence 'selecting them out' before coming into this world seems a better option. Does this imply that quality of life is not relevant for persons with disabilities?

IS QUALITY OF LIFE RELEVANT FOR PERSONS WITH DISABILITIES?

Quality of life is equally relevant for persons with disabilities. It is an important parameter to adopt social justice measures. The quality of life of an individual is not solely tied to material wealth, but to the more elusive, but no less important, aspects of individual happiness and community belonging.[96] It is a multidimensional construct that has the potential to move beyond being the concept of one's personal situation.[97] The 'selecting out' of persons with disabilities, due to quality-of-life perceptions, is problematic because selecting out cannot confer quality of life on anyone. Further, this strategy fails to address the quality of life of existing people with disabilities.

[96] Braddock (2002).
[97] Jones (2003).

Persons with disabilities should be supported to have effective participation, which is equal to all others. Sometimes they may need support for matters that exclusively concerns them. Quality of life cannot be considered as a one-size-fits-all construct. To recall the story of Goldilocks and the three bears,[98] when Goldilocks sampled bowls of porridge that belonged to each of the three bears, she declared one too hot, one too cold, and one 'just right'. However, to the mama bear, the porridge of the correct temperature was the one that Goldilocks had considered too hot. A person's perception is impacted by his or her relationships, age, sex, geographic location, and developmental stage in life.[99] Using quality-of-life reasoning to justify selective abortion on the ground of disability feeds invidious discrimination.

***

The sanctity of life is the fundamental principle that values human life intrinsically. The above analysis of theological and legal ramifications of the sanctity of life shows that it is the principle that produced the fundamental doctrines that protect human life. The theological prohibition on contraception and abortion was prevalent in an era where social Darwinism and eugenic theories postulated the ideology of better human beings through selective breeding. Therefore, it can be ascertained that the sanctity of life received great public policy support in the said period.

The legal ramification of the sanctity of life has been seen in the principles of equality, right to life, punishment for killing human beings, and in the judicial stand on wrongful life and wrongful birth claims. Courts have refused to make a finding that any person would be better off dead and have refused remedies in the wrongful life actions because of their assumption that granting a remedy would inherently involve endorsing such a claim. The rejection of wrongful life claims endorses that such claims would undermine lives with disabilities.

Courts have always acknowledged that states have a significant interest in promoting the sanctity of life, meaning respect for the intrinsic value of human life. Thus, the sanctity of life has been seen as the

---

[98] Cummins (1923).

[99] Felce and Perry (1996).

most fundamental of all ethical and legal principles. However, later public policy ramifications resulted in legal sanctioning of practices that contradict the sanctity of life or diminish the value of human life. As a result, we have seen the overturning of practices and principles based on the sanctity of life. In contrast to the intrinsic value postulated by the sanctity of life, there began the practice of valuing human life based on the quality of life.

Development of science and consequent technological advancement triggered the notion of quality of life. Philosophers who support valuing human life based on its quality have consistently argued for exploitation of technology to improve the quality of life. Where technology failed to improve the quality of human life in tune with medical criteria, the very same quality-of-life argument was postulated to eradicate such lives. Thus, those humans, who are below the threshold of medical quality, became vulnerable to the process of cleaning-up.

The medical practices discussed above, such as withholding of treatment for newborns with disabilities, and prenatal testing and selective termination of foetuses because of disability, detail the notion of quality of life. They explain how science and law marry to import quality of life into human lives. The said medico-legal practices limit the quality of life to individual perfection. Thus, the quality of life promoted under the medical scenario of individual perfection has caused the exclusion of socio-economic developments from the notion of *quality of life*. This has led to the emergence of laws that permit termination of humans who fail to reach the standard of quality postulated by science and medicine. Even though quality-of-life arguments undermine the value of a disabled life, they retain relevance for persons with disabilities. As disability is an integral part of the human condition, disability-selective abortions cannot obviate the need to adopt measures to enhance the quality of life for existing people with disabilities. The unspoken question is whether quality-of-life justifications for disability-selective abortions also dilute obligations to ensure the quality of life of persons with disabilities.

Abortion, prenatal testing and selective termination, and euthanasia laws are examples of such quality-of-life practices. At the same time, the principles of equality, right to life, and inherent dignity of human life postulated under the sanctity of life, clubbed with human rights, have contributed to development of laws that protect humans who were targeted under 'quality of life' or utility. However, this contradiction between the value of human life and rights of human beings can be found in the human rights arena as well. One such prominent contradictory legal position can be found in India's selective-abortion law. In the following chapter, I will analyse the contradictory gender and disability perceptions of laws that permit prenatal testing and selective abortions.

CHAPTER THREE

Varied Perspectives on Sex- and Disability-selective Abortions

· ·

The age in which we live is the 'age of science'. Whilst there is an argument that science and technology are value-neutral, another argument contends that the current technology does not benefit all segments of society equally, and is not meant to do so.[1] Most often, technology is used in a manner that produces or reinforces prejudice in human beings. This prejudice caused by science has more damaging moral and ethical consequences when it is selectively used against certain groups of human beings. The selection may be on the basis of their social or ethnic characteristics. Often, such selections are made on the ground that certain lives are below the threshold of the expected 'standard of perfection'. Whenever a human life is perceived as not being up to the expected societal standard, its existence is put at risk and subjected to the control of others. Science has facilitated

---

[1] Wolbring (2001: 38).

such selective control before birth. In fact, science prescribes 'selecting out', assuming it is good for the society. In the process, it fails to explore alternatives to this strategy.

Thus, science and technology create a division among human beings by talking of two classes of human beings, desired and undesired. Technological advancements are so influential that society internalizes such categorizing and provides legal permission to execute this division. Such legally sanctioned scientific practices contradict the ethical and legal principles of human dignity and equality. Although most modern laws try to prevent discrimination amongst human beings, some result in marrying with technology to achieve a society of *perfect bodies and minds*.

One such science-attributed legal position can be seen in the law that regulates the use of prenatal diagnostic techniques in India. India has enacted the Pre-Natal Diagnostic Techniques (Regulation and Prevention of Misuse) (PNDT) Act, 1994 to prevent sex-selective abortions or female foeticide. Sex-selective abortions are considered the most visible form of discrimination against women. But whilst prohibiting sex selection and thereby prohibiting gender discrimination, it permits selection of foetuses using the characteristics of disability. However, this legal position seems to be in contradiction to ethical and legal principles that accord inherent value, dignity, and equality to all human beings.

How can this paradox be justified? Is it justifiable to deny dignity, equality, and value to one section of people when they possess all those rights equally with other humans? Since both *sex selection* and *disability selection* for the purpose of abortion, display an analogous form of human discrimination, the legitimate question to be asked is: can the 'non-discrimination' norm behind prevention of sex-selective abortions be logically extended to disability-selective abortions? Is it legitimate to draw the principle of 'equality and non-discrimination' from sex-selective abortions to disability-selective abortions in light of the fundamental rights of equality and non-discrimination, and the right to life affirmed by both constitutional and human rights law?

With this as the objective, this chapter will analyse the nuances of prenatal tests and abortion laws in India, which demonstrate a contradicting legal stance on selective abortions. This will be analysed in the light of constitutional and human rights discourse.

PRENATAL TESTS AND SELECTIVE ABORTIONS

Prenatal tests were introduced in the 1960s to monitor high-risk preg-nancies. However, by the 1980s it became a routine medical check-up in many countries.[2] It has furthered the medicalization of pregnancy and childbirth with its various invasive and non-invasive methods. Prenatal tests mainly involve ultrasound, amniocentesis, and cho-rionic villus sampling.[3] This technology is widely used to diagnose neural tube defects or Down syndrome and other genetic deformities of the foetus. These prenatal techniques can be used to diagnose the sex of the foetus as well. Medical professionals prescribe prenatal tests not only as routine but highly necessary and desirable.[4] Consequently, women have accepted them as part of routine obstetric or childbirth care.[5] However, this has facilitated a routine elimination of certain foetuses with 'undesired' traits. Thus, the positive sanction for using prenatal scientific technology has produced a prejudiced selection of foetuses on the basis of certain characteristics such as sex and dis-ability. But these practices have been viewed from two perspectives, both by law and medicine.

Whilst sex-selective abortion is recognized as a malicious social prejudice against the female gender, disability-selective abortion is treated as part of healthcare. The medical profession perceives disability-selective abortions as an inevitable health intervention. They consider this a legitimate medical practice to prevent the birth of a baby with disabilities. Consequently, related laws, health policies, and healthcare programmes focus on the strategy of prevention of disability through prenatal diagnosis and disability-selective abortions. This unquestioned acceptance of disability-linked abortions shows that disability is seen as per se undesirable and human life with disability as not worth living. However, the positive sanction for disability-selective abortions is justified on the ground that it enables women to exercise their reproductive choice. This leads to a presumption that the consequences of

---

[2] Patel (2007b).

[3] For further details, see Kenny (1986).

[4] Ghai and Johri (2008: 298).

[5] Masden (1992).

discrimination or diminishing the value of women from sex-selective abortions cannot be extended to persons with disabilities. It presumes that disability, as an 'undesired' condition, deserves to be eliminated from society.

This contradictory strategy challenges the ethical and legal principles that recognize the value of every human life as equal, including persons with disabilities. Therefore, preventing one kind of discrimination and permitting another kind of discrimination clearly presents a contradictory logic. Explicit prohibition of sex-selective abortions and permission of disability-selective abortions by the very same law demonstrate the contradicting legal perception on disability.

SEX-SELECTIVE ABORTIONS VERSUS DISABILITY-SELECTIVE ABORTIONS

Selective abortions with the aid of medical technology seem like an element of the twentieth-century eugenic philosophy of selection on the basis of genotypes or traits. Selective abortion is a form of eugenic measure directed at the potential offspring identified as containing undesirable characteristics. It involves deciding which characteristic a human being ought to have to be a part of society and which he or she should not. In practice, gender and disability are the two characteristics that are targeted for selection in the Indian societal setting.[6] Thus, selective abortions discriminate against both the female gender and persons with disabilities.

SOCIAL PERCEPTION ON SELECTIVE ABORTIONS

Sex-selective Abortions

Sex-selective abortion is identified as a malicious social prejudice against the female gender, which diminishes her value. The ever-increasing skewed sex ratio of India is attributed to the practice

---

[6] India is one of the few countries that explicitly prevents sex-selective abortions but permits disability-selective abortions.

of sex-selective abortions.[7] Several studies confirm that the phenomenon of female deficit has very likely resulted from the rapid spread of ultrasound and amniocentesis tests in many parts of the country, followed by sex-selective abortions.[8] Studies reveal that the easy availability and simplicity of the tests, combined with the fact of socio-cultural predispositions such as strong son preference and the socio-economic burden of having a female child has promoted female specific abortions.[9] Many studies have shown that the perception of women as being 'burdensome and non-contributors to society' manifested itself in sex-selective abortions. Consequently, sex-selective abortions are condemned as a practice that manifests from gender bias. The bias against the female gender is flagrantly aided by medical technology that helps to detect the sex of the foetus and the liberal abortion law that permits abortion.[10]

A woman's right to reproductive choice not to have a girl child was also challenged because that right would violate gender equality and non-discrimination. An abortion law that promotes the autonomy or reproductive choice of women is also treated as a law that perpetrates gender discrimination. This prominent social pressure has fostered the enacting of laws that prohibit the practice of sex-selective abortions and thereby give special protection to the characteristic of gender. The social movement for gender equality was preceded by principles of human dignity, equality, and non-discrimination. In contrast, the non-discrimination perception of society towards the characteristic of disability and disability-selective abortions is not similar to that of the female gender and sex-selective abortions.

Disability-selective Abortions

Disability-selective abortions are considered an inevitable medical practice to eliminate disability. The medical model perceives disability

---

[7] This is evident from the sex ratio of the population. The number of women per 1,000 men steadily declined from 972 in 1991 to 933 in 2001. As per the latest census in 2011, the female sex ratio in India is 940 per 1,000 males.

[8] Miller (1989).

[9] Visaria (2007: 61).

[10] Visaria (2007: 70).

as an undesired condition or disease. It strongly influences society to perceive disability as an undesired characteristic that should be eliminated. The elimination of disability through disability-selective abortions has thus been taken as a much-needed step for constructing a better society consisting of only 'perfect bodies and minds'. Society has unconditionally internalized this prejudice. Therefore, the arguments that demand the prohibition of sex-selective abortions are unfavourably constructed towards disability-selective abortions. The demand for prohibition of sex-selective abortions as it discriminates against and diminishes the value of women has not been similarly considered for disability. On the contrary, disability-selective abortions are justified on the ground that a human life with disability is not worth living. This contradiction is reflected in the majority of arguments put forward to prohibit sex-selective abortions and allow disability-selective abortions.

One argument used to justify the prohibition of choice based on gender, while allowing those based on disability, is that persons with disabilities are a burden while women are not.[11] Interestingly, sex-selective abortions were not problematic in the Indian patriarchal society, until law and policies said otherwise. The widespread practice of son preference was felt justified considering the vulnerable status of Indian women. She was considered 'burdensome' by her family and society. However, later, law and policies that valued the equal status of women rejected this prejudice against the female gender. Consequently, society has recognized the value of the female gender, including the significant contributions of women to society. But the very same argument of being 'burdensome' still exists against persons with disabilities. They are considered a burden to their family as well as to society. The non-disabled majority also perceives the life of a person with disability as a misery.

Similarly, females were not only considered 'burdensome', but also 'non-contributors'. However, when law and policies started recognizing the equal value of the female gender, sex-selective abortions became an issue. Consequently, this argument was rejected as it produced prejudice against and injustice to the female gender. However, the very same argument is still used against persons with disabilities

[11] Wolbring (2001: 41).

to justify disability-selective abortions. Persons with disabilities are still considered people who cannot make contributions to society. They were referred to as 'useless eaters',[12] to mean persons who would consume resources without contributing to their production. Thus, the argument of 'being a burden on society' has been construed as a justification for disability-selective abortions.

In this context, it is pertinent to note that the reasons given to prohibit prenatal tests and sex-selective abortions are not extended to disability-selective abortions. The practice of sex-selective abortions was primarily challenged on the argument that it violates the right to equality and non-discrimination. Sex selection was thought to be 'a bad practice', mainly because of its apparent gender inequality. Finally, a law that explicitly prohibited prenatal tests to diagnose the sex of the foetus for selective abortion was required to enhance the values of equality and non-discrimination as applicable to women. Hence, a moral line has been drawn on sex-selective abortions. However, this moral line of equality is not extended to disability-selective abortions. Instead, disability-selective abortions are justified as a necessary practice to prevent the birth of persons with disabilities.

The laws that prohibit sex-selective abortions are a recognition of the fact that it lowered the status of women and perpetuated the situation that gave rise to it. The argument of 'diminishing value' by selective abortions was first raised for sex-selective abortions. This argument has never been extended to disability-selective abortions. Instead, disability-selective abortions are viewed as a major prevention strategy. The medical professionals suggest abortion as the sole solution whenever a prenatal diagnostic test gives any indication of disability. The parents are thereby provided with information that undermines the value of a human life with disability. Consequently, disability-selective abortions are carried out for the very same reasons for which sex-selective abortions are prohibited.

The other main argument for disability-selective abortions arises from: first, the obligation to reduce suffering for the affected family and the foetus when a serious and untreatable genetic disorder has

---

[12] The twentieth-century Nazi sterilization programme aimed at eliminating persons with mental and physical disabilities. For further details, see Board of Directors of the American Society of Human Genetics (1999: 337).

been diagnosed, and second, the medical obligation or commitment to prevent genetic disease and its impact on present society and future generations in the absence of effective genetic therapies. However, this argument clearly fails to fit those communities in which female offspring may also be perceived as burdens. If the non-desirability of disability arises from the notion of 'suffering', then the place to begin ameliorating that suffering is with the eradication of social discrimination[13] as in the case of non-desirability of a female child. Eradication of females by preventing their birth to prevent their suffering is not an acceptable argument. Likewise amelioration of suffering in the case of disability also should not be with the eradication of persons with disabilities. Indeed, the perception of 'burden', whether associated with gender or disability, is based on societal perceptions and familial circumstances. Selecting out to ameliorate individual suffering negates social justice obligations.

Since gender and disability face a similar kind of discrimination, this contradictory view raises serious questions as to its logic and justifiability. Hence, if we construe these arguments as not being applicable to 'disability', it suggests that the human condition of 'disability' and the persons who possess this condition do not deserve equality and respect. It also suggests that the principle of 'non-discrimination' cannot be equally applied to all in a society. This becomes serious when this contradictory view is reflected in law.

The relevant laws, policies, and medical programmes support disability-selective abortions. This practice implies that people with disabilities should not be welcomed into the family or the world.[14] This also suggests that abortion is the morally correct choice when a foetus is diagnosed with disability. The medical professionals and policymakers may hold that prenatal testing followed by pregnancy termination, if the foetus is diagnosed with disability, promotes public health. For them disability-selective abortion is simply one more legitimate method of avoiding disability in the world.[15] Thus, advanced medical technologies and related health policies, along with legitimization of abortion, try to prevent disability by preventing the

---

[13] Saxton (2000: 148).
[14] Asch (2001: 307).
[15] Asch, 'Bioethics and Human Rights,' 306.

births of persons with disabilities. Clearly, this contradictory legal position is explicit in the Indian laws that regulate prenatal tests and abortions. They prohibit sex-selective abortions but permit disability-selective abortions.

PRENATAL TECHNOLOGY AND ABORTION LAWS IN INDIA

India pioneered legalization of abortions under the Medical Termination of Pregnancy (MTP) Act, 1971. India has adopted the MTP Act in tune with common law. The legalization of abortion was thought to be a measure to prevent unauthorized abortions to save the lives of pregnant women. The MTP Act legalized abortion within 20 weeks of the pregnancy, on the grounds of saving the life of the mother or to prevent the birth of an 'abnormal' (in terms of physical and mental health) child. Accordingly, abortions can be legally availed if a pregnancy carries the risk of grave physical injury to a woman, or endangers her mental health, or when pregnancy results from contraceptive failure (only for married women), or from rape, or is likely to result in the birth of a child with physical or mental abnormalities.[16] Thus, it is always possible to terminate an undesired foetus with collaboration between the parents and medical professionals. However, apart from creating a supporting environment, the MTP Act does not provide anything explicitly that permits female-specific abortions. But it does provide explicit provisions that legitimize disability-selective abortions.

Disability-selective Abortions and the MTP Act

An analysis of the grounds for abortion provided under the MTP Act shows that they are primarily based on the physical and mental health of the mother. Though the MTP Act does not recognize a woman's right to abortion, it regulates the grounds on which abortions can be performed. A close analysis of these provisions shows that the law has sanctioned abortion for certain pregnancies, if such pregnancies cause grave physical or mental risk to the mother. Even a pregnancy resulting from failure of contraception amounts to causing physical

---

[16] Section 3, MTP Act, 1971.

or mental injury to the mother. These conditions for termination of pregnancy must be decided by a medical practitioner, if the pregnancy does not exceed 12 weeks. If the pregnancy exceeds 12 weeks but does not exceed 20 weeks, two medical practitioners have to form an opinion in good faith that the pregnancy involves risk to the life of the mother. It may be mentioned here that while all the other arguments point to the physical or mental risk to the pregnant woman, abortion on the ground of 'physical or mental abnormalities of the foetus' does not seem to have connection with the risk to life of the pregnant woman. Because, the law reads as follows: 'There is a substantial risk that if the child were born, it would suffer from such physical or mental abnormalities as to be seriously handicapped.'[17]

Thus, it can be seen that the law itself considers disability a substantial risk. But it is pertinent to note that the law is ambiguous to whom the 'substantial risk' belongs. In the face of this ambiguity, it may be assumed that disability is perceived as per se dangerous by the law. It is clear that disability is the most projected justification for abortion under the abortion law. Yet another point to be noticed here is that the 'substantial risk' of the child suffering from physical or mental abnormalities has to be decided by medical practitioners. In short, a positively sanctioned process of disability selection has to be carried out through a medical opinion. The medical profession has perceived disability as an 'abnormal condition' in comparison to the established norms of a 'normal' human being. Hence, the chances of reaching the medical conclusion that any disability involves substantial risk are high. This systemic medical perception of disability makes it easier to form a medical opinion that suggests abortion as the only one solution. Consequently, women are forced to take an automatic decision, denying them the choice of taking an informed decision about their children. Thus, prenatal tests and the explicit ground of disability for abortion make disability-selective abortion the legitimate objective of prenatal tests and the MTP Act. However, this aspect of law remains less visible when compared to sex selection. The issue of disability-selective abortion remains invisible even as it becomes more obtainable through the law that prohibits sex selection.

---

[17] Section 3(2)(b)(ii), MTP Act, 1971.

Sex Selection and Disability Selection in the PNDT Act

The PNDT Act, 1994 was enacted to prohibit sex-selective abortions. The overarching objective of the statute is the regulation of medical diagnostic techniques to prevent sex determination leading to sex-selective abortions or female foeticide. Section 3A of the PNDT Act provides:

> No person, including a specialist or a team of specialists in the field of infertility, shall conduct or cause to be conducted or aid in conducting by himself or by any other person, sex selection on a woman or a man or on both or on any tissue, embryo, conceptus, fluid or gametes derived from either or both of them.

Section 5(2) of the PNDT Act further prohibits communicating the sex of the foetus to any one by words, signs, or in any other manner. Section 6 prohibits the use of any kind of prenatal diagnostic technique including ultrasonography for the purpose of determining the sex of the foetus. The text of these provisions shows the rigid framework of law that prohibits the use of technology for sex selection. It can be seen that all possible restrictions have been created under the law to prohibit sex-selective abortions. This law considers any kind of prenatal diagnostic technique to determine the sex of the foetus as 'misuse' of technology. However, while prohibiting such techniques for sex selection, this law explicitly recognizes such techniques for the purpose of detecting genetic or metabolic disorders or chromosomal abnormalities or certain congenital malformations or sex-linked disorders.[18]

Section 4(2) says 'no prenatal diagnostic techniques shall be conducted except for the purposes of detection of any of the following abnormalities:—

(i)   chromosomal abnormalities;
(ii) genetic metabolic diseases;
(iii) haemoglobinopathies;
(iv) sex-linked genetic diseases;
(v)   congenital anomalies;
(vi) any other abnormalities or diseases as may be specified by the Central Supervisory Board.'

---

[18] Section 4(2), PNDT Act, 1994.

Later, the supervisory board specified that any indication of possible genetic disease or anomaly in the foetus, such as sporadic genetic disease in the couple, a positive screening test for carrier status, or positive screening test for genetic disease or congenital anomaly in pregnancy, etc. would be covered under the above provision.[19] Characteristics such as Tay-Sachs disease, beta-Thalassemia, sickle-cell anaemia, thalidomide, Alzheimer's disease, Phenyleketonuria,[20] mental disability, cystic fibrosis, cerebral palsy, spina bifida, achondroplasia, haemophilia, Down syndrome, coronary heart disease, osteoporosis, etc. would fall under the above 'abnormalities'.

Section 4(3)(iv) of the PNDT Act further provides for conducting prenatal tests if the pregnant woman or her spouse has a family history of mental retardation or physical deformities, such as spasticity or any other genetic disease. This points towards the extreme precaution taken by the law to prevent any birth with disabilities. The case of *Suchita Srivastava* v. *Chandigarh Administration*[21] exemplifies this law. Thus, the PNDT Act, whilst prohibiting sex selection leading to

---

[19] Under S.O.189 (E) dated 12 February 2004, dated 12 February 2004, published in the Gazette of India, notification by Ministry of Health and Family Welfare.

[20] It causes intellectual disability.

[21] AIR 2010 SC 235 (hereinafter referred to as '*Suchita*'). In this case, the Punjab and Haryana High Court ordered the termination of the pregnancy of a woman, about 19–20 years old, who was orphaned and unmarried, with mental disability. She was an inmate of a state-run institution for the mentally challenged in Chandigarh. The court order was reasoned in the best interest of the petitioner, in spite of the medical board's findings that the woman had expressed her willingness to bear a child and was physically fit to do so. However, considering the case on another set of premises, the Supreme Court stayed the order of the High Court with the view that the termination of the pregnancy was not in the best interests of the petitioner. Taking cognizance of reproductive rights, it ruled that a woman's right to reproductive decision-making is a dimension of the fundamental right to liberty under Article 21 of the Constitution. The Supreme Court's ruling is path-breaking, as it unequivocally endorses the respect for autonomy of persons with mental disabilities in the area of reproductive choice. Overcoming the legal struggle, she gave birth to a child without disability, who can medically be referred to as 'perfect' or 'normal'.

female foeticide, explicitly permits and promotes selection by reason of disability.

The above contextualization of disability in the law is intertwined with the medical perception in which any form of disability is treated as a disease. But the difference as to the term 'disease' lies in the medical approach towards 'treatment'. Though the objective of medicine is to treat and cure diseases, 'curing' of disability has been primarily strategized through disability-selective abortion. This medical strategy has married the law to produce the intended eradication of disability. Thus, the PNDT Act and the MTP Act together provide a legal framework to use prenatal tests to first detect 'abnormalities' of the foetus and then to terminate it. So, it can be seen that these laws render a different discourse on persons with disabilities, while assuring equality to women. Does this contradict the rights of equality and non-discrimination accorded by constitutional and human rights law?

EQUALITY, NON-DISCRIMINATION, AND RIGHT TO LIFE FROM THE CONSTITUTIONAL PERSPECTIVE

The principle of absolute equality postulates that everyone is to be treated absolutely equal in every respect. The idea of equality according to the principle of formal equality is that those who are in fact equal in a certain respect are to be treated equally and those who are in fact unequal ought to be treated unequally.[22] The significance of the equality principle can be understood from its legal framework provided in the Indian Constitution. Article 14 provides a negative prescription to the state from denying any person: (i) equality before the law, or (ii) equal protection of the laws within the territory of India. Prima facie, this is a formal declaration of the right to equality without any textual underpinning of recognition of difference amongst persons not equally situated.

However, the Supreme Court of India has on several occasions interpreted Article 14 to state that it is unjustified to treat 'unequals' equally.[23] While Article 14 permits reasonable classification, such

[22] Honderich (1989: 35, 36).
[23] *Onkar Lal Bajaj* v. *Union of India* AIR 2003 SC 2562.

classification cannot be made arbitrarily and without any substantial basis. The classification envisaged under Article 14 is meant to address various needs of different classes of persons and to bring them into the mainstream of the society. Furthermore, the principle of equality encapsulated in Articles 14–16 is now recognized as part of the basic structure of the Constitution.[24] Hence, the constitutional framework places equality on a high pedestal. The high value attributed to the principle of equality is also reflected in the constitutional provisions on non-discrimination.

The Constitution unambiguously prohibits discrimination on grounds of religion, race, caste, sex, and place of birth.[25] The constitutional principles of equality and non-discrimination have been enhanced by the fundamental freedoms and liberty guaranteed under the constitution. The right to protect life and liberty is the most significant among them. Article 21 of the constitution states: 'No person shall be deprived of his life or personal liberty except according to procedure established by law.' The right to life envisaged under Article 21 includes a wide range of rights that enhances human dignity. It has yielded judicial interpretations which have expanded its scope.

Indian courts interpreted the ambit of right to life very narrowly for almost three decades between 1950 and 1977, when, in the landmark ruling of the Supreme Court in *A.K. Gopalan* v. *State of Madras*[26] it was held that the right to life under Article 21 was mutually exclusive of the fundamental freedoms guaranteed under Article 19. This meant that Article 19 was not to apply to a law affecting personal liberty to which Article 21 would apply. It was further held in *Gopalan* that a law affecting right to life and personal liberty could not be declared unconstitutional on grounds of its failure to guarantee natural justice or due procedure. Thus, a law prescribing an unfair and arbitrary procedure could deprive a citizen of his right to life and personal liberty, as long as such law was enacted by a valid legislature.

The Supreme Court's ruling in *Maneka Gandhi* v. *Union of India*[27] brought about a transformation in judicial attitude towards right to

---

[24] *Indra Sawhney* v. *Union of India* AIR 2000 SC 498.
[25] Article 15, Constitution of India.
[26] AIR 1950 SC 27 (hereinafter referred to as '*Gopalan*').
[27] AIR 1978 SC 597 (hereinafter referred to as '*Maneka Gandhi*').

life and personal liberty guaranteed under the Constitution. Judicial activism at its best ensured that the scope of this most crucial right was extended to many areas not expressly laid down in the law and, in the process, read in many more fundamental rights and made it obligatory on the part of the State to fulfil many aspects which were, until then, constituents of the Directive Principles of State Policy. It was held in *Maneka Gandhi* that Articles 14, 19, and 21 of the Constitution were not mutually exclusive. Thus, a law prescribing a procedure or depriving a person of his personal liberty under Article 21 has to meet the requirements of Article 19. Further, the procedure established by law under Article 21 must be in consonance with Article 14 and must not be discriminatory or arbitrary and must be just, fair, and reasonable. It was in this case that the terms 'life' and 'personal liberty' were given an expansive meaning to move beyond mere animal existence. The case also read in several fundamental rights into and as part of the right to life under Article 21, even though those rights were not expressly mentioned in the Constitution.

This trend of expansion of the ambit of right to life was carried forward in subsequent cases. The Supreme Court gave an expansive interpretation to the term 'life' in *Francis Coralie Mullin* v. *Administrator, Union Territory of Delhi and Ors*[28] by extending it beyond mere 'physical or animal existence' and including the right to read, write, and express oneself and to lead a life of dignity. The Court held that 'the right to life includes the right to live with human dignity and all that goes along with it, namely, the bare necessities of life such as adequate nutrition, clothing, shelter over the head, and facilities for reading, writing, and expressing oneself in diverse forms, freely moving about and mixing and commingling with fellow human beings.'[29]

This view of extending the ambit of right to life under Article 21 to beyond mere animal existence (bios) to include political, social, and cultural participation (zoee) was reiterated by the Supreme Court in *Olga Tellis* v. *Bombay Municipal Corporation*[30] where it held that 'the inhibition against deprivation of life extends to those limits and faculties by which life is enjoyed'.

[28] AIR 1981 SC 746.
[29] AIR 1981 SC 746, at 753, Para 7.
[30] AIR 1986 SC 180.

On more than one occasion thereafter, the Supreme Court emphasized the point that the right to life under Article 21 must guarantee to every citizen something beyond just the life of an animal to include the needs of a human being including 'suitable accommodation which allows him to grow in all aspects, viz., physical, mental and intellectual'.[31] The Supreme Court further held in *P. Rathinam* v. *Union of India*[32] that the term 'life' has an expanded scope under Article 21 and defined 'life' as 'the right to live with human dignity and the same does not connote continued drudgery. It takes within its fold some of the fine graces of civilization which makes life worth living and that the expanded concept of life would mean the tradition, culture and heritage of the person concerned'.[33]

This view has been further followed and endorsed by the Supreme Court in *CERC* v. *Union of India*.[34] Another broad formulation of the theme of life with dignity is found in the decision of the Supreme Court in *Bandhua Mukti Morcha* v. *Union of India*,[35] where it was held that the right to life under Article 21 includes '[o]pportunities and facilities for children to develop in a healthy manner and in conditions of freedom and dignity, educational facilities.... These are the minimum conditions which must exist in order to enable a person to live with human dignity. No government can take any action to deprive a person of the enjoyment of these basic rights'.

The court in this case expressly included the provision for educational facilities within the ambit of right to life. It also broadened the scope of the right to life by including, in an overarching statement, 'opportunities and facilities' for children to develop in a healthy manner. These opportunities and facilities, it is submitted, may be interpreted to include educational and teaching aids and reading material, which aid a child in its mental and intellectual development.

---

[31] *Shantisagar Builders* v. *Narayanan Khimalal Totame* (1990) 1 SCC 520, p. 521, Para 9.

[32] (1994) 3 SCC 394.

[33] (1994) 3 SCC 394, p. 409, para 27.

[34] AIR 1995 SC 922.

[35] AIR 1984 SCC 802.

One of the most crucial aspects of the expansion of the ambit of the right to life under Article 21 of the Constitution is the provision for inclusion of the social, political, and cultural life of the person. Thus, the fundamental right to life guaranteed to all persons under the constitution includes the right to live with human dignity and to participate fully in the social, cultural, and political processes of the country. This goes beyond the biological concept of life encompassing only the vegetative state of being alive. As a result of such an expansion, the right to read, write, and fully express oneself becomes an integral part of the right to life under Article 21, because these rights are integral to a person's active participation in the political, social, and cultural processes of the country or of his or her communities.

Access to printed material is one of the most fundamental aspects of the right to read, write, and express oneself in order to form an informed opinion or make an informed choice in one's political, cultural, or social life. When persons with print impairment are denied access to printed material in alternative formats, their fundamental right to life guaranteed to them under the constitution is taken away from them since such denial of access will prevent their participation in the political and social aspects of their lives. Thus, it becomes an obligation on the part of the state to ensure that their fundamental rights are granted to them on an equal basis with other persons, by doing away with any gap which may exist in the law which prevents persons with print impairment from accessing information in the print format. Such action on the part of the state is not only within the framework of the constitution but is also an obligation to be fulfilled on its part.

Thus, the constitutional rights of equality and non-discrimination have much significance in enhancing human dignity and value. These rights are the foundation that eradicate social discrimination and thereby ensure a just society for all. When we examine its implications on gender and disability, it can be seen that 'gender' is abundantly recognized as a prohibited ground for discrimination. But disability is not explicitly covered as a prohibited ground for discrimination in the constitution. But it does not mean that disability is considered a ground for any kind of discrimination against persons with disabilities. On the contrary, judicial interpretation of the above rights renders equal protection to all citizens, irrespective of various classes or characteristics. Hence, evidently, the general formulations around equality and non-discrimination encompass persons with disabilities also. Thus, in a logical application of these fundamental rights, the norm of 'non-discrimination' enshrined in the constitution is equally applicable to disability.

At this juncture of equally applicable constitutional rights, the law that permits disability-selective abortions becomes capable of challenge for its violation of constitutional rights. These contradictory laws that deny fundamental rights to one section of the society are rendered questionable in the context of human rights law that universally confirms equality and non-discrimination to all in general and to women and persons with disabilities in particular.

HUMAN RIGHTS DISCOURSE ON GENDER AND DISABILITY

The universal recognition of inherent human dignity, equality, and non-discrimination is the foundation of human rights law. Human rights instruments respect all the diversities in human beings and protect the rights of all human beings. Article 1 of Universal Declaration of Human Rights (UDHR), 1948 states that 'all human beings are born free and equal in dignity and rights'. Thus, the United Nations (UN) Charter and subsequently, the UDHR, brought forth recognition and affirmation of the inherent dignity and equal and inalienable rights of all human beings. In furtherance of this international commitment, various group-specific international instruments have also been promulgated to safeguard the rights of vulnerable and discriminated groups of people. Women and persons with disabilities are two such discriminated groups. Gender and disability have been dealt with by the human rights law in varied human rights instruments. These human rights instruments affirm and recognize the fundamental rights to life, equality, dignity, and non-discrimination for women and persons with disabilities.

Gender and Human Rights Discourse

The equal status of women has been recognized by specific human rights instruments meant to protect the rights of women. The universal norm of 'gender equality' has been enunciated through many human rights instruments. Non-discrimination on the basis of sex is given equal validity with other prohibitions of discriminations in all human rights instruments. The conceptualization of equality, dignity, and non-discrimination has been further articulated in favour of women in the Convention on the Elimination of All Forms of Discrimination against Women (CEDAW).[36] Article 3 of CEDAW requires state parties: 'To take in all fields, in particular in the political, social, economic and cultural fields, all appropriate measures, including legislation, to ensure the full development and advancement of women, for the purpose of guaranteeing them the exercise and enjoyment of human rights and fundamental freedoms on a basis of equality with men'.

This global sense of gender equality has traversed in nationwide urge of reforming the laws, in order to eradicate discrimination on the ground of sex and to ensure equality to women. India ratified the CEDAW on 9 July 1993. Prohibition of sex selection also specifically forms part of the World Health Organization's Draft Guidelines on Bioethics and the Council of Europe's Convention on Human Rights and Biomedicine. Apart from these specific instruments, other human rights instruments such as the International Covenant on Civil and Political Rights (ICCPR), International Covenant on Economic, Social and Cultural Rights (ICESCR), the Convention on the Rights of Child (CRC), and so on create a legal regime which prohibits sex-based discrimination.

In India, the human rights scenario and the constitutional norm of equality impelled lawmakers to recognize equal status for women. Consequently, female foeticide was identified as blatant discrimination against women that amounted to gender abuse. As a result, the use of prenatal technology to detect the sex of a foetus was denounced and the practice of female foeticide was condemned as a symptom of 'civilizational collapse'.[37] A similar human rights pathway has been traversed to recognize and affirm all the rights of persons with disabilities.

---

[36] The CEDAW was adopted by UN General Assembly on 18 December 1979.
[37] Bose (2007: 80).

Disability and Human Rights Discourse

The human rights model considers disability an integral part of human diversity. It affirms that all human beings, irrespective of their disabilities or abilities, are entitled to certain inalienable rights. Human dignity is the anchor norm of human rights. Each individual is deemed to be of inestimable value and nobody is insignificant. This view is basically constructed upon the spirit of the UDHR, 1948.

The human rights model challenges the traditional medical model view of disability. The human rights model views disability as arising from social oppression which should be addressed as a human rights issue. The rights-based approach to disability essentially means viewing persons with disabilities as subjects of law. The final aim is to empower persons with disabilities and to ensure their active participation in political, economic, social, and cultural life in a way that is respectful and accommodating of their difference. This model has been rooted in the UDHR and other specific soft laws which aim to protect the rights of persons with disabilities. The United Nations Convention on the Rights of Persons with Disabilities (UNCRPD), 2006 is a landmark step towards affirming the right to equality and non-discrimination for persons with disabilities.

The UNCRPD is a culmination of rights affirmed by earlier international human rights instruments. Under the UNCRPD, disability is understood as a human rights issue. Discrimination on the basis of disability is a violation of human rights. This approach challenges inequality and discrimination imposed on persons with disabilities. The human rights approach seeks to promote the quality of socially marginalized groups beyond national borders. The rights-based approach to disability is normatively based on international human rights standards and operationally directed to enhancing the promotion and protection of the human rights of persons with disabilities. The rights-based approach towards persons with disabilities has been accorded full recognition in the UNCRPD. (The significance of the UNCRPD for persons with disabilities will be separately analysed in a later chapter.) However, in order to comprehend the evolution of international law on persons with disabilities, it is necessary to describe the soft laws and binding instruments preceding the UNCRPD. Because, even prior to adopting a specific binding instrument, various soft and hard UN law instruments had shown the concerns related to the rights of persons with disabilities.

PRE-CONVENTION LAWS AND THE RIGHTS OF PERSONS WITH DISABILITIES

Consequent to the desire for democracy and human rights after the Second World War, the UN unanimously adopted the UDHR on 10 December 1948. Although the UDHR has no legal force, its authority is unparalleled, as the single most important ethical statement on human rights. Many legal experts accord the status of international customary law to UDHR. The standards and principles specified by the UDHR have been constantly developed by international conventions on human rights, thus greatly promoting the cause of human rights. After the adoption of the UDHR, the development of human rights has acquired new dimensions. A human rights cooperative system among all countries has been formed, and cooperation and coordination among countries are conducted on the basis of the international conventions on human rights. The appearance of the above new factors has enabled the world human rights cause to make progress in all continents. The UDHR values inform the current human rights law on disability.

Two binding treaties, the ICCPR and ICESCR, are derived from it and both were adopted by the UN General Assembly in 1966. Together, these three texts form the international bill of human rights. The bill continues a tradition of three centuries of human rights thinking and more than two millennia of natural law. In its turn, it has inspired dozens of treaties.

The Declaration on Social Progress and Development, 1969, made an explicit mention of persons with disabilities, where it provided for the protection of rights and welfare of children, the aged, and the 'disabled'. It further made provision for the protection of the physically or mentally disadvantaged.

However, this normative inclusion was not reflected in recognizing the equal rights of persons with disabilities. National laws, which did not recognize persons with disabilities as persons before the law, continued to hold the field. Consequently, a need was felt to have laws which particularly focused on disability.

EARLY EFFORTS TO DEVELOP INTERNATIONAL STANDARDS ON DISABILITY

As an indication of the progress of status of persons with disabilities, the following soft laws, listed in Table 3.1, were adopted by the UN, to develop international standards on disability.[38]

All these soft laws have focused on ensuring the welfare of persons with disabilities, as they were viewed as helpless beings. The ominous silence on civil and political rights of persons with disabilities rendered the rights of persons with disabilities negotiable. The Standard

Table 3.1　Soft laws adopted by the UN

1971	Declaration on the Rights of Mentally Retarded Persons
1975	Declaration of the Rights of Disabled Persons
1981	International Year of Disabled Persons
1982	World Programme of Action concerning Disabled Persons
1989	Tallinn Guidelines for Action on Human Resources Development in the Field of Disability
1991	Principles for the Protection of Persons with Mental Illness and for the Improvement of Mental Health Care[39]
1982–92	International Decade of Disabled Persons
1993	Standard Rules on the Equalization of Opportunities for Persons with Disabilities (Standard Rules)
1993	Proclamation of the Economic and Social Commission for Asia and the Pacific on the Full Participation and Equality of People with Disabilities in the Asian and Pacific Region

[38] Nizar (2015).

[39] It must be noted that this soft law instrument was not included in the preambulatory statement of the UNCRPD. The World Network of Users and Survivors of Psychiatry have explicitly denounced this instrument as it was formulated without the participation of persons with disabilities. See Position paper on 'Principles for the Protection of Persons with Mental Illness', World Network of Users and Survivors of Psychiatry, available online at http://www.wnusp.net/index.php/position-paper-on-principles-for-the-protection-of-persons-with-mental-illness.html (last accessed on 9 February 2016).

Rules[40] provided a voice to persons with disabilities by adopting the right of participation. They defined disability by emphasizing the social conditions which disable a group of individuals by ignoring their need to access opportunities in a manner conducive to their circumstances. The Standard Rules inaugurated a rights-based discourse on disability.

TOWARDS RIGHTS-BASED STANDARDS ON DISABILITY

It is pertinent to note that, except for the Standard Rules,[41] all the other soft laws relating to disabilities endorse the medical model. All these soft laws support the dominance of the medical model. The language used to refer to persons with disabilities shows the medicalized perception of disability. These soft laws mainly adopted a welfare perspective towards disability. Accordingly, these soft laws continued to view persons with disabilities as individuals with medical problems, dependent on social security and welfare. Furthermore, even the entitlements guaranteed by these instruments were only incorporated in declarations, principles, and rules. These soft law instruments had no binding force in international law. Consequently, persons with disabilities continued to face discrimination and were often denied their human rights on an equal basis with others.

The above scenario is reflected in national laws that denied basic rights to persons with disabilities. The PNDT Act and MTP Act provide classic examples of national legislations that devalue the life of persons with disabilities. When compared to 'gender discrimination', the social perception of gender bias was not given legal endorsement. On the other hand, 'disability discrimination' has been accorded positive legal permission. In light of the constitutional and human rights discourse that affirms and accords all fundamental rights to both women and persons with disabilities, the continuing discrimination on grounds of disability is questionable. All law, including the constitution and international conventions, are enlivened by interpretation. While making interpretations, the main question would

---

[40] The Standard Rules were adopted by the General Assembly resolution 48/96 of 20 December 1993.

[41] Adopted by General Assembly resolution 48/96 of 20 December 1993.

be how we can ensure that socially just interpretations are adopted. This is because legal discourse has the power to create social realities. There is a reasonable justification to extend the principles of 'equality and non-discrimination' adopted for sex-selective abortions to disability-selective abortions as well.

***

Sex-selective abortions and disability-selective abortions display many contradictory concerns in their social and legal perceptions. If parents decide to abort a female foetus without disability, society treats that choice as the product of an irrational decision-making process that should not be given effect. At the same time, the abortion of a foetus with disabilities is considered a rational and unproblematic choice. Although disability-selective abortions have the same structure as sex-selective abortions, the law perceives them very differently. Both medical professionals and non-disabled members of the lay public believe that disability has a negative effect on the quality of life of people with disabilities.[42]

Non-disabled people thus readily conclude that the termination of a foetus on the reasons of disability is reasonable because it agrees with their own preconception that disability is unbearable suffering.[43] These biases can be seen in the 'intensely stigmatized language'[44] used in laws, where disability and people with disabilities are referred as defective, deformed, anomalous, and handicapped. This discriminatory and unequal treatment can be contrasted with the dignified outlook adopted in legislations[45] towards the female gender, another

---

[42] Bagenstos (2006: 435).

[43] See Ghai and Johri (2008: 299).

[44] Bagenstos (2006: 435).

[45] This contention is being made exclusively in relation to legislations addressing the matter of sex-selective abortions. I am not oblivious to the patriarchal biases of the law. Because, they get practised despite the law. See Smart (1989); also see Srinivasan (2006) who describes that there are some 350 cases filed under the PNDT Act. Of these, 226 are for running a diagnostic clinic without registration, 26 are for not maintaining accounts. A mere 37 are for communicating the sex of the foetus and 27 are for advertising

vulnerable section of human society. Even technology is not permitted to be misused to encourage gender inequality. In contrast, the justification for special protection of gender, based on the arguments of 'burden, discrimination and diminishing value' is generally perceived positively, but disability has been drawn as a justifiable ground for disability-selective abortion.

The restriction on prenatal tests and abortions in the law are justified in the name of equality and non-discrimination. If a prohibition on sex-selective abortions could be justified on those grounds, then it is contended that the same reasoning should suffice to challenge and prohibit disability-selective abortions. Such a strategy may need to be especially employed when the consequences of this phenomenon on the rights of persons with disabilities are examined. In the following chapter, I will analyse the implications of permitting disability-selective abortions on the rights of persons with disabilities.

---

sex selection. The first conviction involving a prison term was ordered on 28 March 2006, when a doctor and his assistant were sentenced to two years in prison and a fine of Rs 5,000 in Palwal, Haryana. More recently, a sex-selective abortion racket was unearthed in Pataudi, a town 40 km from New Delhi. The police say that A.K. Singh, the quack arrested for the murder of several unborn children and conducting illegal diagnostic tests, confessed to aborting over 260 female foetuses in the past decade.

CHAPTER FOUR

Perfection at the Cost of Excellence

Implications of Disability-selective Abortions

· ·

Disability is perceived as an undesirable trait in humanity. It is treated as a tragedy, similar to acquiring a life-threatening illness. Consequently, scientific efforts, which aim at eliminating disability, are widely welcomed in society. The technology that diagnoses the disability of a preborn child to offer selective abortion is considered an inevitable health intervention to prevent disability. However, this selective pre-birth elimination does not demonstrate the scientific norm of prevention from all the undesired diseases. Selective abortions allow selecting out the kinds of person undesired by society. They are sophisticated means of preventing the existence of one kind of humans. Selective abortions, it can be contended, demonstrate clear prejudice and discrimination against the persons who are being selected out. However, this prejudice differs when it comes to disability and persons with disabilities. Whilst, any other ground for selection is treated as prejudicial against those persons, disability selection is perceived as medically essential.

Scientific information facilitates both sex and disability selections, yet selective abortions on the grounds of disability alone are permitted. Here, law feeds the prejudice served by science. While scientific expertise can facilitate disability-based abortions, it demonstrates how prejudiced it is against persons with disabilities. While applying life-valuing principles, disability-selective abortions would seem to devalue persons with disabilities. When science aims at achieving perfect minds and bodies for human beings, it undermines the significance of having diverse minds and bodies for human kind, and thereby, shuts the door of science to explore diverse lives.

Is creating a model of flawless human beings beneficial to society? When science, law, and policies promote selecting out foetuses with disabilities, do we miss or lose anything? Does it prevent some valuable contributions to humanity? Does this prejudice impact persons with disabilities alone or all of humanity? What do current policies, programmes, and laws around prenatal tests, followed by selective abortions, signal about the social acceptance of diversity? Does society gain anything while law and policies promote selecting out foetuses with disabilities? Does disability-selective abortion deny social justice to persons with disabilities? Legitimacy of disability-selective abortion requires answering these questions.

It is the aim of this chapter to explore the wider implications of prenatal tests and disability-selective abortions in a society already prejudiced against persons with disabilities. Let us first examine the role of prenatal tests in disability-selective abortions.

TECHNOLOGY TO SELECT OUT DISABILITY

Contrary to the initial objective of assisting pregnancies that involved risk to the lives of mothers, the new reproductive technology has been turned into a tool for screening foetal 'defects'. In a country like India, when many low-income women do not have access to any healthcare during pregnancy, millions are being spent on genetic tests and sophisticated ultrasound techniques to detect the genetic conditions of a foetus. It suggests that persons with disabilities are still viewed as inadequate beings, destined to have miserable and unproductive lives.[1] Hence, to many of the 'able-bodied' individuals, it seems rational to use prenatal tests and, based on the results, resort to disability-selective abortions. However, when science promotes disability-selective abortion as a primary mode of disability prevention, it actually promotes getting rid of persons with disabilities. In this manner, disability-selective abortions aim for a society consisting of flawless human beings. The question then is creating a model of flawless human beings beneficial to society? The historical origin of the human urge for perfect bodies and minds indeed limelight the persisting societal intolerance towards diverse minds and bodies. It is interesting that while suffering associated with disability is assigned a negative value, suffering that is inflicted voluntarily on the self in order to achieve physical perfection is valorized. As Welsch puts it,

> The current aestheticization seems to attain its consummation in individuals. We are experiencing everywhere a styling of body, soul and whatever else these fine people might want to have (or acquire for themselves). In beauty salons and fitness centres they pursue the aesthetic perfection of their bodies, and in mediation courses and Toscana seminars the aesthetic spiritualisation of the souls. Future generations should then have it easier straight away: genetic technology will have come to their aid ahead of them; this new branch of aestheticization which holds the prospect of a world full of perfectly styled 'mannequins'.[2]

THE PURSUIT OF HUMAN PERFECTION

The idea of human perfection can be traced back to evolutionary theories, which set forth nature's role in perishing weaker traits and preserving better traits. As discussed in a previous chapter, evolutionary theories created many paths to study the phenomenon of genetic determinism. The said biological explanations were later used as quality-control measures to seek control over the reproductive realm. By the end of the nineteenth century, those theories evolved into

---

[1] Blumberg (1994a: 138).
[2] Welsch (1996: 6).

eugenic measures that controlled the quality of population.[3] Thus, well before the science of genetics, scientists proposed eugenic measures to stem the perpetuation of 'defects'.[4] The diabolical impact of human efforts to create flawless human beings can be seen from the Holocaust.

The Nazi regime launched eugenically-motivated measures to control the quality and purify the population. Under the Nazis, people with disabilities were persecuted with ruthless efficiency.[5] Sterilization was carried out on 5 per cent of the population, and upon the outbreak of war, a ferocious euthanasia programme led to the death of 200,000–275,000 people, a majority of them with mental or learning difficulties.[6] Medical professionals were at the forefront of Nazi eugenic and euthanasia programmes.[7] It reminds us of the danger in attempting to improve the 'stock' of the population.[8]

Thus, earlier attempts to achieve a perfect society filled with perfect bodies and minds have destroyed many lives. They also perpetuated diminishing the value of people who were targeted for their different traits. Therefore, when new reproductive technology is used for selecting out particular kinds of foetuses because of their associated disability, it represents a quality-control measure as in the old eugenics. The eugenic nature of current prenatal tests and selective abortions raises a wide range of implications for contemporary society, which is constructed on the principles of equality and non-discrimination. A major area where it causes conflict is in the reproductive realm.

REPRODUCTIVE CHOICE IN THE DISABILITY CONTEXT

The decision to abort any foetus obviously brings major ethical considerations with it, both for the parents and the society. Therefore, selective abortion is not only the choice of an 'unwanted pregnancy',

---

[3] See Chapter 1 of this volume: 'The Interplay between Natural and Social Selection'.

[4] Hubbard (2006: 93).

[5] Gallagher (1995); Shakespeare (2006: 86).

[6] Burleigh (1994); Gallagher (1995); Shakespeare (2006).

[7] Lifton (1986).

[8] Bailey (1996: 144).

but it also involves the choice of 'the kind of children' that the parents wish to have. Therefore, medical professionals often represent genetic testing, especially prenatal diagnosis, in terms of empowerment. They claim that science has created technology that provides prospective parents with information empowering them to make choices. The medical community, pro-choice advocates, and feminists argue that prenatal tests and abortions are integral to enhance women's reproductive rights. They believe that such absolute freedom for women over their bodies is essential for their empowerment. They also use an emotional argument that restriction of the right to abort a foetus with possible disability would be like forcing women to have 'defective children', in violation of reproductive choice. The selectiveness involved in such abortions limits women from having a meaningful choice over their bodies. Surprisingly, right-to-life activists are also frequently willing to 'compromise' and exempt 'deformed' foetuses from their anti-abortion stance.[9] If this argument is sound, then it should also be contended that the non-sanction for sex-selective abortions restrict women's reproductive choice. After all, decisions to abort both foetuses with disability and of the female sex are taken on the basis of almost similar social and economic reasons.

In a country such as India, often, parents decide not to have a female child, considering the societal treatment meted out to her. Non-recognition of such justification for sex-selective abortions suggests that the law does not sanction social prejudice. Therefore, when science promotes preventing the birth of persons with disabilities, certainly it asks women to ratify the social prejudice that persists against persons with disabilities. Hence, the reproductive choice to abort foetuses for probable disability cannot be seen as expansion of women's reproductive right. Instead, in this choice-making process, women are actually becoming 'quality control gate keepers' of human perfection.[10] Therefore, as long as disability-selective abortions represent the social prejudice subsisting against persons with disabilities, they cannot be seen as part of the reproductive rights of women. In this context, it is significant

[9] Blumberg (1994a: 138).
[10] Gregor (2001: 45).

to examine whether disability-selective abortion reflects the social prejudice against persons with disabilities.

DISABILITY-SELECTIVE ABORTIONS: A PERSISTING PREJUDICE?

The choice involved in both sex- and disability-selective abortions is selecting out foetuses with undesired traits. It suggests that one should possess a certain desirable standard of perfection in order to be welcomed into this world. It indicates that people who do not meet the standard of perfection should be prevented from existing in this world. Thus, selective abortions express negative or discriminatory attitudes not merely against the undesired trait, but against those who carry it. The selection on the basis of a particular characteristic of the foetus is problematic because it sends the message that those individuals should be excluded from society.

As the ease of testing increases, so does the perception within the medical and broader communities that prenatal testing is a logical extension of good prenatal care.[11] The idea is that prenatal tests help prospective parents to have healthy babies. It is claimed that many disabilities are considered avoidable, as prenatal tests provide information about it. The availability of prenatal tests and their potential to predict possible disability creates a moral responsibility on prospective parents to avoid births of children with disabilities. This has particular impact on the Indian cultural context, where disability is depicted as punishment for sins of previous births. Therefore, prenatal tests are perceived as a chance to detect such 'cursed lives' before their birth.

The utilization of prenatal tests for selecting out disability thus reinforces the social prejudice subsisting against persons with disabilities. The justification that disability-selective abortions enhance women's reproductive choices is not only morally problematic but also counterproductive. The availability of these tests and the legal sanction to use them for screening, in fact, restrict the choice of women to decide what kind of children they should give birth to. Women will no longer be seen as mothers of their children, who belong to them, but as mothers of society that mandates them to have a perfect child. Then it

[11] Parens and Asch (2000b: 4).

is only logical to think that it will not take too long to manipulate the purpose of these tests and selective abortions to eliminate or enhance other presumed genetic but socially charged characteristics, such as sexual orientation, race, attractiveness, height, intelligence, and so on.[12]

This trend has already started in society, which can be seen from the attempts to design babies. The selective strategy of science in prenatal tests provides a better opportunity to avoid the 'risk' of giving birth to a child who would live as a person with disability. Not accessing the expertise available with science is considered irresponsible. Consequently, it is a social necessity that women should only give birth to perfect children. This social pressure not only makes the parents responsible for the kind of children they give birth to, but pressurizes them to utilize technology to design the kind of babies that society sees as desirable. In this manner, disability-selective abortions are demonstrated as unavoidable or the sole solution left with the parents, if the foetus is detected with a disability.

THE BRAVE NEW WORLD THAT DESIGNS HUMANS

Today, genetic engineering makes it possible to test for genes that determine the physical and psychological behaviour of a human being.[13] Parents who want to determine several aspects of their child's personality and talents could do it through embryo screening.[14] The possibilities of these tests to provide parents with all kinds of information regarding the characteristics of the foetus opens up the brave new world of designer babies. The availability of such techniques obviously would obligate parents to opt for such babies, rather than giving birth to 'bad babies'.[15] Julian Savulescu, an eminent Oxford academician, says that creating so-called designer babies could be considered a 'moral obligation' as it makes them grow up into 'ethically better children'.[16] According to him, we should actively give parents the

[12] Saxton (2006: 111).

[13] Alleyne (2012).

[14] Alleyne (2012).

[15] Blumberg (1994a: 139). Blumberg refers to the words of a speaker at a reproductive right conference.

[16] Alleyne (2012).

choice to screen out personality flaws in their children as it meant they were then less likely to 'harm themselves and others'.[17] He suggests that genetic selection to determine how our children would look, think, and act is a gift to future generations. He further argues that genetic selection aims to bring out a trait that clearly benefits an individual and society, and parents should be allowed that choice. He refers to such screening as 'rational designs'.

This suggests that the justification of disability-selective abortion as a rational choice of parents could be expanded to design the genetic as well as ethical characters of foetuses. But, what if a genetically corrected foetus become ethically bad or vice versa? It reflects society's views and its degree of intolerance towards diversity.

This is an evidence of the deep prejudice about persons with disabilities. This is ethically problematic and unjustifiable as it embodies discrimination against persons with disabilities. Particularly when such decisions are taken based on misconceived ideas of disability and persons with disabilities, it raises the moral question of the value of persons with disabilities. It underpins the rights and worthiness of persons with disabilities and fundamentally challenges the most basic claim for justice and equality. Do science and law promote disability-selective abortions based on a complete understanding of what is a life with disability and what is the value of persons with disabilities? Have they ever listened to or observed what a life with disability is for persons with disabilities and their families? Why do members of the disability community oppose prenatal diagnosis and selective abortions?

THE DISABILITY-RIGHTS CRITIQUE OF DISABILITY-SELECTIVE ABORTIONS

A vast majority of theorists and health professionals still argue that prenatal testing followed by selective termination if 'impairment' is detected, promotes family well-being and public health.[18] Utilitarian philosophers such as John Harris and Peter Singer have argued strongly

---

[17] Jackson (2013).
[18] Asch (2001: 306).

for permitting parents to go in for screening followed by abortion of foetuses with disabilities.[19] Therefore, disability-selective abortions are simply used as one more legitimate method of preventing disability in the world.[20] Since this has been promoted and accepted as a preventive method, the implications of such tests on persons with disabilities and the society have not been subjected to much public scrutiny. It should be noted that the active promotion and use of prenatal tests for sex-selective abortions was largely debated and objected to by feminist groups, disability-rights activists, and academics.

The disability-rights critique has raised objections to prenatal tests and disability-selective abortions mainly on the grounds of discriminating attitude, eugenic impulse, parental attitude, and misinformation. It would be worthwhile to examine these grounds to analyse the implications of prenatal tests and selective abortions on the ground of disability. Since the eugenic implication has already been discussed, I will examine the remaining objections raised by the disability-rights critique.

Objection on the Ground of Discrimination

The disability-rights critique argues that prenatal tests and selective abortions on the ground of disability are morally problematic. It is because it expresses a negative or discriminatory attitude against persons with disabilities. It is discriminatory, because it targets not only the trait of disability, but persons who carry the trait. This line of objection is known as the expressivist argument or expressivist objection. The central claim of this argument is that prenatal tests to select against the trait of disability express a hurtful attitude against persons with disabilities. It sends a hurtful message to the people who live with disability that their life is not worth living. They ask 'under what conditions is it morally permissible to kill a foetus with disability or to prevent its being born?'[21] What message does this send to the rest of society about the value placed on its disability community?[22]

---

[19] Kuhse and Singer (1985).
[20] Asch (2001: 307).
[21] Wendell (1989) quoted in Asch (2001: 297).
[22] Ward (2002: 194).

The expressivist argument could be interpreted in non-consequentialist and consequentialist ways. The non-consequential interpretation suggests that selective abortion expresses a discriminatory attitude and this would be wrong even if no person with disability were negatively affected. The latter and more powerful version of the expressivist argument grounds the wrongness of selective termination in the harms resulted from it. It harms existing people with disabilities. For example, the policies and practices that allow people to terminate pregnancy to avoid having children with disabilities have negative consequences. Clearly, many persons with disabilities and their supporters feel offended by prenatal diagnoses.[23] It reflects society-imposed hardships; learning that the world one lives in considers it better to 'solve' problems of disability by prenatal detection and abortion, rather than by expending those resources in improving society.[24] Marsha Saxton puts the expressivist argument this way:

> The message at the heart of widespread selective abortion on the basis of prenatal diagnosis is the greatest insult: some of us are 'too flawed' in our very DNA to exist; we are unworthy of being born.... Fighting for this issue, our right and worthiness to be born, is the challenge to disability oppression; it underpins our most basic claim to justice and equality. We are indeed worthy of being born, worth the help and expense, and we know it.[25]

The expressivist objection conveys a strong argument against prenatal tests and selective abortions, and this can be drawn for sex-selective abortions as well.

Discrimination and Sex-selective Abortions

Theorists and professionals oppose sex-selective abortions because, when prospective parents select against an otherwise wanted child because of its gender, it implies that people who exist with these characteristic (female gender) might be less desirable to others. Therefore

---

[23] Shakespeare (2006: 96).
[24] Asch (2003: 333).
[25] Saxton (2006: 115).

sex-selective abortions reflect the discrimination that prevails against women. It demonstrates that having no child is preferable to having a female child.[26] In the context of sex-selective abortions, it is argued that abortion decisions based on the 'gender characteristic' of the child is morally problematic. It is emblematic of a larger belief of the undesirability of women. Therefore, even dissemination of information regarding the sex of the foetus is considered morally wrong. They support prohibition of sex-selective abortions mainly on the ground that it discriminates or disvalues the life of females. A decision related to selective abortion always expresses disdain for a form of life that has consequences for how their community and society will welcome difference.[27]

Thus, sex-selective abortions represent the relationship between abortion and wider social discrimination. It can be seen that the social context in which people choose to raise or not raise children who would have disabilities is similar to the social context in which people choose to raise or not raise a female child. Both the female child and a child with disability are considered burdensome. Both of them require higher costs. Despite preventive laws, women should pay dowry to men to get married. The additional resource required to accommodate a child's disability is almost similar to an Indian parent's investment for dowry.

However, the above arguments have not been recognized to continue with sex-selective abortions. Instead, the aforesaid discriminatory social environment is the reason to prohibit prenatal tests and sex-selective abortions. However, the difference is in how both selective abortions are perceived. Sex-selective abortions are considered to stem from a discriminatory societal structure, whereas disability is constructed as a problem intrinsic to the individual.[28] Consequently, the disadvantages experienced by women are considered not as being caused by the intrinsic characteristic of being female, but by the behaviour of male-dominated societies towards her. At the same time, the disadvantages experienced by people with disabilities are viewed as problems caused by the intrinsic

---

[26] McKinney (2009: 8).
[27] McKinney (2009: 18).
[28] Wolbring (2001: 25).

characteristic of disability. This contradicting attitude towards human selection is ethically and morally problematic. It sends a hurtful message to persons with disabilities that 'it is better to be dead than disabled'. Consequently, when one kind of humans is selected out on misconceived ideas, it demonstrates a clear discrimination against them. Adrienne Asch clarifies what this hurtful message is: 'As with discrimination more generally, with prenatal diagnosis, a single trait stands in for the whole, the trait obliterates the whole. With both discrimination and prenatal diagnosis, nobody finds out about the rest. The tests send the message that there's no need to find out about the rest.'[29]

This can be interpreted as, 'because of the presence of some single trait that a foetus with disability bears, prenatal tests are letting that part stand alone for the whole'.[30] This impairment overpowers any positive qualities there might be in being alive. This underscores how incomplete the information provided by prenatal testing is. Writing in 1987, a woman with disability shares:

> I know that amniocentesis can't tell any parents what kind of child they will have. It can only tell what disability might exist in that child. Amniocentesis could never have told my mother that I would have artistic talent, a high intellectual capacity, a sharp wit and an outgoing personality. The last thing amniocentesis would tell her is that I could be physically attractive.[31]

Thus, in disability-selective abortions, the whole individual is viewed from the lens of the disabling trait. Since the trait of disability is generally perceived as undesirable, knowledge of this single trait is sufficient to warrant the abortion of an otherwise wanted child. A major consequence of this choice is that we miss the other values that are attached to those individuals. Thus, prenatal tests seem to be more discriminatory, by valuing the life of a whole individual only on the basis of a single trait of disability. This reinforces the idea that only some traits warrant the attention of parents. Thus, disability-selective

---

[29] Parens and Asch (2000b: 13); Asch (2000b: 234).
[30] Asch (2000a: 962).
[31] Noe (1987); also quoted in Asch (2000b: 235).

abortions involve implications to parental attitude that changes along with developing technology.

Selective Abortions and Parental Attitude

In selective abortions, parental attitude becomes significant, as it involves an altered decision of an otherwise wanted pregnancy to an unwanted one. Therefore, a decision of abortion taken by the parents based on a particular characteristic of the foetus indicates a problematic conception of, and attitude towards, parenthood. Whether this is to select a foetus on the basis of its female sex or disability, both point towards parental attitude towards accepting their children. In fact, a particular trait of their children has no importance to the prospect of parenthood and the concomitant moral obligation.

The parental attitude argument suggests that prenatal tests are rooted in a 'fantasy and fallacy' that 'parents can guarantee or create perfection' for their children.[32] The prospective parent who wants to avoid raising a child with a diagnosable disability forgets that along with the disabling trait come other traits, many of which are likely to be as enjoyable, pride-giving, positive (and as problematic, annoying, and complicated), as any other child's traits.[33] At the moment of decision regarding whether to abort the foetus or not, knowledge of an otherwise desired child's talents, interests, and personality are entirely unknown. The decision to select out a foetus on the reason of its disability can therefore be characterized as allowing the trait of a predisposition to disability to override the entirety of that prospective child's rich personal complexity.

When parents choose a child on the basis of a particular trait, it expresses the 'selective mentality'[34] of parents. Parenting entails the values of unconditional nurturing, loving, and caring of children, where traits are not accounted for their appreciation. The attention to particular traits indicates a morally troubling conception of parenthood, a preoccupation with what is trivial and an ignorance of

---

[32] Parens and Asch (2000b: 17); Asch (1996: 88).

[33] Asch (2000a: 963).

[34] Parens and Asch (2000b: 18).

what is profound.[35] One may legitimately ask the question whether these tests lead us to commodify our children rather than treating them as 'ends in themselves'?[36] When female members of society are confronted with sex selection, they often raise concerns about this selective mentality.

Availability and the potential of prenatal tests to detect the disability trait have brought changes in our attitude towards parenthood. Even modern reproductive technology cannot guarantee 'perfect babies'. Children who are born medically perfect may later lose their physical and mental abilities. Does this mean that the parents should abandon their children on account of their acquired disability?

Every prospective parent may agree to the fact that all possible ailments of the future child cannot be detected, nor can its future existence without disabilities be assured.[37] Despite this recognition of improbability, parents are not inclined to accept a child with disability. This gives rise to a developing ideology that foetuses have to pass a quality test before parents acknowledge them as their babies and assume parental responsibilities towards them.[38] Even modern reproductive technology cannot inform the parents 'who' or 'what' the child is before or after her birth. This means 'who' or 'what' the baby is cannot be the reason for the parent–child relationship.[39] Therefore, it can be said that if prospective parents imagine that disability precludes everything else that could be wonderful about the child, they are likely to be acting on misinformation and stereotype. No human child is fit for survival without the support of elders.[40] Prenatal screening and selective termination drawing the line about how much support they should need is extremely problematic. It challenges the ethics of parental attitude. In particular, when such decisions are taken on the basis of misinformation or incomplete information. Hence, the disability-rights critique uses the argument

---

[35] Parens and Asch (2000b: 18); Parens and Asch (2012: 64).
[36] Parens and Asch (2000b: 18).
[37] Vehmas (2002: 476).
[38] Vehmas (2002: 477).
[39] Vehmas (2002: 475).
[40] Asch (2000b).

of misinformation to establish the problematic part of disability-selective abortions.

The Misinformation Argument

The misinformation argument is based mainly on the implications of the medical model of disability. Within the medical framework, disability is considered a biological condition that limits an individual's species typical functions. The medical profession perceives that a certain level of health and functioning serves as the prerequisite for the 'normal opportunity range'[41] for an accepted life. Therefore, in the medical model, health is highly prized, because 'impairments' reduce the range of life opportunities open to the individual to construct 'plan of life' or 'conceptions of good'.[42] This medically oriented understanding of disability contains erroneous assumptions. First, it fails to recognize the fact that disability per se is not the condition that limits or obstructs the life opportunities of a person with disabilities. The disadvantages experienced by persons with disabilities arise from society's lack of accommodation to different methods of performing valued activities such as learning, communicating, moving, or living in this world.[43] More clearly, as Adrienne Asch puts it: 'The opportunities which are lost to a person with disability are to be attributed not only to the species-atypicality of the person's biology, but also to the architectural design of the buildings in which some of those opportunities reside.'[44]

This world has been constructed by the non-disabled majority without acknowledging the presence of persons with disabilities in this world. Consequently, the quality of a life with disability is dealt on the basis of a cost–benefit analysis, rather than on the value of individual life. It can be said that such assessments are made without taking into account the perspective of persons with disabilities in their life. Adrienne Asch raises this issue when she asks, '[i]f people with disabilities consistently indicate that their lives—even with

---

[41] Asch (2001: 322).
[42] Daniels (1985: 27).
[43] Asch (2001: 297).
[44] Asch (2003: 319).

problems—are more satisfactory to them than non-disabled people or health professionals believe, should their judgements be used in measuring life quality?'[45]

This points towards medical and societal perceptions that invalidate 'disabled bodies', based on self-perceived ideas of disability and persons with disabilities. In fact, life with disability is not the unremitting tragedy as generally portrayed by medical and bioethics literature.[46] Even on 'quality-of-life' measures, a life with disability can be rewarding.[47] The claim that certain impairments preclude valuable experiences does not mean that they thereby make life any less rich or valuable overall; it may rather support the conclusion that there is an indefinite variety of ways in which human lives can flourish.[48] It can be enabled only by recognizing the dignity of all human beings.

Of course, this does not undermine the associated inconvenience of having disabilities. It is true that disability, pain, and the need for compensatory devices and assistance can produce considerable inconvenience. Quality-of-life initiatives are required to enable persons with disabilities to overcome the social prejudice that subsists against them. However, these inconveniences are minimal compared to the discriminatory and insensitive attitudes, thoughtless behaviour, ensuing ostracism, and lack of accommodation and understanding that make life with disability more difficult.[49] It is worthwhile to note that, in reality, persons with disabilities lead productive lives and do contribute to humanity.

Therefore, it can be argued that disability, 'physical', 'cognitive', or 'intellectual', cannot be perceived as a condition that should limit or foreclose the 'opportunities' of individuals. Having disabilities does not necessarily mean that such individuals are worthless. Indeed, for many persons with disabilities, it is part of their identity and they are proud of it. This could be deduced from the reluctance of persons with disabilities to receive treatment for certain disabilities. Thus, for

[45] Asch (2001: 317).
[46] Asch (2001).
[47] Asch (2001).
[48] Wasserman (2001: 222).
[49] Saxton (2006: 107).

example, persons with manic-depressive illness feel that the temperament associated with the condition also contributes to their creativity,
and treatment of the condition could cause loss of their creative skill
and imagination.[50]

PERFECTION AT THE COST OF EXCELLENCE

We have seen that the debates about sterilization and forced abortion
have been replaced by more sophisticated prenatal testing and therapeutic and voluntary abortions. But the ethical problems remain the
very same. We forget the fact that imaginative minds and bodies
brought invaluable contributions. This also involves some difficult
issues with respect to the uncertainty of science. Larry Gostin, the
director of the American Society of Law and Medicine, has addressed
some of those issues. He says:

> Complex and often pernicious mythologies emerge from public igno-
> rance of genetically based diagnostic and prognostic tests. The com-
> mon belief is that genetic technologies generated from scientific
> assessment is always accurate, highly predictive and capable of iden-
> tifying an individual's offspring's inevitable pre-destination of future
> disability. The facts are diametrically opposed to this common belief.
> The results of genetic-based diagnosis and prognosis are uncertain for
> many reasons. Predicting the nature, severity and course of disease
> based upon a genetic marker is an additional difficulty.[51]

MANIC-DEPRESSIVE ILLNESS AND ITS RELATION
TO ARTISTIC TEMPERAMENT

Manic-depressive illness or bipolar disorder is a genetic disease, which
encompasses a wide range of mood disorders and temperament.[52]
Kay Redfield Jamison, a professor of psychiatry, in her book about
manic-depressive illness explains the compelling association between
artistic creativity and manic-depressive illness. Indeed, the specific

---

[50] Jamison (1994: 241).
[51] Committee on Government Operations (1992: 24).
[52] Jamison (1994: 13).

role of 'mania' in artists and genius is considered normal or fine madness.

Therefore, a possible link between madness and genius is one of the oldest and most persistent of cultural notions.[53] At the same time, it is one of the most controversial as well. History shows that an intimate relationship between the ancient gods, madness, and the creators was described in pre-Grecian myths. This is evident from speech of Socrates on divine madness. He said:

> Madness, provided it comes as the gift of heaven, is the channel by which we receive the greatest blessings ... the men of old who gave things their names saw no disgrace or reproach in madness; otherwise they would not have connected it with the name of the noblest of arts, the art of discerning future, and called it the manic art.... So, according to the evidence provided by our ancestors, madness is a nobler thing than sober sense ... madness comes from God, whereas sober sense is merely human.[54]

According to Socrates, if a man comes to the door of poetry untouched by madness, he will never reach perfection in his work. Socrates and Plato considered 'madness'[55] as encompassing a wide range of states of thought and emotions, not just psychosis. Their emphasis was clearly upon a profoundly altered state of consciousness and feeling. However, by the beginning of the eighteenth century there emerged a renewed interest in the relationship between genius and madness.[56] Individual attitudes, balancing, and rational thoughts were seen as the primary components of genius.[57] But this brief period was reversed by the nineteenth-century Romantics, who once again emphasized the melancholic side of genius.[58] In the twentieth

[53] Jamison (1994: 50).

[54] Plato (1974: 46, 47).

[55] In the human rights era, 'madness' in fact is not a politically right term. Here, however, it refers to the earlier philosophical understanding of mental disability. But, it is worthwhile to note the beneficial perspective of disability, with the earlier non-political term.

[56] Jamison (1994: 52).

[57] Jamison (1994: 52).

[58] Jamison (1994: 52).

century, Emil Kraepelin, a clinical psychologist, and William James, a psychologist, emphasized the positive features associated with certain kinds of 'madness' and speculated about how these features might combine with other talents to produce an extraordinarily creative or accomplished person.[59]

Various biological studies and life-study investigations of prominent writers, artists, and composers provide corroborative scientific evidence that supports a correlation between manic temperament and creativity. Studies show that the cognitive aspects of mania might benefit imaginative thought. Runco and Pritzker said, 'An examination of cognitive aspects of creativity has been presented in this work through a number of research papers, particularly about transitional states, analogies, cognitive style and divergent thinking.'[60] Jamison analyses the lives of many artists who could be possessed of a manic temperament. Alfred Lord Tennyson, Robert Schuman, Henry James, Herman Melville, Samuel Taylor Coleridge, Virginia Woolf, Ernest Hemingway, Mary Wollstonecraft, Mary Shelley, Samuel Johnson, James Boswell, and Vincent van Gogh are prominent among them. During their manic period, most of the artists displayed high fluency, rapidity, and flexibility of thought.[61] Their classic works were produced during their manic period. It is important to note that most of them acknowledged their experience with mood disorders and its significance to their work. This evinces the inevitable relation between creative skills and manic-depressive illness.

Weighing the adversities associated with this mood disorder,[62] still strong scientific and biographical evidence links manic-depressive illness and its related temperament to artistic imagination and expression.[63] It is pertinent to know that, since the creativeness is the product of the manic, they fear that psychiatric treatment

---

[59] Jamison (1994: 54).

[60] Runco and Pritzker (2011).

[61] Jamison (1994: 105).

[62] The fluctuating mood may lead them to do drug and alcohol and sometimes it also drives them to suicide. Goodwin and Jamison (2007: 255–62).

[63] Jamison (1994: 240).

will transform them into normal, well-adjusted, dampened, and bloodless souls who are unable or unmotivated to write, paint, or compose.[64]

Manic-depressive illness appears to convey its advantage not only through its relationship to 'artistic temperament and imagination', but through its influence on many eminent scientists as well as business, religious, military, and political leaders.[65] Thus it can confer advantages on both the individual and the society. Such consequences yet again cause us to query prenatal tests and selective abortion on the ground of disability. Then, as asked by Jamison, the legitimate question is, when disability can confer advantages on society, is it possible to justify disability-selective abortions on the ground of disability being harmful to society?[66]

The above analysis on beneficial aspect of mental disabilities was required, because mental disability is perceived as the most undesired condition. However, disability-selective abortion is not only chosen for reason of mental disabilities, it has been done even for a cleft lip.[67] This also provides justification to eliminate persons with disabilities, as we can see from many such arguments. For instance, Jeff McMahan puts forward a justification of 'time relative interest' to explain why the killing of certain human beings is less seriously objectionable, like killing animals, as both of them have less psychological capacities.[68] He refers to three groups of people whose psychological capacities are no more advanced than those of animals. They are: (i) foetuses whose physiological capacities are yet to mature; (ii) those with acquired cognitive capacities or who have lost cognitive capacity; and (iii) congenitally cognitively impaired human beings.[69] The argument also closes the chances for future cognitive psychological development, in particular for a foetus, since the psychological ties

---

[64] Jamison (1994: 241).

[65] Jamison (1994: 252).

[66] Jamison (1994: 8).

[67] Claire (2011) and Weiss (2007).

[68] McMahan (2002: 204).

[69] McMahan (2002). Accordingly, impairment of cognitive functioning includes loss of memory, perceptual disturbance, deterioration of rational capacities, etc.

of the foetus with its future is weaker.[70] This polarization brilliantly covers any pre- and post-born or acquired disabilities. Among these three groups, he refers to persons with less-cognitive psychological capacity as 'severely retarded' and says:

> These human beings have cognitive and emotional capacities no higher than those of certain animals. As a consequence their time relative interest in continuing to live is no stronger than that of their non-human counterparts.... Therefore it is no more wrong, other things being equal, to kill a severely retarded human being than it is to kill an animal with comparable psychological capabilities.[71]

However, drawing no difference between killing those persons with weak time relative interest to animals needs to be viewed through the mirror of advantages or benefits of such a condition. Moreover, when disability-selective abortions are promoted on the grounds of undue burden and non-productiveness of persons with disabilities, they raise questions about achievements in a society where only reciprocal relationships are accepted on the basis of ability, intellect, and economic worth. However, reciprocal advantages or individual achievements are not the basis to value human life. Moreover, the original invaluable contributions made by persons with disabilities disproves the 'non-contributors' and 'time relative interest' argument. Those contributions are more valuable as they could achieve it in so much hostility, where persons with disabilities are perceived to be incapables. An examination of the work of great scientists causes us to come up with a row of personalities, from Isaac Newton to Stephen Hawking, who have made invaluable contributions to science and humanity.

The groundbreaking theory of gravity emerged from a mind gripped with manic depression or what is now called bipolar disorder. Newton's psychological problems during 1693s culminated in nervous breakdown, the term we use now for such conditions.[72] Perhaps

[70] McMahan (2002: 205).

[71] McMahan (2002: 205).

[72] The Newton Project, 'His Personal Life', available online at http://www.newtonproject.sussex.ac.uk/prism.php?id=40 (last accessed on 20 February 2016).

he was the first person who thought about why, when the apple fell on his head, and not on the sky. His theories on gravity, calculus, and optics laid the foundation for physical science as is known today. In 1705, Newton was the first scientist to be knighted by Queen Anne for his great scientific contributions.[73] Can this original and invaluable contribution be rendered invalid, because it was discovered by a person with mental disability?

The music composed by Ludwig van Beethoven, the greatest eighteenth-century composer, yet again weakens the diminishing perception about disability. Speaking and hearing are considered essential abilities for humans. Anyone who does not have these capabilities is perceived as a lesser being. But the music created by Beethoven, with his disabilities, remains classic forever. Scholar Maynard Solomon has characterized Beethoven as having had 'sudden rages, uncontrolled emotional states, melancholic disposition, and frequent feelings of persecution'.[74] These 'manic' episodes were part of his creativity.

Dyslexia or learning disability did not prevent Albert Einstein from developing the general theory of relativity and the energy equivalence formula. He is the most renowned twentieth-century scientist, and a Nobel laureate.[75] He is regarded as the father of modern physics. Whilst there are disagreements about whether Einstein had a learning disability, researchers agree to his speaking difficulties during his childhood.

Similarly, we consider people with autism as persons who cannot do anything for themselves. But, Paul Dirac, a twentieth-century British theoretical physicist, who was known as 'Britain's Einstein', was autistic. He was a pioneer of quantum mechanics and quantum electrodynamics. He was the youngest theoretical physicist to win a Nobel Prize. Many of the abilities that we consider essential to have a valued life are not so for persons with disabilities. Helen Keller and

---

[73] The Renaissance Mathematicus, 'A Knighthood for Science', available online at https://thonyc.wordpress.com/2012/04/16/a-knighthood-for-science/ (last accessed on 20 February 2016). Also see Westfall (1983: 625), makes a statement that the honour was not for Newton's contributions to science, but for greater glory of party politics in the election of 1705.

[74] Solomon (1988: 146).

[75] Langtree (2005).

her life with disabilities just demonstrates her perception of life that, 'the best and most beautiful things in the world cannot be seen nor even touched, but just felt in the heart'.[76]

Abraham Lincoln, 16th president of the United States (US), suffered from severely debilitating and on occasion suicidal depressions, as recorded by Carl Sandburg in his comprehensive six-volume biographical analysis of his life. Lincoln, with his disabilities, ruled a state and contributed to political reforms in the US. To consider some more examples, John Nash, the mathematical genius, was diagnosed with schizophrenia.[77] Emmy Noether, another distinguished mathematician, had communication disability—a lisp—and was nearsighted. Well-known personalities such as Henry Ford, Graham Bell, Walt Disney, Winston Churchill, and Thomas Alva Edison were all persons with learning disabilities.

Frida Kahlo is the most famous woman artist with physical disabilities. Stephen Hawking from the contemporary period is the most renowned person with disability who has enormously contributed to the field of science by his theories related to space. All these contributions have come in the face of hostility, and in a world where disability and persons with disabilities are not accommodated. It suggests that society de-prioritizes the contributions made by persons with disabilities in various fronts of humanity. It also implies the imperialistic attitude that accepts the contributions, but submerges the individual condition of disability.

If such contributions can come from persons with disabilities, in a totally hostile environment where their disability has not been accommodated, it is necessary to imagine what could emerge in a conducive environment. Valuable as these contributions are, the case for disability inclusion cannot be built on instrumental foundations. It needs to be built on principles of social justice. Social justice endorses treating all human beings as ends in themselves and not as means to others. A liberal democratic society is based upon the ideal of civic responsibility in which we care for the most vulnerable, not because of their potential economic productivity, but because of their intrinsic worth. When society values human life on the basis of its potential

---

[76] Keller (1902).

[77] Nasar (2001).

economic productivity, it demonstrates devaluing human beings. However, in order to construct a just society and to accommodate the excluded requires resource distribution. But it can be seen that such realization has been viewed as resource-intensive. Consequently, the utility justification for disability-selective abortion raises the question of social justice for persons with disabilities.

THE PARAMETER OF SOCIAL JUSTICE FOR PERSONS WITH DISABILITIES

When it comes to the question of social justice for persons with disabilities, theorists negate distribution of resources based on the reason of higher 'conversion costs' required for it. The argument of 'extra cost' that a non-selection entails for the parents and the society attempts to justify disability-selective abortions. For Amartya Sen, a profound social philosopher, disability is an example to demonstrate the limitation of the income-based approach to measure poverty.[78] Amita Dhanda criticizes Sen's position on income-based approach as it would not take into account the higher amounts persons with disabilities need to expend to convert capabilities into functioning.[79] She further criticized Sen's argument that conversion costs are an inflexible perennial truth and he sets up the case for rights of persons with disabilities within the prevention paradigm.[80] She also counters this on the point that it is sin of omission as he failed to refer to the jurisprudence of universal design.[81] Because the higher conversion costs to accommodate persons with disabilities was Sen's reason to justify primary prevention of disability. He states: 'It is extremely important to understand that many disabilities are preventable, and much can be done not only to diminish the penalty of disability but also to reduce its incidence. Indeed, only a fairly moderate proportion of the 600 million people living with disabilities were doomed to these conditions at conception, or even at birth.'[82]

---

[78] Sen (2009: 258). Dhanda (2010a).
[79] Dhanda (2010a: 135).
[80] Dhanda (2010a: 135).
[81] Dhanda (2010a: 135).
[82] Sen (2009: 259).

This social intervention justifies viewing life with disability as an economic liability for both the family and society. Such a life is perceived to contribute little and require disproportionate investment from society. Therefore, this transcendental approach justifies preventing the birth of persons with disabilities on the ground that society has to bear the cost of the disability. However, this is unjustifiable on account of inaccessible social and infrastructural environment constructed by the non-disabled majority, disregarding the presence of persons with disabilities. [83]

Further, people with disabilities often require more resources than other people because they need assistance, or assistive devices, or adaptation of social practice to engage in some of the fundamental activities of life.[84] A standard illustration of the added expenses imposed by disability is the individual who must acquire a wheelchair to traverse distances ordinary citizens travel across on their legs.[85] However, as previously mentioned, most accommodations are necessary only because of the manner that society has chosen to organize the structured environment to accommodate only the non-disabled majority. With compromised productivity or larger than typical needs, persons with disabilities have been portrayed by twentieth-century social contract theory as problematic for justice.[86] Anita Silvers and Michael Ashley submit that it is because the contributions of persons with disabilities are thought inadequate to offset their needs.[87] Consequently, they have not been sought after as equal members by social contract theorists in developing definitive fundamental principles and procedures for justice.[88]

---

[83] Dhanda (2010a: 136).

[84] Stein (2003: 79); Silvers, Wasserman, and Mahowald (1998: 13, 73–5). They discuss that most accommodations are necessary only because of the manner that social convention has chosen to organize the structured environment.

[85] Sen (1980: 217–8). (Discussing about the reduced marginal utility of a 'cripple'.)

[86] Rawls (1971).

[87] Silvers and Stein (2007: 1616).

[88] Silvers and Stein (2007: 1616).

The traditional social contract theories assume that the individuals in the 'original position' are equal, free, and independent. Rousseau's social contract theory is an account of moral and political evolution of human beings over time. Consequently, the progression of a natural society to a civilized one produced inequalities. The social contract idea is that justice is the outcome of an agreement among persons.

In the Kantian idea of social contract, each individual has a dignity that demands respect come what may, and that each person is an 'end in itself' that may not be used merely as a means for the advancement of the purposes of others.[89] However, since this original state of nature equality presupposes equal natural powers and capacities,[90] it excludes individuals who are dependent on others.[91] Therefore, all these assumptions excluded persons with disabilities. Even the contemporary social justice proponents conform to the whole social contract tradition. In *A Theory of Justice*, Rawls does not cater to special needs of persons with disabilities in the original position but only in the post-contractual stage. This theory justifies postponement of social justice for persons with disabilities. Accordingly, persons with disabilities cannot be included, because 'it would not be appropriate to measure the well-being of the disabled who might require more resources to achieve the same level of well-being as of non-disabled. Index of primary goods based on income and wealth can measure adequately the well-being of the non-disabled'.[92]

In Rawls' account of the social contract, rational parties choose mutually advantageous arrangements through a process of coming to agreement about the fundamental principles of justice.[93] To make the agreement plausible, the participating parties are presumed to be roughly equivalent to each other in strength, abilities, intelligence, sensibilities, and status. They are also presumed to resemble each other in desiring to exercise sovereignty over themselves and of being

---

[89] Kant (1996).

[90] Nussbaum (2004: 51).

[91] Couto (2007).

[92] Rawls (1971: 73).

[93] Rawls (1971: 15) mentioned in Silvers and Stein (2007: 1618).

capable of doing so.[94] Behind a 'veil of ignorance', all parties are similarly well-positioned to convince the others to leave the state of nature by accepting their collectively agreed-on ideas regarding basic tenets of justice.[95]

Thus, Rawls' account of justice is procedural in nature. Rawls emphasizes homogeneous reciprocity. Commentators concerned about justice for women and racial minorities have insisted that social contract theory incorporating this feature is flawed.[96] The thrust of their arguments is that the social contract model places such outliers, either individually or collectively as out-group members, beyond the reach of equal justice. Social contract theory, understood as a process of bargaining for mutual advantage, excluded persons with disabilities. The idea of social contract in mutual advantage among approximate equals failed to address questions of social justice posed by unequal parties. Social contract theorists thus exclude persons with disabilities from the social contract, as they believe that persons with disabilities could not be active contributors in social cooperation.[97] This perception of disability held by non-disabled people and the decision to exclude persons with disabilities does not affect them as it is articulated in unproblematic terms.[98]

Martha Nussbaum challenges this liberal belief that mutual advantage is the only basis for social cooperation.[99] She holds that a just contract would not only include terms which favour the parties to contract. Social justice demands that the concerns of all members of the society should find voice in the contract whether or not they

---

[94] Rawls (1971: 12). Among the essential features of this situation is that no one knows his place in society, his class position or social status, nor does one know his fortune in the distribution of natural assets and abilities, his intelligence, strength, and the like.

[95] Rawls (1971: 139).

[96] See for example, Mills (1997: 63, 69), averring that social contract theory positions African Americans at a disadvantage where justice is concerned; Williams (1991: 224), 'Contract law reduces life to fairy tale … activity is caged in retrospective hypotheses about states of mind at the magic moment of contracting'.

[97] Gombos and Dhanda (2009: 74).

[98] Gombos and Dhanda (2009: 75).

[99] Nussbaum (2006: 23).

participate in the making of such contract. This contemporary capability approach theory of justice seeks to extend justice and dignified life condition to the excluded group.

In particular, the capability approach proposed by Nussbaum proposes a basis for justice on which the needs of non-disabled and disabled people are equally[100] taken account of. According to this approach, responding positively to their needs is of equal political as well as moral value. The capability theory is a substantive alternative to the proceduralism of traditional social contract theory for understanding what obligations states owe to persons with disabilities.[101] The philosopher identifies persons with disabilities as people who have not as yet been included in existing society, or as citizens, on a basis of equality with other citizens.[102] Since the capability approach specifies what goods are fundamental to all humans' interests, these resources are core human entitlements that a just society has an overriding obligation to provide to everyone.[103] This is regardless of individuals' different abilities to represent themselves in shaping mutually advantageous arrangements or to contribute materially to the implementation of those cooperative arrangements.[104]

Central capabilities are the key determinants of the quality of individuals' lives because they are essential to people being able to execute 'universal' functions and so live a 'truly human' existence.[105] Thus, to be considered just political arrangements under Nussbaum's capabilities scheme, states must provide sufficient resources to enable people to be raised up to the basic functional levels. Further, since each capability is a separate component in her theory, states ought not to provide for one capability beyond the threshold at the expense of denying or limiting some or all people's reaching the threshold

---

[100] Nussbaum (2006: 23).

[101] Nussbaum (2006: 409).

[102] Nussbaum (2006: 2).

[103] Silver and Stein (2007: 1621).

[104] Silver and Stein (2007: 1621).

[105] Nussbaum (2006: 76–8). To give substance and direction to fulfilling entitlements to capabilities, Nussbaum enumerates a list of 10 central capabilities that individuals require to flourish. These are essential, she avers, because being able to exercise all of them at a threshold level is a uniquely human mode of existence.

level for any other capability. States must provide resources to each individual to develop threshold levels of each of the proposed 10 central capabilities to enable each to flourish in a truly dignified human manner.[106] In the case of persons with disabilities, some may need more resources than their non-disabled peers to achieve roughly equivalent capabilities as measured against species-typical threshold level.[107] Hence, differential distribution of resources, recognizing differences among people, may be needed to achieve the good equally for everybody. The capabilities approach endorses allotting greater resources to persons with disabilities if relatively greater distributions are able to bring those individuals up to average baseline levels of capabilities, that is, to the thresholds for species-typical flourishing.[108]

The capability scheme therefore distributes resources, which individuals can convert into the functioning that is of central importance for their flourishing. Society's obligation to achieve these goods reaches people unable to be parties in a contractual process or otherwise represent themselves effectively in developing principles of resource distribution. Nussbaum thus transforms the contemporary philosophical approach to a distributive justice one. Justice for persons with disabilities requires that each one be brought up to threshold levels of capabilities. Social contract theory reaches this conclusion by conflating the dynamics of being the subject of justice (those who choose just principles) and being the object of justice (those who benefit from just principles), and making the latter dependent on the former. It thereby provides an account of the good in terms of core human entitlements to resources that are necessary in view of their functional outcomes. The Capability approach explicitly rejects assessing well-being through welfare metrics, because this approach mandates the state to provide each person with means to exercise the capabilities.[109]

Thus, capability approach requires that each and every person be treated as an end in themselves, rather than as the instrument

---

[106] Nussbaum (2006: 85).

[107] Nussbaum (2006: 87–8).

[108] Nussbaum (2006: 116–8).

[109] Silvers and Stein (2007: 1624).

or agency of the ends of others.[110] Accordingly, the expense or the higher conversion costs are justified because everyone deserves being brought as close as possible to the minimal level needed for a dignified life.[111]

Thus in contradiction to contract theories of mutual benefit, the capability theory ascribes human dignity to all humans regardless of their ability to identify their personal good, or to contribute to other people or society's good.[112] This means that a state cannot disregard any member of the society for extra resource allocation, which is an absolute responsibility of the state in the scheme of capability approach. Because the search for absolute value should set or suggest principles of priority in case resources are insufficient to discharge all public obligations under justice.[113]

This approach is significant for 'quality-of-life' initiatives for persons with disabilities. Otherwise, even if we allow them to get born, for their inherent value, absence of quality-of-life provisions would progressively kill them. Then, there will be no difference in respecting inherent value but not having quality of life. Social justice measures to ensure quality of life is significant for persons with disabilities. It is significant, because any one of us may acquire this condition of disability at any point in our lifetime. Quality-of-life parameters would provide a conducive environment for persons with disabilities. This would lead to a social perception where anyone can think that disability is a fine human condition.

Consequently, a just society is one that values the inherent value of persons with disabilities. Similar to the human rights approach, the capability approach requires all humans to be treated as ends in themselves.[114] The critical underpinning of treating all humans as ends in themselves is that everyone must have the freedom to achieve. However, freedom is non-negotiable whether with or without achievements. It obligates a just society to distribute resources to persons with disabilities, who are excluded as lesser human beings. This would

---

[110] Silvers and Stein (2007: 1624–5).

[111] Silvers and Stein (2007: 1625).

[112] Silvers and Stein (2007: 1631).

[113] Silvers and Stein (2007: 1638).

[114] Nussbaum (2006: 78).

acknowledge them as ends in themselves, deserving of treatment that affirms their human dignity. Freedom, as the most primary virtue, entitles persons with disabilities to be valued for their inherent dignity and not on the basis of their contributions.

The above analysis shows that disability and its travails are the products of an inadequate social justice discourse. By preventing the birth of persons with disabilities, the law takes the stance that certain kinds of lives are not worth living. This legal order is wrongly constructed on prejudiced perception about disability and persons with disabilities. If persons with disabilities require more resources to perform equally like all others, it is just because the world has been constructed by the non-disabled majority to accommodate themselves alone, and not persons with disabilities too. This draws on the failure of social justice to reach persons with disabilities to recognize them as ends in themselves. Then it can be analysed that disability-selective abortions are a means to reach the 'social end' to prevent the existence of persons with disabilities. Thus, it implies the failure of social justice to value the presence of persons with disabilities in humanity.

***

The blanket prohibition on prenatal tests and sex-selective abortions is an attempt to provide equal justice to women. It is contended that disability-selective abortions are problematic. We may never know the role of an individual with or without disability in the world. When we select out, on the reason of disability, we forget the truth that disability is an inherent part of human life. Therefore, the entire prospect of prenatal tests and disability selective-abortions raises the question of whether preventing the birth of persons with disabilities does any good to society or deprives humanity of something valuable? The paradigm of prevention envisaged under disability-selective abortion laws in fact categorizes and exclude persons with disabilities, denying them social justice. This outlook emanates from the vision of medical profession, which views human beings as 'stable machines' that could not be designed differently.

The social objective of prenatal tests reduces the fact of disability from humanity, which is unethical, unjustifiable, and wrong. First, it will never possible for society to eliminate disability from humanity.

Disability is an inherent human condition, which cannot be eradicated from humanity. It should also be noted that not all disability is preventable, and also that many disabilities are acquired during the course of one's lifetime. Second, as long as the reasons in favour of disability-selective abortions are not justifiable, such selective practices become unjustifiable. If prenatal tests aim to ameliorate the suffering of persons with disabilities, selective abortions are not the place where we should begin such amelioration. As in sex-selective abortions, amelioration of suffering and discrimination should begin from challenging the social system and not by letting them screened and killed before birth.

If science and medicine can take away all the fallibilities in human beings, how many of us could inhibit this world? When disability-selective abortions are carried on with a general perception that disability is an unproductive trait, it diminishes the value of some of the most extraordinary humans and their immortal contributions to the humanity. While disability is an 'undesired' trait for the society, we disvalue their life. It is undeniable that the lives of persons with disabilities, whether they make contributions or not, be valued like anyone else's. They are ends in themselves, not the means to ends. Yet, legally sanctioned prenatal tests and selective abortions suggest that, the first right of persons with disabilities is a claim to life itself, along with social recognition of the value and validity of the life of someone with disabilities. Value based upon the abilities is to buy into a disadvantaged idea of humanity. Every human being should be inherently valued. The inherent value mandates celebrating disability as part of being. The disability human rights paradigm has introduced an approach that should respect the dignity of persons with disabilities as persons who need to be valued for themselves. The mandate of social justice requires quality-of-life provisions to be made to provide a conducive environment for all human beings, including persons with disabilities. The United Nations Convention on the Rights of Persons with Disabilities (UNCRPD), 2006 has introduced this paradigm by endorsing inherent dignity to persons with disabilities, thereby making their status equal to that of all other human beings. In the following chapter, I will examine the UNCRPD rights paradigm, to analyse the legal legitimacy of prenatal tests and disability-selective abortions.

CHAPTER FIVE

The Equality–Non-discrimination Gaze on the Right to Life

· ·

The medical profession is a social institution that has been ethically charged with respecting and enhancing the value of life of all human beings. It is expected that the ethics of protection or preservation of human life be applied equally to all without discrimination. Healthcare interventions are intended to promote the health of human beings and thereby protect human life. Yet the healthcare system perceives disability-selective abortion as an acceptable health intervention. Laws, health policies, and healthcare programmes focus on the strategy of prevention of disability through prenatal diagnosis and disability-selective termination of pregnancy. Healthcare programmes related to prenatal care have routinized prenatal screening for foetuses with disabilities. The law has sanctioned its use and the subsequent termination of such foetuses. This unquestioned acceptance of disability-linked abortion shows that disability is seen as undesirable per se and life with disability as not worth living. This diminishes the value of persons with disabilities by presenting the prevention of their birth as a justifiable healthcare intervention.

This strategy is contrary to ethical and legal principles that recognize the value of every human life as equal, including the lives of persons with disabilities. In particular, the United Nations Convention on the Rights of Persons with Disabilities (UNCRPD), 2006, recognizes the inherent human dignity and right to life of persons with disabilities.

In this chapter, I will examine the question of whether disability-selective abortion as a prevention strategy diminishes the value of persons with disabilities, in the context of right to life and dignity of life accorded by the UNCRPD to persons with disabilities. Does this legal strategy violate the universal law of UNCRPD?

UNCRPD: DISABILITY-RIGHTS PARADIGM

The rights-based approach towards persons with disabilities has been accorded full recognition in the UNCRPD. The UNCRPD can thus be introduced as the most recent member of the human rights family.[1] However, the move to persuade the United Nations (UN) to adopt a human rights convention for persons with disabilities was not the first of its kind. But the previous efforts[2] were turned down on the reasoning that disability is in no way excluded from general human rights instruments; consequently, there was no need to adopt a special convention on disability rights.[3]

---

[1] Dhanda (2008: 44).

[2] Sweden and Italy had earlier made efforts to obtain a disability-rights convention.

[3] The Universal Declaration of Human Rights (UDHR), 1948 and the Declaration on Social Progress and Development (DSPD), 1969 are the two pre-UNCRPD general soft law instruments. The International Covenant on Civil and Political Rights (ICCPR), 1966 and the International Covenant on Economic, Social and Cultural Rights (ICESCR), 1966 are the two pre-UNCRPD general and binding international instruments. The UDHR was adopted by the General Assembly of the UN in 1948 and it specified human rights standards accepted by all member states. The UDHR

These claims of normative inclusion in no way matched the ground-level experience of persons with disabilities. Even as the international community did not accede to the claims of persons with disabilities for a special convention, it admitted to these ground-level difficulties encountered by persons with disabilities by adopting the Standard Rules on the Equalization of Opportunities for Persons with Disabilities (henceforth Standard Rules)[4] and the World Programme of Action Concerning Disabled persons.[5] As discussed in Chapter 3, the Standard Rules provided a voice to persons with disabilities.

These soft law instruments, which were adopted without the participation of persons with disabilities, signify how the non-disabled world perceived disabilities and hence created a lower standard of rights for persons with disabilities.[6] For instance, the Principles for the Protection of Persons with Mental Illness and for the Improvement

emphasized the inherent dignity and equal rights of the human family. The UDHR proclaimed the right to life and liberty of all human beings. These values of the UDHR inform the current human rights law on disability.

The DSPD made an explicit mention of persons with disabilities, where it provided for the protection of the rights and welfare of children, the aged, and the 'disabled'. It further made provision for the protection of the physically or mentally disadvantaged.

The ICCPR listed several rights that were of relevance to disability. It is however, debatable whether persons with disabilities were within the conceptualization of the state parties whilst negotiating the Convention. Illustratively, Article 26 of the treaty states that all people are equal before the law and have the right to equal protection of law. And yet, national laws that did not recognize persons with disabilities as persons before the law continued to hold the field.

The ICESCR recognizes the right of everyone to the enjoyment of the highest attainable standard of physical and mental health. The Covenant did not explicitly refer to disability. Article 2(2) prohibits discrimination on the ground of race and colour, and 'other status'. However, it could be contended that disability can be included under 'other status'.

[4] Adopted by the UN General Assembly on 20 December 1993.
[5] Adopted by the UN General Assembly on 3 December 1982.
[6] Dhanda (2008: 45).

of Mental Health Care (henceforth Mental Health Care Principles)[7] built on unproven assumptions about the biomedical nature of 'mental illness'. The medical term 'patient' was used throughout the document to mention persons with mental disabilities. The Mental Health Care Principles supported the dominance of the medical model. This soft law instrument endorsed involuntary detention and treatment for persons with mental disabilities. The Mental Health Care Principles were developed without significant involvement of users and survivors of psychiatry. The World Network for Users and Survivors of Psychiatry has explicitly denounced this instrument, and this seriously reduces the credibility of the Mental Health Care Principles.[8]

The unenforceability of these soft laws and an ominous absence of civil and political rights compounded the discriminatory status and deprivation of persons with disabilities. Even the general and binding instruments drew a line between first-generation and second-generation rights.

Although the UDHR was a composite document incorporating both rights, the succeeding conventions introduced a divide between two sets of rights.[9] International human rights law has conferred immediacy and justifiability as two qualities important to civil and political rights. This has contributed to the non-negotiable visage of civil and political rights.[10] Therefore, no need was felt to guarantee to persons with disabilities the right to life, the most relevant civil right. Consequently, persons with disabilities continued to suffer from discrimination and were often denied their rights. In this vacuum, the UNCRPD recognizes the right to life of persons with disabilities on an equal basis with others.[11] This affirmation

---

[7] Adopted by the UN General Assembly in its resolution 46/119 of 17 December 1991. It should be noted that this soft law was not included in the preambulatory statement of UNCRPD.

[8] World Network of Users and Survivors of Psychiatry (2001).

[9] Dhanda (2008: 50).

[10] Dhanda (2008: 46). In the absence of a civil and political rights regime, persons with disabilities were unable to assertively claim their rights; they had to continually negotiate for the same.

[11] Article 10, UNCRPD.

challenges the stereotypical perception that a life with disability is a less valued life. In this context, it would be appropriate to describe the significance of the UNCRPD on the value and status of the lives of persons with disabilities.

SIGNIFICANCE OF UNCRPD

The UNCRPD is significant in many respects. It is not a mere anti-discrimination convention. It provides a wide range of basic rights to persons with disabilities. The convention breaks away from the state-centric model of negotiation,[12] by according pride of place to persons with disabilities in the negotiation process. The UNCRPD was adopted in the presence of persons with disabilities and their representative organizations from different parts of the world.

The UNCRPD, together with its Optional Protocol, was adopted on 13 December 2006 and came into force as an international human rights law on 3 May 2008. As the first human rights convention adopted in the twenty-first century, the UNCRPD seeks to protect the rights of all persons with disabilities. It identifies the rights of persons with disabilities as well as the obligations on state parties to the UNCRPD to promote, protect, and ensure those rights. It considers the lives of persons with disabilities as valuable as that of any other human being.

The states that become parties to the UNCRPD agree to promote, protect, and ensure the full and equal enjoyment of all human rights and fundamental freedoms to all persons with disabilities, and to promote respect for their inherent dignity. The convention effects a paradigm shift in its approach towards disability. It is a shift from a model in which persons with disabilities are treated as objects of medical treatment, charity, and social protection, to one in which persons with disabilities are recognized as having a standing that is accountable in the human rights arena.[13] Significantly, it recognizes the inherent value of persons with disabilities.

---

[12] Melish (2007: 37).
[13] Nizar (2011: 227).

VALUE OF LIVES OF PERSONS WITH DISABILITIES IN UNCRPD DISCOURSE

The UNCRPD provides a wide range of basic rights to persons with disabilities. It recognizes the inherent dignity of all human beings. Along with equality and non-discrimination as the general principles informing the convention, Article 3 provides for dignity, individual autonomy, full and active participation and inclusion, respect for difference, and accessibility. The provision of reasonable accommodation and positive action measures under Article 5(3) of the convention also reflects the substantive approach to equality and non-discrimination. Thus, the UNCRPD has introduced a paradigm shift by affirming both 'sameness and difference' for the rights of persons with disabilities. Thus, while they are entitled to the same dignity and respect as the rest of humanity, they are also entitled to reasonable accommodation of their difference.[14]

Right to Equality and Non-discrimination

Article 5 of the UNCRPD explicitly addresses the right to equality and non-discrimination. It states:

1. States Parties recognize that all persons are equal before and under the law and are entitled without any discrimination to the equal protection and equal benefit of the law.
2. States Parties shall prohibit all discrimination on the basis of disability and guarantee to persons with disabilities equal and effective legal protection against discrimination on all grounds.
3. In order to promote equality and eliminate discrimination, States Parties shall take all appropriate steps to ensure that reasonable accommodation is provided.
4. Specific measures which are necessary to accelerate or achieve *de facto* equality of persons with disabilities shall not be considered discrimination under the terms of the present Convention.

The right to equality in general affirms that all human beings are born free and equal. The right to equality for persons with disabilities

[14] Dhanda (2008: 47).

envisages the same rights and respect for the diversity to accommodate persons with disabilities. This means that laws, policies, and programmes should not be discriminatory, and also that public authorities should not apply or enforce laws, policies, and programmes in a discriminatory or arbitrary manner. Non-discrimination is an integral part of the right to equality. Hence, in this Article, the UNCRPD embraces both the formal and substantive approaches to equality.

The formal approach recognizes that all are equal before the law.[15] The more substantive approach specifically prohibits discrimination on the basis of disability.[16] State parties are required to combat any form of discrimination as defined by Article 2. Accordingly:

> Discrimination on the basis of disability means any distinction, exclusion or restriction on the basis of disability which has the purpose or effect of impairing restriction or nullifying the recognition, enjoyment or exercise, on an equal basis with others, of all human rights and fundamental freedoms in the political, economic, social, cultural, civil or any other field. It includes all forms of discrimination, including denial of reasonable accommodation.

The UNCRPD aims to apply the principle of equality and non-discrimination to every human right. Human equality is central to the system of basic freedoms postulated by human rights law. Its core premise is that all persons not only possess inherent self-worth but are also inherently equal in terms of self-worth, regardless of their difference. It means that a just society is one that has a positive approach towards human differences.[17] Valuing human difference is validated by the human rights perspective of the UNCRPD. From one angle, equality focuses on the need for even-handedness by parliaments when they create distinctions in law and policy. This interpretation of formal or juridical equality is, of course, vital and it will continue to form the bedrock of any understanding of equality.[18] It seems equality and non-discrimination are necessary rights to make other rights meaningful and to produce real change. The human rights paradigm

---

[15] Article 5(1), UNCRPD.
[16] Article 5(2), UNCRPD.
[17] Quinn and Degener (2002).
[18] Quinn and Degener (2002).

of the convention has been further strengthened by the right to life and health.

Right to Life

Article 10 of the UNCRPD states: 'State Parties reaffirm that every human being has the inherent right to life and shall take all necessary measures to ensure its effective enjoyment by persons with disabilities on an equal basis with others.'

The terms 'reaffirm' and 'shall take all necessary measures' have been used to strengthen the text and to make it clear that the 'right to life' includes the 'right to survive'. The right to life was included in the convention mainly in view of the stereotypes prevailing in society against a life with disability. The lives of persons with disabilities are under threat because others think that their lives are not worth living.

This right also has a bearing on the issue of when life begins, and whether legal protection to life is available both before and after birth. The International Disability Caucus (IDC), representing people with disabilities and civil society organizations, chose not to address this question and only insisted that the value of a life with disability should be recognized and all persons with disabilities should have the right to live.[19] The negotiations over this article shows that the IDC sought to introduce a text stating that disability should not be a justification to terminate life.[20] This was to highlight the reality where people use disability as the justification to end life rather to live with disability. Therefore, the affirmation of the right to life itself challenges the belief that a life with disability is a less valued life and hence it does not need to be protected.[21] The right to life and right to health are interlinked, as both aim to dignify the lives of persons with disabilities.

---

[19] Schulze (2009: 57). Also see UNCRPD, Daily summary of discussion at the seventh session, 17 January 2006, available online at http://www.un.org/esa/socdev/enable/rights/ahc7sum17jan.htm (last accessed on 28 February 2016).

[20] Marianne Schulze (2009: 57).

[21] Quinn and Degener (2002: 46).

Article 25 of the convention states: 'State parties recognize that persons with disabilities have the right to enjoyment of the highest attainable standard of health without discrimination on the basis of disability.'

It further provides persons with disabilities the right of access to gender-sensitive, equal, and non-discriminated health services. The reference to reproductive health in Article 25(a) of the convention is crucial, as there is an apprehension of international legitimization of abortion.

A combined reading of the rights to life and health provided in the UNCRPD shows that the convention only provided for secondary prevention of disability. Prevention envisaged under the right to health refers to minimizing further disabilities of persons with disabilities. Secondary prevention means and includes actions aimed at preventing impairments from causing permanent functional limitations or disability. No article in the convention provides for primary prevention of disability, as aimed for by disability-selective abortion.

A study of the convention's preparatory papers shows that this difference in approach was caused by the active participation of persons with disabilities in the process of negotiation. The stakeholders took the stand that primary prevention may have significance for society at large but had no place in a convention concerned with the rights of persons with disabilities.

The convention accords unequivocal rights of equality and non-discrimination to persons with disabilities. The rights to life, inherent dignity, equality, and non-discrimination accord high value to the lives of persons with disabilities. Equality and non-discrimination form the touchstone on which national legal frameworks must be assessed. When viewed through this lens, the right to life combined with right to equality and non-discrimination renders disability-selective abortion questionable. It is the 'selectiveness' in the abortion that is problematic. A woman should decide about the baby within the confines of her right to choose. But, disability-selective abortions are systemic when social prejudice forces her hand to choose selectively. To remove this persisting prejudice against one group of humans requires appreciating the significance of the equality on the right to life.

PRO-LIFE AND RIGHT TO LIFE

Stefan Tromel, who represented the European Disability Forum, testifies:

> When it was first proposed to have an article on the right to life, this proposal met with some opposition. The right to life is a hugely controversial issue, as there is no agreement within the UN on when life starts, and to open such a debate immediately becomes a debate about the right (or not) to abortion and euthanasia. The presence of pro-life activists throughout the negotiation process was a permanent reminder of the delicate nature of this discussion.[22]

'Is the foetus a person?' is an oft-debated question in relation to the right to life. Pro-life advocates argue that the right to life begins from the conception of an embryo. They argue that a foetus has the same value of a human being and it has the right to life. Catholic legal theory and other pro-life religious groups propound the view that the foetus is a human being. Biological facts evidence the genetic identity and individuality of the unborn child from the moment of conception.[23] Since pro-lifers advocate for the right to life of the foetus, they consider abortion to be murder, as it takes away the life of a human being. Consequently, pro-lifers seek a total ban on abortion. Pro-choice theorists do not ascribe life to the foetus and contend that it is the right of pregnant women to decide whether to continue the pregnancy or not.

The presence of members from different countries holding these divergent views meant there was no way to have an explicit article to outlaw 'forced abortion' based on the prenatal diagnosis of disability. The right to life endorsed by the UNCRPD does not explicitly mention the thematic issue of selective abortion on the reason of disability, as it was not possible to cover it without entering the delicate and never-settled discussion on whether life starts at conception or at birth.

But, the right to life accorded to persons with disabilities by the UNCRPD is a far-reaching right which recognizes the life of

---

[22] Tromel (2009: 124).
[23] Kreeft (1997).

a person with disability as inherently worthwhile. Consequently, when it comes to disability-selective abortion the right of the foetus or the pregnant woman has no relevance, as it involves the question of the value of life of the stakeholder, the kinds of persons who are selected out. This is significant, as can be analysed from the silence maintained by the UNCRPD on primary prevention of disabilities. It was based on the reasoning that primary prevention is not a disability-rights issue and hence should not find a place in a disability-rights charter.

RIGHT TO LIFE AND PRIMARY PREVENTION OF DISABILITY

Right to life as a civil right has been categorized as basic, as without this right the realization of all other rights is a non-starter. Right to life is an assertion that the difference of disability contributes to the richness and diversity of human condition and is not a deficit that has to be selected out.[24] Right to life legally establishes the right of people with disabilities to live in the world. The preparatory papers of the UNCRPD show that there was an assertion regarding the lives of all persons with disabilities in the future. The term 'ensure its effective enjoyment' specifically proposed to maintain life by securing physical survival as well as participatory and inclusive life.[25] Otherwise right to life would be confined within narrow interpretations. That is why the developments in bioethics and prenatal testing were also discussed, as they would feed into the intolerance towards diversity.[26]

It can be seen that the right to life was majorly negotiated as a right to be born and the right to be different. The UNCRPD is totally silent on primary prevention of disabilities, as prevention is not a disability rights issue, and hence, it did not find place in the

---

[24] Dhanda (2008: 46).

[25] Schulze (2009: 57).

[26] 'Comprehensive and integral international convention to promote and protect the rights and dignity of persons with disabilities', 9 August 2002, Working paper by Mexico, New York, available online at http://www.un.org/esa/socdev/enable/rights/adhocmeetaac265w1e.htm (last accessed on 2 March 2016).

convention on the rights of persons with disabilities. The inclusion of a primary prevention provision would stigmatize persons with disabilities. Because, it is virtually saying that persons with disabilities do not have the right to live.[27] It is also incoherent to deal at the same time with termination of disability and promotion of the rights of persons with disabilities. Besides, primary prevention is against the spirit of the UNCRPD, as it interferes with the right to life enshrined in it.[28]

Stefan Tromel comments: 'It is very important to highlight that the convention does not refer to the prevention of disability. This was a deliberate decision taken by the Ad Hoc Committee and is one of the elements that reflect [sic] the paradigm shift from "disability" as an object to "persons with disabilities as subjects".'[29]

The commentator adds that it is important for states to draw the relevant conclusions from this decision and therefore exclude the issue of prevention of disability/impairment from any legislation or policy to promote the rights of persons with disabilities.[30] Accordingly, he opines that the application of non-discrimination principles and the references found in Article 4[31] should ensure that abortion legislations do not discriminate on the basis of disability. The controversial nature of the right contributed to the UNCRPD's silence on disability-selective abortions. Despite this silence, it is necessary to examine whether the legitimization of disability-selective abortions undermines the right to life and reinforces the stereotype that a life with disability is not worth living.

In the wake of the UNCRPD, is making disability-selective abortion a preventive strategy for disability ethically and legally justifiable? Does it not devalue the lives of persons with disabilities?

---

[27] Dhanda (2010: 214).

[28] Dhanda and Raturi (2010: 111).

[29] Quinn and Waddington (2009: 120).

[30] Quinn and Waddington (2009: 121).

[31] 'State Parties undertake ... (a) To take all appropriate measures, including legislation, to modify or abolish existing laws, regulations, customs and practices that constitute discrimination against persons with disabilities; (b) To take into account the protection and promotion of the human rights of persons with disabilities in all policies and programmes.'

DOES DISABILITY-SELECTIVE ABORTION DEVALUE PERSONS WITH DISABILITIES?

Ending a life is not a function of medical science as a mode to prevent any disease. Yet, selectively preventing the birth of a child with disability is an approved medical mode for preventing disability. This strategy does not prevent or treat disability in an existing human being or in a foetus. Advanced medical technology is being utilized, not to maximize the lives of persons with disabilities, but to prevent the birth of people with disabilities by medically terminating foetuses diagnosed with disability. While medical technology has made it possible to detect problems in the foetus, it has also made it possible to prevent disability through the diagnosis and treatment of problems in utero.[32] Though foetal care is still in its nascent stage, it is possible to make efforts to develop the field to treat the problems of foetuses.[33] However, medical professionals justify termination of pregnancy for 'severe anomalies', because they consider non-treatable defects to be lethal.[34]

Disability-selective abortion is justified as enabling women to exercise their reproductive choice. The existing principles, policies, and laws diminish the value of persons with disabilities by presenting the prevention of their birth as a justified healthcare intervention. This challenges the ethics of the value of lives of persons with disabilities. It also infringes upon the right to life and right to health of persons with disabilities as accorded by the UNCRPD.

This type of prevention is an explicit form of denial of the right to lives of persons with disabilities. The right to health envisaged under the UNCRPD mandates states to spend resources to minimize further disabilities of persons with disabilities. But the health policy promoting prevention through disability-selective abortion diverts resources from minimizing disability to diagnosing disability and terminating it. Resources and technology are used not to empower the lives of persons with disabilities, but to diminish their value by denying them the right to life. Preventing the birth of an individual with a disease

32 Ram (2010).
33 Suresh (2010).
34 Nizar (2011: 228).

is morally different from preventing a disease. It sends the message that persons with disabilities are not entitled to the rights to life and equality and implies that the lives of persons with disabilities are not worth living.

As right to life involves controversial issues, the participating countries and various groups with different approaches to those controversies made UNCRPD silent on disability-selective abortion. Nevertheless, certain groups such as the World Federation of the Deaf (WFD) expressed the view that abortion based on disability should be prohibited in recognizing the right to life.[35] The IDC provided clear examples of situations where the lives of persons with disabilities had been put in danger, because of the perceived low quality and value of life. The IDC also wanted the convention to outlaw forced abortion based on the prenatal diagnosis of disability.[36]

As the UNCRPD recognizes persons with disabilities as subjects of law, and to confirm this 'new rights paradigm', a well-studied silence has been maintained in the convention about disability-selective abortions. However, this silence cannot be presumed to mean that the UNCRPD has permitted disability-selective abortions. This can be seen as strengthened by the concluding observations of the UN committee in the case of Spain.[37] The Sexual and Reproductive Health Act of Spain[38] allows extended time for termination of pregnancy on the basis of foetal disability.

This law, which decriminalizes voluntary termination of pregnancy, allows pregnancy to be terminated up to 14 weeks. However, it provides an extended time limit for abortion if the foetus has disabilities. It permits abortion up to 22 weeks of pregnancy if there is 'a risk of serious anomalies in the foetus'. If 'an extremely serious and incurable illness is detected in the foetus', it inter alia permits

[35] Quinn and Waddington (2009: 27).

[36] Quinn and Waddington (2009: 124).

[37] Concluding observation no. 18: 'The Committee recommends that the State party abolish the distinction made in Act 2/2010 in the period allowed under law within which a pregnancy can be terminated based solely on disability' (Committee on the Rights of Persons with Disabilities: 2011).

[38] Organic Act 2/2010 of 3 March 2010 on Sexual and Reproductive Health.

abortion beyond 22 weeks. Thus, this law provides two specific cases in which the time limits for abortion are extended if the foetus has a disability.

Noticing the longer time limits allowed for terminating pregnancies when the foetus has a disability, the UN committee has raised the question of whether the Government of Spain considered this to be in line with Article 4, paragraph 1(d), of the UNCRPD. When the committee considered the reports submitted by Spain under Article 35 of the Convention, it recommended that Spain 'abolish the distinction made in the law in the period allowed within which a pregnancy can be terminated based solely on disability'.[39] The committee addressed the problem not by referring to the right to life but to the right to equality and non-discrimination.

The above observation of the committee strongly makes the point that a distinction in an abortion law on the basis of disability is inconsistent with the convention. Interestingly, the convention has explicitly not commented on any time limit or prohibition of abortion on the basis of disability. However, the recommendation of the committee to abolish the law that permitted extended time for abortion on the basis of disability brings the human rights violation of such laws into focus. It also reinforces the interpretation of the rights under the convention from a disability-rights perspective. Consequently, the political, but brilliant silence maintained by the UNCRPD cannot be presumed to mean that the UNCRPD has permitted disability-selective abortion. Instead, states should draw relevant conclusions from this decision to inherently value the lives of persons with disabilities.

It is also significant to note that the UNCRPD ensures equal respect for human rights regardless of the difference of disability. It accords value to the lives of persons with disabilities. The assertion of value of life was accorded a narrow interpretation. The right to life accorded to persons with disabilities needs to be interpreted from a disability-rights perspective. Gerard Quinn considers the right to life to be a right for existence.[40] He submits that the right to

---

[39] 'Consideration of reports submitted by States parties under article 35 of the Convention', Concluding Observations 18, UN Committee on the Rights of Persons with Disabilities, 6th Session, 19–23 September 2011, p. 3.

[40] Quinn and Degener (2002).

life accorded by the UNCRPD has been violated through abortion on the basis of disability.[41] Therefore, disability-selective abortion laws are controversial because such laws permit the elimination, or prevent the existence of the persons who have disability.[42] In effect, such laws inform that it would have been better if every person with disability had never been born. Consequently, disability-selective abortion, which is inconsistent with the equal status accorded by the UNCRPD, diminishes the value of persons with disabilities. The UNCRPD's right to life stance is strongly endorsed for the stakeholders of other core human rights instruments. This can be confirmed by examining the right to life for other groups of people.

RIGHT TO LIFE AND ITS DISCOURSE UNDER OTHER HUMAN RIGHTS TREATIES

The text of the right to life in the UNCRPD is consistent with that in core human rights treaties such as the UDHR, ICCPR, Convention on the Rights of the Child (CRC), and the Convention on the Elimination of All Forms Discrimination Against Women (CEDAW). After the horrors that human kind experienced in the first half of the twentieth century, in particular after the genocidal Nazi regime, there was an obvious need to reassert the overriding importance of respect for human life.[43] Consequently, the right to life was reaffirmed in Article 3 of the UDHR as, 'Everyone has the right to life, liberty and security of person'.

The paramount importance of this right was reiterated while drafting the ICCPR. Article 6(1) of the ICCPR provides, 'Every human being has the inherent right to life. This right shall be protected by law. No one shall be arbitrarily deprived of his life.'

The adjective 'inherent' emphasizes the high hierarchical position of the right. The right has been seen as the outflow of a pre-positive stratum of law, namely *jus naturale*.[44] The state responsibility envisaged

---

[41] Quinn and Degener (2002).

[42] Glover (1992); also, Harris (2004: 431).

[43] Tomuschat, Lagrange, and Oeter (2010: 4).

[44] Bossuyt (1987: 119).

is very explicit in the ICCPR committee's general comment, which notes:

> The right to life enunciated in article 6 of the Covenant has been dealt with in all State reports. It is the supreme right from which no derogation is permitted even in time of public emergency which threatens the life of the nation (art.4). However, the Committee has noted that quite often the information given concerning article 6 was limited to only one or other aspect of this right. It is a right which should not be interpreted narrowly.[45]

The committee further states:

> The right to life has been too often narrowly interpreted. The expression 'inherent right to life' cannot properly be understood in a restrictive manner, and the protection of this right requires that States adopt positive measures. In this connection, the Committee considers that it would be desirable for States parties to take all possible measures to reduce infant mortality and to increase life expectancy, especially in adopting measures to eliminate malnutrition and epidemics.[46]

The Treaty on Civil and Political Rights (ICCPR) thus holds that the right to life is a right to provide for the inherent value of all human beings. It is a right not to be arbitrarily deprived of life. If we look into other treaties and their stance on the right to life, we can see that this right is rather a right that recognizes the inherent value of human beings.

Article 6(1) of the CRC explicitly states that state parties recognize that every child has the inherent right to life. The statement of the CRC committee on the right to life of children with disabilities shows the significance of the right to life for children with disabilities. It states: 'States must create an environment that respects human dignity and ensures the holistic development of every child. In the assessment and determination of the child's best interests, the

[45] Human Rights Committee (1982).
[46] Human Rights Committee (1982).

State must ensure full respect for his or her inherent right to life, survival, and development.'[47]

This points to state responsibility to protect the right to life of every child, respecting his or her inherent value of life. It explicitly states that the right to life is the right to survive and develop. Thus, the right to life can definitely be interpreted as the right to exist and survive decently in this world. However, disability-selective abortion, and the narrow application of the right to life in such cases, implies that persons with disabilities have no right to survive. The committee further expands this right in connection to children with disabilities.

The inherent right to life, survival, and development is a right that warrants particular attention where children with disabilities are concerned. In many countries of the world, children with disabilities are subject to a variety of practices that completely or partially compromise this right. The Committee on the Rights of the Child reports that, 'In addition to being more vulnerable to infanticide, some cultures view a child with any form of disability as a bad omen that may "tarnish the family pedigree". Accordingly, a certain designated individual from the community systematically kills children with disabilities. These crimes often go unpunished or perpetrators receive reduced sentences.'[48] States parties are urged to undertake all measures that are required to put an end to these practices including raising public awareness, setting up appropriate legislation, and enforcing the law that ensures appropriate punishment of all those that directly or indirectly violate the right to life, survival, and development of children with disabilities.[49]

Here, the right to life of children with disabilities has been viewed from the perspective of infanticide, which is after birth. When we

---

[47] Committee on the Rights of the Children, General Comment No.14, 29 May 2013, p. 11, paragraph 42, available online at http://www2.ohchr.org/English/bodies/crc/docs/GC/CRC_C_GC_14_ENG.pdf (last accessed on 23 February 2016).

[48] Report of the UN Committee on the Rights of the Child, (2006), p. 38. Also see Angel et al. (2014). General Comments by UN Treaty Body System, p. 1298.

[49] General Comment No. 9 (2006), UN Committee on the Rights of the Child, CRC/C/GC/9, 43rd session, 2006, p. 9.

add this to the previous comment of the committee about the inherent right to life and survival and development, disability-selective abortions deny such right to children with disabilities, prior to their birth.

The CRC committee, as part of the plan of action to report the implementation of the CRC, decided to produce examples of good practices for legislations that uphold the convention. In particular, the committee uphold legislations which ensure that children with disabilities enjoy the equal right to life, survival, and development and condemned laws which abolish discriminatory laws on abortion and healthcare. It shows that the CRC considers abortion laws that prevent the birth of children with disabilities as discriminatory and inconsistent with right to life accorded by it.[50]

Thus, evidently, right to life occupies a high position in the hierarchy of human rights legal norms. The right to life in human rights jurisprudence is based on the need to protect the dignity and value of human life. Therefore, in the UNCRPD, the clause 'ensure its effective enjoyment' deviates from the standard clauses on the right to life, for broad interpretation of the right. The main cause for this formulation is the fact that regularly the lives of persons with disabilities are devalued as not 'worth living' and thereby their elimination is justified. Right to life accorded in the UNCRPD thus reinforces the 'respect for inherent dignity' of persons.[51]

Since the value of life strengthens the right to life, the legitimacy of disability-selective abortions should be interpreted as diminishing value to life with disability. Therefore, disability-selective abortion and its inconsistency with right to life should be examined on the basis of its implication on the value of life of persons with disabilities. A reasonable interpretation of the right to life obligates states to recognize the value of persons with disabilities in their laws, which facilitate the application of scientific advances as well.

However, the UNCRPD envisages right to life by combining it with right to equality and non-discrimination. The UNCRPD committee's response to the abortion law in Spain, which grants more time to abort a foetus with disability, is a strong indication of how the right

[50] Quinn and Waddington (2009: 27).
[51] Article 3(a), UNCRPD.

to life is tied up with equality and non-discrimination. When law and policy devise strategies based on medical perception, they need to be assessed on the parameter of equality and non-discrimination. Disability-selective abortions are rendered questionable because they discriminate and deny the equal status of persons with disabilities.

Scientific developments in the area of genetics and prenatal technology are used for selecting out disability. As Marxa Saxton said:[52]

> Scientists and physicians apparently accept screening technologies based on the 'commonsense' assumption that prenatal screening and selective abortion can potentially reduce the incidence of disease and disability and thus improve the quality of life. A deeper look into the medical system's views of disability and the broader social factors contributing to disability discrimination challenges these assumptions. Prenatal screening results can turn a 'wanted baby' into an 'unwanted foetus'.

However, Asch has pointed out the contradiction between bioethicists' goals of inclusion and equality for people with disabilities and primary prevention of disability through selective abortion.[53] Bonnie Steinbock has empathetically explained this contradiction:

> Disability activists have a laudable goal: to change society so that it is welcoming and accepting of people with disabilities. However, there is no reason why society cannot both attempt to prevent disability and to provide for the needs of those who are disabled. As a matter of fact, the rise of prenatal screening has coincided with more progressive attitudes toward the inclusion of people with disabilities, as evidenced in the United States by the passage of the Americans with Disabilities Act.[54]

Peter Singer, a contemporary bioethics scholar, says: 'On the one hand we are naturally sympathetic to the claims of a disability rights movement that models itself on movements defending the rights of women and ethnic minorities, and, on the other hand, we all accept

---

[52] Saxton (2000: 158).
[53] Asch (2003: 317).
[54] Steinbock (2000: 121).

that to have a disability is to be worse off than to be without the disability.'[55]

He uses the following argument to justify genetic testing and subsequent termination of a foetus with disability. According to him:

> There are many things that people who are paralyzed below the waist could not do in any society, no matter how constructed. They cannot visit untracked wilderness, go ice skating, or play football. And many other things that they can do, they can do only with difficulty and with more time than it would take those who have the use of their legs. The decision to abort a foetus, that has, say, Down syndrome, is not a decision that is 'anti-children', still less 'anti-life'.[56]

We can see that bioethicists argue that it is better not to have a disability than to have one, and that it is preferable to select against the foetus with a disabling trait. This argument is explicit in the questions raised by certain bioethicists that, 'Shouldn't parents seek the best—even through genetics—for their offspring? Don't we expect them to?'[57]

Thus, the bioethics and the medical profession perceive that 'disabilities are not generally advantageous, not something to be hoped for; indeed, they are to be avoided, if possible. They are not merely neutral forms of variation.'[58] Consequently, in disability-selective abortions scientific advances are legally facilitated to prevent the existence of people with disabilities. Such practices are promoted as part of 'quality of life' or 'deteriorating suffering'. In any situation, it ultimately prevents the existence and right to life of persons with disabilities. As Adrienne Asch asks, 'Is it possible to espouse the goals of CRPD of including persons with disabilities as fully and equal participating members and simultaneously promoting the use of prenatal tests and selective abortion to prevent the birth of those who would live with disabilities?'[59] This is crucial in the wake of the rights paradigm introduced by the UNCRPD.

[55] Singer (2000: 247).
[56] Singer (2000).
[57] Buchanan et al. (2001: 156).
[58] Bossuyt (1987: 113).
[59] Asch (2003: 315).

Prenatal testing and disability-linked selective abortions certainly prevent individuals who would be born with disability from coming into existence. While it is done on the imperialistic opinion of medical profession, it is in fact offending the rights perspective perceived under the UNCRPD. This offending part of disability-selective abortion has been put forth by Thomas William Shakespeare. He said: 'Bioethical and biomedical versions of prenatal diagnosis also fail to account for the complexity and vulnerability of human embodiment.'[60] As long as frailty and impairment are inherent facts of human life, the drive for 'perfect baby' is a futile attempt. Selecting the 'best foetus' also cannot assure you that the child will be free from any such conditions in the future. Approximately 1–2 per cent[61] of births are affected by congenital disability, while between 10–20 per cent of people acquire disability after birth.

As prenatal diagnosis followed by disability-selective abortions is viewed as a legitimate medical and public health practice, there is an acknowledgement that the characteristic of disability is not desirable. If public health espouses the goals of social justice and equality for people with disabilities, it should reconsider whether it is ethically correct to promote this practice. All other medical conditions or diseases are addressed with health interventions aimed at reducing the impact of, or treating, the condition. This approach is adopted even in relation to incurable diseases. Interventions that reflect the preference for perfect bodies and minds offend the dignity of people with disabilities. Moreover, when abortion is promoted for one particular group to eliminate characteristics they receive in the natural lottery, this results in apparent discrimination.[62]

At this juncture, it is important to state that not all disability is preventable, and also that many disabilities are acquired during the course of one's lifetime. Is it not then more desirable that the

---

[60] Shakespeare (2011: 40).

[61] This percentage can be argued as a very negligible number, which does not warrant grappling with its legality. However, disability-selective abortion and its wrongness lie not with the number selected out, but with the social prejudice involved in the decision.

[62] Nizar (2011: 228).

medical profession learns how to deal with diverse human minds and bodies? It is important that professionals learn much more than they know at present about a life with disability, in order to disseminate correct information to prospective parents and the society at large. If professionals recognize, respect, and affirm disability as part of the human condition, it would be easier to incorporate disability into the familial and social landscape. Disability would be one more aspect of human diversity as envisaged under the UNCRPD.[63]

The UNCRPD has introduced a dramatic shift in the perception towards disability. In essence, the human rights perspective on disability means viewing persons with disabilities as subjects and not as objects. It entails moving away from viewing persons with disabilities as problems and viewing them as holders of rights. It signifies the value of human diversity in the context of bioethics. It affirms the core values of human rights—dignity and equality. Right to dignity deems each individual to be of inestimable value and nobody is insignificant. The UNCRPD focuses on the inherent dignity of persons with disabilities and it accords the right to equality by valuing difference. But the legal order on disability-selective abortion is paradoxical and violates the rights accorded by the UNCRPD. Consequently, screening out and selective abortion on the basis of disability diminishes the value of life of persons with disabilities.

***

The UNCRPD recognizes that state parties are required to take substantial measures to protect and respect all rights. The convention aims at empowering persons with disabilities. All these rights are accorded to achieve the goal of making persons with disabilities self-reliant and full members of society. In order to enjoy any of these rights, they should be permitted to born. But disability-selective abortion not only prevents persons with disabilities from coming into existence, but it also diminishes their value. It embodies the view that there is something undesirable about being a person with disability, so

---

[63] Nizar (2011: 228).

undesirable that it is better that such people are not born. Consequently, disability-selective abortion discriminates against persons with disabilities.

Disability-selective abortion is therefore unquestionably inconsistent with the UNCRPD and its new disability–human rights paradigm. The convention is brilliantly silent about disability-selective abortion, so as to not make an incoherent deal by simultaneously endorsing the value of life and its termination. The recent recommendation of the UNCRPD committee to abolish the Sexual and Reproductive Health Act of Spain strongly establishes the inherent value of life accorded to persons with disabilities under the UNCRPD. The committee's observation, that a law that provides extended time for abortion on the basis of disability contrasts with the UNCRPD, clearly provides a wider meaning of the right to life from a disability perspective, combining it with equality and non-discrimination. Therefore, it can be concluded that disability-selective abortion laws that diminish the value of persons with disabilities are explicitly inconsistent with UNCRPD.

India is under an international obligation to espouse the goals of including people with disabilities as fully equal and participating members, but its laws simultaneously facilitate selective abortion to prevent the births of those who would live with disabilities. This contradiction denies the inherent value and equal status to persons with disabilities. If they are not permitted to be born for no other reason than their disability, then the legitimacy of these legislations should be revisited.

Reasonably, it raises the following questions: is it not more desirable to give to humans the best kind of life with the kinds of minds and bodies they possess than chasing the mirage of the perfect mind and body? Is it not possible to accept disability as an integral part of the human condition? If disability is accepted as an integral part of the human condition as stated by the UNCRPD, policymakers can focus on planning a society which would accommodate disabilities, as we do for many other human conditions. Then resources can be allocated for building a just society rather than being expended on waging a losing battle.

Disability-linked abortions need a re-examination because they diminish the value of persons with disabilities and obstruct the social acceptance of persons with disabilities. Legally permitted disability-selective abortions indirectly suggest that people have to prove their worth before they are born. In the wake of India's ratification of the UNCRPD, it is the state's responsibility to protect the rights, equal status, and inherent value of persons with disabilities to ensure equality and non-discrimination. In the following chapter, I will examine whether India can continue with such laws that diminish the value of persons with disabilities.

CHAPTER SIX

Disability-selective Abortions in National and International Law

. . . .

The process of disability-selective abortions seems to demonstrate that deep prejudice subsists against persons with disabilities. Whilst law permits this selection, it diminishes the status of persons with disabilities. Disability-selective abortion has a demonstrative effect, as it feeds into pre-existing prejudice. Disability-selective abortion is problematic, because it is an unquestioned process. Disability is seen as a medical condition. Consequently, a person who possesses this condition is considered a carrier of an undesired condition. Once a person is born with disability or once anyone acquires disability, that person begins to be seen as a problem instead of an individual. Disability-selective abortions seem like a part of the same process.

The UNCRPD's rights paradigm recognizes the equal value of persons with disabilities. The convention has dislocated the medical model of disability. It makes a shift from treating persons with disabilities as 'medically flawed' beings. In the UNCRPD paradigm, disability is no more a diminishing medical condition, but an inherent human condition to be celebrated. India has both signed and ratified the UNCRPD, which came into force in May 2008. In fulfilment of India's international human rights obligation under the treaty, India should revisit its laws to harmonize them with the convention. In this chapter, I will examine the legal status of disability-selective abortions under the Pre-Natal Diagnostic Techniques (Regulation and Prevention of Misuse) (PNDT) Act, 1994 and the Medical Termination of Pregnancy (MTP) Act, 1971 in the wake of India's ratification to the UNCRPD.

Technological advancements such as prenatal diagnostic tests have contributed to further the long-persisting social prejudice against female child in India. A similar situation had prevailed against women in India. Until the law intervened, such practices were unproblematic in our society. It would be worthwhile to explore the long-persisting social prejudice against the female gender in India. This is to analyse how law has intervened to remove the social opprobrium on girl child.

SELECTIVE KILLING OF GIRL CHILD

Female infanticide has been prevalent in India from the early nineteenth century, so it is evident that such selective killing of girl child was never a problematic practice in India. Even though such practices were offensive to Western sensibilities, the British government instructed the East India Company officials to avoid all interference. Especially, if it was determined that religious sanction supported the practice or custom in question. It was the first venture of the company to opt for a full-fledged legislation in the form of Bengal Regulation VI of 1802,[1] to prohibit the sacrifice of children to the sharks on Saugor

---

[1] In compliance with the desire expressed by G.H. Barlow, the Governor General in Council, in his letter dated 18 February 1802, the Nizamat Adwalat prepared a draft to stop the sacrifice of children at Saugor and other places. The draft was submitted to His Excellency Richard Marquis Wellesley, Governor General and it was passed on 20 August 1802. These correspondences are available in *Parliamentary Papers: Papers etc.* (East India Company: Third Part, vol. IX, 1813: 429–30).

Island at the mouth of the river Ganga. The case of sati[2] was much more difficult for the company, as this custom enjoyed scriptural sanction.[3]

While sati was practised publicly, female infanticide was almost a private household act.[4] Even the advantage of lack of scriptural sanction for the practice of female infanticide was offset by complex factors.[5] An effective policy against female infanticide depended upon a free-flowing social intercourse between the rulers and ruled, which was non-existent. Any zeal for reform was further frustrated by the British government's reluctance to interfere in the private affairs of Indian subjects. Its infanticide policy was the infanticide fund, composed of fines collected from infanticide chiefs,[6] to be distributed to families who had preserved their daughters.[7]

However, an aggressive anti-infanticide policy undertaken by the company, at first, seemed successful, with rewards from the infanticide fund for informers and infanticide chiefs who helped to secure three infanticide convictions by the Bombay High Court in 1834–5. But this success quickly turned sour, as the most prominent chief to

[2] A Hindu religious custom that forced the widow to immolate herself in the funeral pyre of the deceased husband.

[3] Cassels (2010: 157).

[4] Cassels (2010: 159).

[5] Cassels (2010: 159).

[6] The company made the Chiefs (native rulers of the provinces and clans) to sign agreements for suppression of infanticide. Alexander Walker, who framed this policy, called it as 'infanticide engagements' (Bhatnagar, Dube, and Dube 2005: 107). Thus infanticide chiefs were the chiefs who entered into such agreements with the East India Company. Jahreja chief was one among the very first to enter into such an agreement (Cassels 2010: 159). The Chiefs who permitted infanticides were considered failed to keep such promises or agreements and thus levied with fines. The infanticide funds were offered to pay dowries of surviving daughters to encourage families to preserve their daughters and not consider them financial burdens (Bhatnagar, Dube, and Dube 2005: 5).

[7] Elphinstone Minute, 9 January 1821, Bombay Political Consultations 21 February 1821, in *Parliamentary Papers* (1824), XXIII, paper 426, p. 116, Parliament of India. All the parliamentary papers are available for access in the Parliament Library of the Parliament of India.

be convicted became a martyr among his own people and some of the informers were murdered. Consequently, the district officers came to the conclusion that female infanticide 'was not a safe subject to investigate and legislate upon'.[8] Instead, they shifted their anti-infanticide policy towards education with grants from the infanticide fund for essay contests in schools. This hostility among officers towards any idea of legislation on the subject of infanticide was reinforced by the Law Commission of 1837 in Kolkata, which rejected proposals for fresh infanticide legislation. The Law Commission rejected the proposals with the abrupt comment: 'This is a subject which belongs to the Penal Code'.[9]

Meanwhile, district officers in Rajputana and the North Western Provinces (NWP) had discovered that female infanticide was flourishing even among Rajputs who had originally signed engagements with the company renouncing the practice. However, a fresh legislative initiative was brutally interrupted by the rebellion of 1857. The immediate result was the replacement of Section 13 of the Bengal Regulation XXI of 1795[10] with the simplified Sections 315 and 317 of the Indian Penal Code enacted in 1860. It prescribed certain punishments for the 'exposure of infants and concealment of births'. The simplified and generalized penal law appeared to be a solution to the problem of female infanticide among the Rajputs. But in NWP, the penal code was inadequate to prohibit female infanticide.

[8] J. Erskine, Political Agent in Kattywar, to Chief Secretary, Bombay Government, 30 June 1837, Bombay Political Consultations 20 February 1839, No. 5, in *Parliamentary Papers* (1843) XXXV, p. 198, Parliament of India.

[9] J.P. Grant, the official Secretary of Indian Law Commission had reported this to R.D. Mangles, the officiating Secretary to Government in the Legislative Department on 30 March, 1838. (I.O.R., pp. 206–96); this stand is also clear from the letter dated 14 April 1837 from the Chief Secretary to the Government of St. George. (Indian Legislative Proceedings of 15 May 1837, Nos 1–2, IOR, pp. 206–88. These papers are preserved and available at N.A.I, Delhi); see Cassels (2010: 126).

[10] Bengal Regulation XXI for preventing Brahmins in Province of Benares Establishing Kooehs, Wounding or Killing their Female Relations or Children, or sitting Dhurna and for Preventing the tribe of Raujekoomars in That province Killing Their Female Children (passed on 27 March 1795), I.O.R.,V/8/17, p. 138.

However, when the central government (colonial) surveyed the presidencies and princely states for the need of a new special infanticide law, the response was overwhelmingly negative.[11] It took an alarming report from R.T. Hobart, joint magistrate of Bastri district, to force a call for special legislation for the suppression of female infanticide. Thus, Act VIII for the Prevention of the Murder of Female Infants became law in April 1870. It was a flexible law open to the complexity of the multifaceted nature of the crime. The local governments were made responsible for taking census. If necessary, these local governments were authorized to raise a special police force and limit the marriage expenses among the specially designated clans who were involved in female infanticide. The legislation was considered to be an indication that female infanticide had been successfully suppressed. But, the practice had become endemic by the twentieth century, spreading far beyond the control of law. The 1921 census report, which provides figures from 1901 to 1921, refers to the much lower number of females in certain caste groups,[12] which were classified as 'castes having a "tradition" of female infanticide'.[13]

It can be analysed that the colonial efforts to suppress female infanticide were not successful, as it was perceived a justifiable practice. Starting from Jonathan Duncan's efforts among the Rajkumar Rajputs of Jaunpur district in 1789, to the passing of the Female Infanticide Prevention Act in April 1870, British efforts to stop female infanticide covered a period of nearly 100 years.[14] However, female foeticide became a subject ultimately enshrined in the penal code, with subsequent special legislation enacted in response to apparent need.

PRENATAL DIAGNOSTIC TECHNIQUES AND SELECTIVE FOETICIDE

Prenatal diagnostic techniques were introduced in India in the late 1970s to detect foetal 'abnormalities'. The feminists were very quick

---

[11] Cassels (2010: 161).

[12] Marten (1924: Appendix VI). In this report, in Punjab the Hindu Rajputs are shown as having 822 (1901), 756 (1911), and 796 (1921) females per 1,000 males.

[13] Viswanath (2007: 270).

[14] Viswanath (2007: 279).

to point out that the same techniques were also capable of providing information about the sex of the unborn child.[15] It was evident that in a society where female infanticide was unproblematic, such techniques were more likely to be used for sex-selective abortions. The declined sex ratio was not really an issue of number. But it reflected the social prejudice that subsists against women. Law has been a powerful weapon to question and stop it, bringing a remarkable change in the unproblematic perception towards female foeticide. However, due to medical lobbying, the use of prenatal tests were used to diagnose disabilities, instead of a total ban.

The exception for screening disability was defended and glorified as it was used to detect diseases. It was argued that:

> Members of all the parties have supported this law that shows that it is a good law but it should be implemented also. It has been done to cure diseases; it should not prove to be a malady itself. It should be resorted to, to detect certain deformities only and not for termination of pregnancy.[16]
>
> ...
>
> Medical science is to relieve pain, is to relieve distress, is to remedy sickness, and not to kill people and not to take life.[17]

The medical advancement that helped detect foetal sex was seen as an abuse of the technique. Permitting such medical advancement was recognized as discriminatory towards the female sex, affecting the dignity and status of women in society. However, a complete ban was never considered a feasible idea and these tests were defended with the arguments that ban would prevent the maximum use of available know-how,[18] perceive the right perspective of the scientific development,[19] and ultimately detect some diseases.[20] The medical

---

[15] Masden (2002).

[16] Statement of Ramashray Prasad Singh, Parliament of India (1994: 591).

[17] Statement of Syed Shahabuddin, Parliament of India (1994: 555).

[18] Statement of Lakshminarayan Pandeya, Parliament of India (1994: 558).

[19] K.D. Jeswani, Parliament of India (1994: 577).

[20] D. Venkateswara Rao, Parliament of India (1994: 576).

profession convinced others that we need such tests. Thus, rejecting an absolute ban of prenatal tests, the exception was carried out, even ignoring the apprehension expressed by certain medical profession- als regarding the chances of them being continued for sex selection. A member of the joint committee reported:

> A famous gynaecologist, who runs a major genetic centre, informed us that the law should be enacted but banning the test will not serve any purpose. The tests are carried out for one reason or the other such as to check the abnormality of the child, the heredity disease, and the side effects of medicine on woman etc. But it is difficult to say that these tests will not be carried out to know the sex of the foetus.[21]

The legislative process to enact a special law to ban prenatal tests to prevent sex selection faced the unproblematic societal attitude towards female infanticide or female foeticide. Certain medical pro- fessionals also acknowledged this technological approval of social prejudice. In the parliamentary debate, K.D. Jeswani, a medical doctor, submitted: 'Scientific developments have only transferred the elimination of the girl child from the born to unborn stage. Sex determination tests are a powerful example of what can happen when modern technology colludes with the force of a traditional society.'[22]

However, it can be seen that medical professionals justified these scientific advancements on the basis that they were introduced by the medical fraternity because of social demand. It is evident from the argument discussed below that medical professionals were providing sex selection as a service.

> There are a variety of modalities which are in vogue and they are meant for pre-natal diagnostic techniques. Most of these tests are used for the sex determination and a few are only used for the sex determination and then a few are only used for the intrauterine status of the foetus. And this has been going on before the eyes of the administration and the Government. In fact, when the MTP Act was introduced in 1971 and the embryonic death was legalised, the medical fraternity brought

---

[21] D. Venkateswara Rao, Parliament of India (1994: 602).

[22] Parliament of India (1994: 579).

home the techniques of prenatal intrauterine sex determination on the criminal demands of the society.[23]

Reflecting on this unproblematic approach to female foeticide/infanticide, arguments were raised against enacting a law that would prevent sex selection. One of the arguments that supported sex selection was that it was important for a 'balanced family'. The other argument that justified female foeticide was relatively new; it said that it is the right of the parents to choose their children. It was argued that if the PNDT Act were passed, it would infringe the right to parenthood. Such a law would also contradict the MTP Act, the law that permits abortion for failure of family planning. When a mother conceives a girl child, which she had not intended, that causes mental anguish and therefore, female foeticide is justified.[24] However, this argument was also not accepted as it cannot be a right to decide not to have a child simply because it is female. And the problem of family planning failure cannot occur only for conceiving a female child. The third argument was that the advance of research in the medical sphere should not be curtailed.[25] This argument was negated, based on the exception given for prenatal tests for screening disability or 'deformity or diseases'. Consequently, the PNDT Act came into force.[26]

However, despite the legal regulation, the 2001 census showed an alarming decline in the sex ratio. In 2003, a public interest litigation (PIL)[27] prompted the central government to place the onus of action against the providers of sex-selective abortions.

---

[23] K.D. Jeswani, Parliament of India (1994: 577).

[24] Parliament of India (1994: 569).

[25] Parliament of India (1994: 570).

[26] It came into force on 1 January 1996 (G.S.R. 706, dated 20 December 1995).

[27] *Centre for Enquiry into Health and Allied Themes (CEHAT) and Others* v. *Union of India and Others*, (2003) 8 SCC 398. The PIL was initiated in February 2003 by three petitioners: Sabu George, the Centre for Enquiry into Health and Allied Themes (CEHAT), Mumbai, and the Mahila Sarvangeen Utkarsh Mandal (MASUM), Pune, in the Supreme Court of India. In this PIL, the Supreme Court has clearly directed the Central Government and State Governments to take a number of measures to prevent sex-selective

The patriarchal biases to law still carried on. But, we can see that the law became a challenge to the indifferent attitude that had resulted in the widespread acceptance of female foeticide. Thus, it can be analysed that social opprobrium towards girl child was taken into account to intervene in the case of female foeticide. The PNDT Act reveals the social prejudice that disvalued female gender. In fact, the same law reveals the social prejudice that persists against persons with disabilities as well. Prenatal tests and selective abortions are prejudicial to both gender and disability. However, while intervening against such prejudice, the legislature has permitted it to sustain against disability. This less visible aspect of the PNDT Act was not questioned on various grounds. It is analogous to the gender construction in a patriarchal society, where females are devalued. This diminishing gender perception, which justified female infanticide or foeticide, persists against disability as well.

It can be seen that disability has been unequivocally perceived as a medical condition. It is embedded within the medical model. The medical model considers any disability as a biological limitation that limits individual opportunities. Thus, the medical profession treats disability as something to be avoided at all costs. Consequently, the availability of scientific technology, such as prenatal diagnosis, is seen as a blessing that may pre-empt and prevent disability. Therefore, medical professionals adopt a directive approach and do not consider the individual value of a person with disability. Thus, medical professionals tend to medicalize non-medical conditions such as pregnancy to project prenatal diagnosis as highly necessary and desirable to erase disability. This rationale is, however, flawed. It is an illusion that advancements in genetics will wipe out disability. While a very small per cent of all births are affected by disability in the womb, the rest of disability occurs after birth. Disability may occur at any time during the lifespan of an individual.

---

abortion. Survey of bodies specified in Sec. 3 and its registration action taken against non-registered bodies operating in violation of Sec. 3 of the Act. The amendment was to made the punishments more stringent so as to serve as a deterrent for minimizing violations of law. Sec. 22 and Sec. 23 of the PNDT Act.

The widespread practice of son preference and sex-selective abortion in Indian society was justified on the basis of the high cost involved in the form of dowry. Similarly, apart from the psychological costs experienced by the mother, a child with disability is viewed as an economic liability, as raising such a child would invariably entail more expenses and suffering for the child as well as the family.[28] Disability-selective abortion is analogous to the practice of sex-selective abortion.

Another rationale offered in support of prenatal screening is the enrichment of parental autonomy or the reproductive right of the women to choose a particular kind of child. However, in the selective abortion discourse, the choice to determine the nature or quality of the foetus is constructed as a parental right. This right has not been recognized to choose a child with a desired sex, because such choice would prejudice the existence of the undesired sex, which is not welcomed to this world. At this juncture, it would be appropriate to examine the reproductive aspect of Indian abortion laws to understand the legitimacy of disability-selective abortion.

LEGAL STATUS OF REPRODUCTIVE RIGHTS IN INDIA

The MTP Act was enacted in 1971 with the objective of legalizing abortions undertaken by registered medical practitioners on the grounds provided under the act. Prior to the legislation, such medical practices were punishable under criminal law. The MTP Act was enacted in the background of loss of women's lives by reason of backdoor abortions. Therefore, the MTP Act legalized abortions under certain circumstances, and protected medical practitioners from criminal liability.

The continuance of the pregnancy that would involve a risk to the life of the pregnant woman is a permissible ground for abortion. However, this law does not permit women to terminate unwanted pregnancies, except on two conditions: pregnancies caused by

[28] Ghai and Johri (2008: 300). The authors argue that, in a globalizing context, where the profit paradigm predominates, the justification for preventing the birth of children with disabilities is that society has to bear the cost of disability.

rape[29] and contraceptive failure (used to limit the number of children) in the case of married women.[30] This shows that the MTP Act does not provide an absolute right to women to decide about continuing their pregnancy. Disability-linked abortion is legal under this law if two doctors consider that 'there is a substantial risk that if the child were born it would suffer from such physical or mental abnormalities as to be seriously handicapped'.[31] Yet, what this permits and, in particular, how much scope it allows for parental input into the decision-making process is uncertain. The law, by treating disability as a substantial risk, does not weigh a prospective parent's views in decisions about foetal disability. In turn, it makes the mothers responsible to bear only perfect children. It is a question of the appropriate scope of 'reproductive autonomy'.[32]

In the case of sex-selective abortion, the choice has been taken away from women. The same has been done with disability-selective abortion as well. But for disability-selective abortion, it is presumed that women would wish to abort. Therefore, the MTP Act does not provide much choice to women to decide about their pregnancy. Moreover, abortions are permitted in India only up to 20 weeks of pregnancy. The conditions and the period of abortion provided by this law show that it does not confer any reproductive choice on women. This law mainly protects medical practitioners from penal liability for abortions performed under legally permitted medical grounds.

Thus, it can be seen that, in India, an abortion on the basis of the characteristic of the foetus is permissible only on the basis of

[29] Section 3(2) Explanation 1, MTP Act 1971. Where any pregnancy is alleged by the pregnant woman to have been caused by rape, the anguish caused by such pregnancy shall be presumed to constitute a grave injury to the mental health of the pregnant woman.

[30] Section 3(2) Explanation 2, MTP Act 1971. Where any pregnancy occurs as a result of failure of any device or method used by any married woman or her husband for the purpose of limiting the number of children, the anguish caused by such unwanted pregnancy may be presumed to constitute a grave injury to the mental health of the pregnant woman.

[31] Section 3(2)(ii), MTP Act 1971.

[32] Scott (2005b). This would make the women responsible to decide the quality of life of the child.

potential disability of the child. It is pertinent to note that disability-linked abortions are permitted by these laws not to affirm reproductive rights of women, but to focus on the strategy of prevention of disability through prenatal diagnosis and disability-selective termination of pregnancy.

Interestingly, the PNDT Act and the MTP Act appoint the service provider as the decision maker for disability-selective abortion. Medical professionals are perhaps one of the most biased sections of the population against disability.[33] Hence, the chances of reaching the medical conclusion that any disability involves substantial risk are high. Because, the medical perception of disability is that it is something to be avoided at all costs.

Prenatal tests and the explicit ground of disability for abortion make disability-selective abortion a legitimate objective of prenatal tests and the MTP Act. Thus, it is clear that according to Indian abortion law, the possibility of a child being born with disability is a justifiable reason for abortion. Both laws explicitly prevent the birth of persons with disabilities, by permitting abortions on the foetal attribute of disability. This legal permission provided for disability-linked abortions becomes more contentious as evident from sex-selective abortions. Legal permission was categorically denied for sex-selective abortion on the basis of an attribute of the foetus. The law prohibits sex-selective abortions, compromising the reproductive right of women. Feminist scholars believe that the critical factor in all abortion debate is the woman's uncontested right to choose. However, they do acknowledge the fact that choice is not always unconditionally autonomous and free.[34] It is important to note that feminists challenge sex-selective abortions, while retaining the right to abortion. This is because the choice is always driven by social prejudice.

This legal position of India demonstrates how law intervenes in social prejudices by taking into account the social opprobrium on vulnerable groups of people. However, it is paradoxical that the very same law that prohibits prenatal technology for sex-selection permits it to screen out disabilities. The MTP Act permits abortion

---

[33] Addlakha (2010).
[34] Ghai and Johri (2008: 292).

of foetuses identified with possible disabilities. Thus, these laws facilitate the prevention of the birth of persons who would live with disabilities. Though the very same scientific information facilitates both sex-selective abortion and disability-selective abortion, the difference is in how the law treats both pieces of information. Whilst scientific information is not legally supported or permitted for sex-linked abortions, it is recognized and used for disability-linked abortions. This explicitly contradicts the international convention that recognizes the inherent human dignity of all human beings and treats persons with disabilities on an equal basis with all the other human beings.

EQUAL STATUS OF PERSONS WITH DISABILITIES AND INDIAN DISABILITY-SELECTIVE ABORTION LAW

The inherent dignity and equality of all human beings form the core of human rights jurisprudence. In international human rights law, equality is founded on the principle of non-discrimination. While all conventions substantively affirm inherent human dignity, Article 5 of the UNCRPD explicitly addresses the right to equality and non-discrimination. The substantive approach specifically prohibits discrimination on the basis of disability. Thus, the convention confirms equal status for persons with disabilities.

Consequently, the contradictory position adopted by Indian selective-abortion laws against the female gender and persons with disabilities becomes contentious. The PNDT Act, an anti-discrimination law, whilst prohibiting selection or screening out on the basis of sex, permits it for disability. Sex selection and subsequent termination of female foetuses have been prohibited to ensure the right of equality to women. Therefore, by explicitly prohibiting sex-selective abortion, the law enhances the right to equality and non-discrimination of women. When the law prohibits the use of prenatal techniques and selective abortion to affirm equality to one group of human beings and permits the same for another group of human beings, does this law not demonstrate discrimination against the latter group of human beings?

Article 5(1) of the UNCRPD reaffirms all persons' right to equality before the law and their entitlement to equal protection and equal benefit of the law.[35] Article 5(2) further provides for a substantive approach from state parties to promote equality and eliminate discrimination. The UNCRPD affirmed the objective of non-discrimination evidenced in the right to equality.[36] The recognition of this right may raise questions as to the discourse of equality such as: 'What do persons with disabilities want? Do they want the same rights and treatment as the non-disabled world or do they want different rights and treatment?' However, the UNCRPD affirmed this right to equality by seeking both 'same rights and different treatment' to accommodate persons with disabilites. Consequently, whilst persons with disabilities are entitled to the same respect and dignity as the rest of humanity, they are also entitled to reasonable accommodation of their difference.[37] Article 5(3) of the convention reaffirms the right to recognize disability as a human condition and its accommodation. In contrast, the PNDT Act and the MTP Act permit selecting out disability. Consequently, these legislations discriminate against persons with disabilities.

The discriminatory aspect of the law is more visible from its position towards sex-selective abortions. The law that strongly objects to selective abortion for one human condition facilitates it for another. Selective abortion is not permitted by law to ensure equality from the gender perspective. This legal position can be understood as a strong anti-discriminatory status to enhance equality. Therefore, when the

---

[35] Article 5 states:

1. States Parties recognize that all persons are equal before and under the law and are entitled without any discrimination to the equal protection and equal benefit of the law.
2. States Parties shall prohibit all discrimination on the basis of disability and guarantee to persons with disabilities equal and effective legal protection against discrimination on all grounds.
3. In order to promote equality and eliminate discrimination, States Parties shall take all appropriate steps to ensure that reasonable accommodation is provided.
4. Specific measures which are necessary to accelerate or achieve de facto equality of persons with disabilities shall not be considered discrimination under the terms of the present Convention.

[36] Dhanda (2008: 46).
[37] Dhanda (2008: 47).

same law facilitates selective abortion for another human condition, it can be assumed that the law discriminates against persons with such conditions. Sex-selective abortions demonstrate avoiding children of a non-desired sex. Abortion to avoid having a child with disability is on par with abortion to avoid having a child of the 'wrong' sex.

It reinforces the prejudice against persons with disabilities. It embodies the view that there is something undesirable about being a person with disability, so undesirable that it is better that such people are not born. Thus, evidently, when the PNDT Act provides explicit permission to select out foetuses with disabilities, it discriminates against persons with disabilities, by treating their life as not worth living. Therefore, it can be submitted that the PNDT Act denies equal status to persons with disabilities in relation to other human beings. The discrimination displayed by the law becomes particularly questionable as selective abortions are recognized as dangerous and prevented to eradicate discrimination against women. While the PNDT Act facilitates screening out disabilities, the MTP Act permits the medical practitioners to terminate such pregnancies.

The MTP Act explicitly permits abortion, if the child would be born with disabilities. This law treats the birth of a human being with disabilities as a substantial risk. It specifically includes both physical and mental disabilities, referring to them as abnormalities.[38] The legal criteria, which are related to the terms of the disability ground in the MTP Act, more obviously seek to avoid the birth of a child with disability. Consequently, this law acts as a measure to prevent the birth and existence of persons with disabilities.

This contradictory legal position towards disability means legal discrimination against persons with disabilities. The characterization of disability as a medical condition becomes challengeable, as the UNCRPD recognizes disability as an inherent human condition. Therefore, treating disability as an abnormality and preventing the births of infants with disabilities discriminates against persons with disabilities. Consequently, both the PNDT Act and MTP Act and their provisions that permit disability-selective abortions violate Article 5 of the UNCRPD. Unlike these provisions, the convention accords equal value to the lives of persons with disabilities.

---

[38] Section 3(2)(ii) of MTP Act, 1971.

RIGHT TO LIFE IN UNCRPD AND DISABILITY-SELECTIVE ABORTION LAW

The convention stresses on the inherent value of a life with disability, and it is this emphasis which informs the construction of the right to life under the convention. The negotiations surrounding this article show that the right to life was introduced to state that disability should not be a justification to reduce the value of a life with disability. However, under international law the question whether a foetus is recognized as the bearer of the right to life and consequent state regulation of abortion is most contentious. Since international courts or tribunals have not addressed the difficult philosophical issue of when life begins, it should be considered on the basis of the core language of the international instruments.

A close examination of the UNCRPD reveals that the right to life is an assertion that the difference of disability contributes to richness and diversity of the human condition and is not a deficit that has to be selected out.[39] All efforts to include a primary prevention provision in the convention were shot down by persons with disabilities during the negotiations on the basis that disability prevention is a common concern of human development, and could not be viewed as a part of disability rights. Mentioning primary prevention is almost like contending that persons with disabilities are unwelcome members of the human community.[40] The right to life under the convention is enriched by its combination of right to equality and non-discrimination.

Therefore, the PNDT Act and the MTP Act that facilitate selecting out and termination result in depriving the right to life of persons with disabilities. The right to life under the convention explicitly values the lives of persons with disabilities.

Under international law, the right to life occupies a high position. It is non-derogable under various human rights treaties. The Human Rights Committee has commented on it as a right which should not be interpreted narrowly.[41] The UNCRPD envisages explicit protection

[39] Dhanda (2008: 46).
[40] Dhanda (2010a: 136).
[41] United States Human Rights Committee, General Comment 6, Article 6 (16th session, 1982), Compilation of General Comments and General

for persons with disabilities. Thus, it further elaborates on the normative scope of human rights. The negotiation and preparatory papers
show that the right to life was proclaimed as indispensable for the
realization of inherent dignity and value of life of persons with disabilities. Accordingly, disability cannot be considered as justification
to terminate life.

Moreover, the reference to reproductive health in Article 25(a) of
the UNCRPD is crucial, as it concerns the international legitimization of abortion. Indian abortion laws permit disability-selective
abortion as a primary mode of preventing disability. However, the
convention does not contain any provision in respect of prevention,
as it envisages prevention under the right to health as minimizing
further disabilities of persons with disabilities.[42] The convention, as
a rights-based instrument, does not mention primary prevention.
The silence maintained by the UNCRPD on primary prevention
should be treated as a positive affirmation which confirms 'right to
live and survive' for persons with disabilities. Therefore, when both
the PNDT Act and MTP Act facilitate disability-selective abortions,
it is clear that they avoid the existence of persons with disabilities.
Consequently, it gives a message to society that the existence of such
persons is undesirable.

Therefore, in the wake of the convention that accords unequivocal rights to life, inherent dignity, equality, and non-discrimination
to the lives of persons with disabilities on an equal basis with others,
it is apparent that India's disability-selective abortion laws become
unjustifiable. Research also shows that disability-selective abortions
diminish the value of persons with disabilities, and thereby contradict
the UNCRPD. Consequently, the PNDT Act and the MTP Act challenge India's international human rights obligation. This raises the
question: can India promote these laws in the wake of its ratification
of the UNCRPD?

Recommendations Adopted by Human Rights Treaty Bodies, UN Doc.
HRI/GEN/1/Rev.1 at 6 (1994). Available online at http://www.ohchr.org/
EN/NewsEvents/Pages/DisplayNews.aspx?NewsID=16687andLangID=E
(last accessed on 29 February 2016).

[42] Article 25(b), UNCRPD.

RATIFICATION OF UNCRPD AND INDIA'S HUMAN RIGHTS OBLIGATIONS

The UNCRPD came into force in May 2008. India has both signed and ratified the convention.[43] Consequently, the convention has become an operative and binding international law for India. It is an established proposition in international law that a state is bound by its provisions after it depositing the instrument of ratification. As states are bound by the treaties they ratify, they should discharge their obligations in good faith.[44] Moreover, the international human rights obligation has a 'special character', as it deals with obligations of a state towards individuals rather than between the states.[45] Especially since more explicit protection of specific groups of people is envisaged under specific human rights instruments. The UNCRPD and its human rights discourse has emanated as part of the rights-based strategy on behalf of marginalized and excluded groups. Therefore, it can be said that the UNCRPD is an outcome of the 'struggle for new human rights'.[46] The paradigm shift introduced by the UNCRPD deepens and broadens the rights-based approach in support of persons with disabilities. It enunciates the right to inclusion and full participation of persons with disabilities. Thus, ratification of the UNCRPD created a strong legal obligation on India to ensure the enjoyment of human rights to persons with disabilities.

States assume obligations and duties under international human rights law to respect, protect, and fulfil human rights. The obligation to respect means that states must refrain from interfering with or curtailing the enjoyment of human rights. The obligation to protect requires states to protect individuals and groups against human rights abuses. The obligation to fulfil means that states must take positive action to facilitate the enjoyment of basic human rights.

In turn, ratification obligates the states to provide a substantive framework for the application of rights within domestic law and

---

[43] While ratification brings in a positive obligation, signature inducts a negative duty in the ratified states.

[44] Moeckli, Shah, and Sivakumaran (2010: 125).

[45] Moeckli, Shah, and Sivakumaran (2010: 127).

[46] Bob (2009).

policy.[47] Civil and political rights are broadly framed to include prevention of state interventions with rights, such as the right to life,
movement, thought and expression, association, religion and political
participation, commonly referred to as negative rights.[48] The indivisibility of rights is an integral theme that runs right through the treaty
and systematically highlights both the negative and positive dimensions
of all rights.[49] For example, Article 5 of the UNCRPD, guaranteeing
equality and non-discrimination, states in paragraph 3 that '[I]n order
to promote equality and eliminate discrimination, States Parties shall
take all appropriate steps to ensure that reasonable accommodation is
provided'. It has become clear that, without a positive duty to promote
substantive equality, patterns of discrimination and social exclusion will
remain unchanged.[50] The convention incorporates highly disability-
specific interpretations of existing human rights, which transform
negative rights into positive state obligations.

GENERAL OBLIGATIONS OF STATE PARTIES UNDER UNCRPD

Article 4 of the UNCRPD requires state parties to promote the full
realization of human rights and fundamental freedoms for all persons
with disabilities, without discrimination of any kind by:

1. Adopting legislative, administrative, and other measures to
    implement the rights contained in the UNCRPD.
2. Adopting legislative, administrative, and other measures to
    abolish discrimination against persons with disabilities.
3. Not engaging in any act or practice that is inconsistent with the
    UNCRPD and ensuring that the public sector acts in confor-
    mity with the UNCRPD.
4. Taking measures to eliminate discrimination on the basis of
    disability.
5. Involving persons with disabilities in developing and imple-
    menting legislations and policies and in all decision-making
    processes related to persons with disabilities.

---

[47] Kayess and French (2008: 1).
[48] Kothari (2010: 66).
[49] Kothari (2010: 66).
[50] Fredman (2005: 199).

Accordingly, as a state party, it is India's obligation to eliminate discrimination on the basis of disability. If the laws of the state discriminate on this basis, it should take steps to abolish such laws. This can be supported by the UNCRPD committee's recent recommendation to Spain to abolish the distinction made in its law over the period allowed within which a pregnancy can be terminated based solely on disability.[51] The committee also asked whether the Government of Spain considers this to be in line with Article 4, paragraph 1(d), of the convention, which obligates state parties to refrain from engaging in any act or practice that is inconsistent with the convention and to ensure that public authorities and institutions act in conformity with the convention. Apart from these general obligations stipulated by the UNCRPD, an international obligation is a constitutional mandate for India.

CONSTITUTIONAL ASPECTS OF INTERNATIONAL OBLIGATION

The Indian Constitution contains provisions related to compliance with international treaties and conventions. Article 51 of Indian Constitution, as part of promotion of international peace and security, states: 'The State shall endeavour to ... (c) foster respect for international law and treaty obligations in the dealings of organised people with one another.'

Article 253 further provides the power to make any law as part of an international obligation. It states: 'Notwithstanding anything in the foregoing provisions of this Chapter, Parliament has power to make any law for the whole or any part of the territory of India for

---

[51] UN Committee on the Rights of Persons with Disabilities, Sixth session, 19–23 September 2011, CRPD/C/ESP/CO/1, Consideration of reports submitted by States parties under article 35 of the Convention, Concluding observations of the Committee on the Rights of Persons with Disabilities, Spain. Available online at http://www.google.co.in/url?sa=tandrct=jandq= andesrc=sandsource=webandcd=2andcad=rjaanduact=8andved=0ahUKE wibzsjSlJ7LAhWMjo4KHZ_UCd4QFggnMAEandurl=http%3A%2F%2F www2.ohchr.org%2FSPdocs%2FCRPD%2F6thsession%2FCRPD-C-ESP-CO-1%2520.docandusg=AFQjCNHwVuEfx6WO1aC1h37Fj1T6WSnE tQandsig2=MiYhlX1PGgF19E9Ij_uvpQandbvm=bv.115339255,d.c2E (last accessed on 1 March 2016).

implementing any treaty, agreement, or convention with any other country or countries or any decision made at any international conference, association or other body.'

Despite several international conventions and treaties not having been enacted into municipal law, courts have been relying on the principles of international treaties, especially human rights treaties, to interpret domestic law. In *Gramophone Company of India Ltd* v. *Birendra Bahadur Pandey and Others*,[52] the Supreme Court held that due regard must be given to international conventions and norms for construing domestic law. The Supreme Court passed a landmark judgement in *Vishaka and Others* v. *State of Rajasthan and Others*,[53] where it relied on the provisions of the Convention on the Elimination of All Forms of Discrimination against Women (CEDAW) to apply the principle of the right to life and dignity for women at the workplace. The Supreme Court went so far as to recognize the concept of legitimate expectation of observance of international obligations if there is a void in the domestic law. The Court made reference to Article 11 of the CEDAW and General Recommendation 19 particularly in framing guidelines for the prevention of sexual harassment and abuse of women. In this landmark judgement, the Supreme Court addressed the relevance of international sources to the interpretation of the constitutional guarantees as follows:

> In the absence of domestic law occupying the field, to formulate effective measures to check the evil of sexual harassment of working women at all workplaces, the contents of International Conventions and norms are significant for the purpose of interpretation of the guarantee of gender equality, right to work with human dignity in Articles 14, 15, 19(1) (g) and 21 of the Constitution and the safeguards against sexual harassment implicit therein. Any International Convention not inconsistent with the fundamental rights and in harmony with its spirit must be read into these provisions to enlarge the meaning and content thereof, to promote the object of the constitutional guarantee. This is implicit from Art 51(c) and the enabling power of the Parliament to enact laws for implementing the International Conventions and norms by virtue of Article 253 read with Entry 14 of the Union List in Seventh Schedule of

---

[52] AIR 1984 SC 667.
[53] (1997) 6 SCC 241 (hereinafter referred to as '*Vishaka*').

the Constitution. Article 73 also is relevant. It provides that the executive power of the Union shall extend to the matters with respect to which Parliament has power to make laws. The executive power of the Union is, therefore, available till the Parliament enacts legislation to expressly provide measures needed to curb the evil.[54]

Following *Vishaka*, in *Apparel Export Promotion Council* v. *A.K. Chopra*[55] the Supreme Court observed that 'international instruments (such as CEDAW) cast an obligation on the Indian State to gender-sensitise its laws and the courts are under an obligation to see that the message of the international instruments is not allowed to be drowned'.[56] In *T.N. Godavarman Thirumalpad* v. *Union of India*,[57] the Supreme Court observed that it is necessary for the government to take into account the international obligations and act on them, unless there are 'compelling reasons' to depart from them.

The Indian courts have also used international law as a guide to interpret domestic law. In *Mackinnon Mackenzie and Co Ltd* v. *Audrey D'Costa*,[58] in which a female shorthand typist challenged the discriminatory pay system in her firm between women and men, the Supreme Court relied extensively on the International Labour Organization's (ILO) convention no. 100 to interpret Article 39(d) of the Indian Constitution and the Equal Remuneration Act, 1976. Article 39(d) says: 'The State shall, in particular, direct its policy towards securing that there is equal pay for equal work for both men and women.' Interpreting national legislation in conjunction with the ILO convention, the Supreme Court granted relief to the petitioner by holding the employer's action to be an unconstitutional violation of the principles of equal pay for equal work. This judgement was later followed by the Delhi High Court in *Smt Bimla Rani and Others* v. *Appellate Authority, Equal Remuneration Act and Others*.[59]

A recent judgement of the Bombay High Court has taken the principle of reasonable accommodation enshrined in the UNCRPD and

---

54 *Vishaka*, at 248.
55 AIR 1999 SC 625 (hereinafter referred to as '*Chopra*').
56 *Chopra*, at 634.
57 (2002) 10 SCC 606.
58 AIR 1987 SC 1281.
59 113 (2004) DLT 441.

The Contradiction in Disability Law

applied it in the domestic context in the case of *Ranjit Kumar Rajak* v. *State Bank of India*.[60] In this case, the petitioner was declared medically unfit for employment as an officer in the State Bank of India. He had previously undergone a renal transplant, but was fully capable of carrying out the duties of the job he had applied for. The respondent bank refused to select him on the ground that his monthly medical expenses, which would be borne by the bank, would be substantially high as he had undergone a renal transplant. The Bombay High Court rejected the bank's contention and directed it to appoint the petitioner for the job by providing reasonable accommodation in the form of medical expenses. The court held that 'reasonable accommodation if read into Article 21 of the Indian Constitution guaranteeing the right to life, based on the Disabilities Convention, would not be in conflict with municipal law and on the contrary it would give added life and dimension to the ever expanding concept of life and its true enjoyment'.[61] Right to life is a fundamental right provided by the Indian Constitution. Article 21 of the Constitution declares: 'No person shall be deprived of his life or personal liberty except according to procedure established by law.'

Right to life in India is perceived as not restricted to 'mere animal existence', but imports human dignity into its peripheries.[62] Right to life was interpreted and extended to many rights, such as the right to live with human dignity,[63] right to free and compulsory education,[64] right to privacy,[65] right to healthy environment,[66] right to health,[67] and right to medical treatment.[68] It may be assumed that the expanded

---

[60] 2009(5) Bom.C.R. 227, MANU/MH/0452/2009, p. 235 (hereinafter referred to as 'Ranjit Kumar').

[61] *Ranjit Kumar*, 2009(5) Bom.C.R. 227, p. 235.

[62] *Francis Corlie Mullin* v. *Administrator, Union Territory of Delhi* (1981) 1 SCC 608; AIR 1981 SC 746.

[63] *Bandhu Mukti Morcha* v. *Union of India* (1984) 3 SCC 161; AIR 1984 SC 802; *Charles Sobharaj* v. *Supdt. Central Jail Tihar* 1978 Cr LJ 1534.

[64] *Unnikrishnan* v. *State of Andhra Pradesh* [1993] 1 SCR 594.

[65] *Kharak Singh* v. *State of U.P.* 1963 Cr LJ 329.

[66] *M.C. Mehta* v. *Union of India* 1988 AIR 1037; [1988] 1 SCR 279; 1987(4) SCC 463.

[67] *Consumer Education and Resource Centre* v. *Union of India* (1995) 3 SCC 42.

[68] *Paschim Baga Khet Mazoor Samiti* v. *State of West Bengal* (1997) 1 SCC 388.

formulation will also be applicable to persons with disabilities. There are not many cases where the Indian courts have deliberated upon the content of the right to life for persons with disabilities. The courts have however been required to address right to life in its survival manifestations for persons with disabilities. The Bombay High Court's decision in *Niketa Mehta*,[69] on disability-linked abortion has a bearing on the right to life of persons with disabilities.

However, in this case, Indian judiciary was not concerned with the question of the value of a life with disability which informed the induction of Article 10 in the UNCRPD. In *Niketa Mehta*, Niketa Mehta was 26 weeks' pregnant when her doctor diagnosed the foetus as having a congenital heart block. Since her pregnancy had crossed the legally permitted time limit of 20 weeks under the MTP Act, the petitioners (Mr and Mrs Mehta and the doctor) approached the Bombay High Court, seeking judicial interference under the specific provisions of the MTP Act in order to permit medical termination. The court appointed a committee of doctors to submit a report, based on which it concluded:

> [T]aking into consideration the opinion expressed by the doctors' committee from J J Group of Hospitals as well as the two-expert committee of doctors constituted by the petitioners themselves, there is no categorical opinion before us from the medical experts to the effect that 'if the child were born, it would suffer from physical or mental abnormalities as to be seriously handicapped.' Apart from the fact that already the period of 26 weeks of pregnancy has passed, even the requirements of the provisions of law under Section 3(2)(ii) read with Section 3(2)(b) are not satisfied. In other words, even if the petitioners were to approach this Court before the expiry of 20 weeks of pregnancy, based on the medical opinion placed before us, it would not have been possible for this Court to issue direction for exercise of right in terms of Section 3 of the said Act.[70]

It is clear that the court rejected termination on technical grounds as legitimately it was possible[71] for the court to allow termination of

---

[69] *Nikhil D. Dattar and Others* v. *Union of India* (2008)110(9) BOM.L.R. 3293 (hereinafter referred to as '*Niketa Mehta*').

[70] (2008) 110(9)BOMLR 3293, p. 3302.

[71] In a recent case, the Supreme Court of India has permitted a minor rape victim to abort her pregnancy, even though it had crossed the permissible 20 weeks' time limit (Nair 2015).

pregnancy beyond the time limit of 20 weeks. However, the court also stated that the requirements of the law, to term the condition as being seriously handicapped, were not satisfactory to permit termination. That may be the reason, apart from the technical reason, that the court stated that it would not have permitted it, even if was sought within the statutorily permitted time, as the medical report did not show that the disability was such that it would cause a 'serious handicap' to the unborn child. This in turn will need interpretation of what constitutes 'serious handicap'.[72]

The verdict, however, generated demands from a section of society for an extension of the prescribed period of abortion to enable parents to terminate foetuses with disabilities. This case demonstrates the social attitude towards disability. This has resulted in non-adjudication of the issue in the light of UNCRPD-accorded value of lives to persons with disabilities. The implication of this adverse legal position is also evident from the silence of the proposed new law on disability regarding disability-selective abortion.

In view of the rights guaranteed under the UNCRPD, India has initiated revisiting all related laws in order to harmonize them with the convention. India is on its way to preparing a new law for persons with disabilities. In the proposed draft, the right to life has found an appropriate place in an expanded manner.[73] Accordingly, right to life and living was framed to mean that:[74]

---

[72] Whilst a social prejudice subsists against any disability condition, a polarization between simple and serious disabilities would thwart grappling on the question of its wrongness first and finally celebrating disability as an inherent human condition.

[73] Working Draft of Persons with Disabilities Act 2011, dated 9 February 2011, available online at http://socialjustice.nic.in/pdf/workdraftdd.pdf (last accessed on 4 March 2016). A working draft is the preliminary form of a possible future document prepared by a working committee. It indicates commitment on the part of the legislature to do further work on the working draft. The draft put out by the ministry to seek stakeholder or public opinion is the final draft.

[74] Sec.10, Right to Life and Living, Working Draft of Persons with Disabilities Act 2011, dated 9 February 2011, available online at http:// socialjustice.nic.in/pdf/workdraftdd.pdf (last accessed on 4 March 2016).

1. Every person with disability has the inherent right to life. The State shall take all necessary measures to ensure its effective enjoyment by persons with disabilities on an equal basis with others.

Explanation:
The term 'State' here has same meaning as the term 'state' under Article 12 of the Constitution of India.

2. Right to life includes the right to live with dignity, which includes but is not limited to:

   (a) Adequate nutrition, clothing, and shelter;
   (b) wellness and healthcare;
   (c) access to facilities for reading, writing and expressing one-self in any form or language whether written, spoken, unspoken, or sign language; and
   (d) freedom of movement, association, participation and living and sharing with other persons and communities;
   (e) opportunity to acquire personal, social, educational and vocational skills required to function as a person with disability;

3. Any act or omission which damages or injures or interferes with the use of any limb or faculty of persons with disabilities either permanently or temporarily will be punishable under this Act.

Any contravention of this Section shall be penalized under Section 30F.[75]

However, the Rights of Persons with Disabilities Bill, 2014 shows how hard it is for persons with disabilities to avail civil and political rights. Section 3(1) of this Bill enunciates the right to life, not taking account of the needs of persons with disabilities. Accordingly, 'the appropriate Government shall ensure that persons with disabilities enjoy the right to equality, life with dignity and respect for his or her integrity equally with others'.

---

[75] Sec. 30F Punishment for contravention of Section 10(3) provides that, '(1) Whoever voluntarily injures, damages or interferes with the use of any limb or faculty of a person with disability, permanently or temporarily shall be punishable with imprisonment for a term which shall not be less than six months but which may extend to eight years, or with fine, or with both.'

The Bill was originally drafted to bring Indian laws in line with international obligations, following a thorough pre-legislative deliberative process with the stakeholders.[76] Yet, the legislation approved by the Cabinet has no relationship with the original draft, a progressive rights-based law. When embedded in a regressive law, even progressive provisions will fail to see adequate implementation.[77]

In this context, we can see the dilution of reproductive rights of persons with disabilities in the pending Bill 2014. It encapsulates the socio-legal prejudice persists against them. The reproductive rights of persons with disabilities and its ground reality had been deliberated in the sub-group of law committee, during the drafting of the new disability law. The sub-group looked at the nature of the CRPD guarantee as provided under Article 6 of the CRPD, which recognizes that women and girls face multiple discrimination and require extra resources and programmatic intervention to realize the right. The sub-group decided to tackle the issue of double discrimination by adopting the twin-track approach for women and girls with disabilities by inclusion of their concerns and their rights in the preamble and in provisions relating to equality and non-discrimination,[78] education,[79] employment,[80] health,[81] abuse and violence,[82] home and family.[83] When the committee finalized the drafting of law after state

---

[76] Dhanda (2014: 9). A legislation, which was drafted on a consistent deliberation with the stakeholders, finally became a rehabilitation document in the hands of the executive.

[77] Dhanda (2014: 9).

[78] Sec. 6, Working Draft of Persons with Disabilities Act, 2011, dated 9 February 2011.

[79] Sec. 7B, Working Draft of Persons with Disabilities Act, 2011, dated 9 February 2011.

[80] Sec. 7C, Working Draft of Persons with Disabilities Act, 2011, dated 9 February 2011.

[81] Sec. 7E, Working Draft of Persons with Disabilities Act, 2011, dated 9 February 2011.

[82] Sec. 7D, Working Draft of Persons with Disabilities Act, 2011, dated 9 February 2011.

[83] Sec. 7F Working Draft of Persons with Disabilities Act, 2011, dated 9 February 2011.

consultations, the reproductive rights of persons with disabilities and its significance for women with disabilities were well provided in a section on right of women with disabilities in Home and Family. Section 7F(2) of the draft law stated: 'the right of each woman with disability to retain her fertility and shall not be subjected to any medical procedure which leads to infertility or termination of pregnancy without her express consent.'

However, most recent copy of the Bill on the Rights of Persons with Disabilities published by the Ministry of Social Justice and Empowerment on 7 February 2014[84] shows that the reproductive rights of women with disabilities have been included as part of a general article on reproductive rights. Section 9(2) of the pending Bill says, 'no person with disability shall be subject to any medical procedure which leads to infertility with his or her free and informed consent.'

Also, the reproductive right of women with disabilities has been diluted as a socio-economic right in the provisions for Social Security and Health.[85] Accordingly, the appropriate government shall provide support to women with disability for livelihood and for upbringing of their children, but within the limits of its economic capacity.[86] The government shall also provide sexual and reproductive healthcare, especially for women with disabilities.[87]

This shows that reproductive right has been manipulated to a welfare right which has to be availed from the hands of the state. But the Indian society has internalized the medical model to select out disability before birth through disability-selective abortion. In such a state, where disability is not welcomed before birth, 'economic capacity' of the state would easily be justified on allocation of extra resources. This negotiation shows the ground-level reality of persons with disabilities to avail their basic and fundamental rights.

---

[84] The Rights of Persons with Disabilities Bill, 2014, Bill No. 1 of 2014, as Introduced in the Rajya Sabha, India, available online at http://www.prsindia. org/billtrack/the-right-of-persons-with-disabilities-bill-2014-3122/ (last accessed on 3 March 2014).

[85] Chapter V of the pending bill.

[86] Sec. 23(2)(d) of the pending bill.

[87] Sec. 24(k) of the pending bill.

Thus, losing its pith and substance, the pending Disability Rights Bill of 2014, the bureaucratic welfare legislation, compensates the reproductive rights of women with disabilities—the doubly disadvantaged. It does not take on board the vulnerability of the most disadvantaged and their struggle to be recognized as equal persons before law, in par with all others. UNCRPD has signaled the change from welfare to rights perspective. The journey of inclusion of every excluded group was through non-discrimination evidenced in right to equality. When the vulnerability is based on more reasons, the originally drafted progressive law was the better way to address the issue of double discrimination subsists against women with disabilities. Whilst the UNCRPD, the universal law, brought a paradigm shift from welfare to rights, the bureaucracy brought this shift in the pending new Bill, but by diluting a rights-perspective law to welfare-perspective. It shows the complete failure of the state's constitutional and international obligation to harmonize the laws with the Universal law and to compensate the doubly discriminated. Amita Dhanda points out: 'It would be infinitely preferable to build consensus around a robust legislation instead of spending the next few decades hoping for positive judicial interpretation and clamouring for legislative amendments.'[88]

The UNCRPD becomes important, as it has several provisions for protection of persons with disabilities in India. It declares the basic rights of equality and non-discrimination and protection of the right to life and dignity for all persons with disabilities. The convention, much like the Indian Constitution, propounds the interdependence and indivisibility of both social, and civil and political, rights. The constitutional guarantee interpretation is made to suggest that disability discrimination is prohibited as an extension of the idea that equality and non-discrimination are linked to human dignity. When this socially just interpretation was given to equality and non-discrimination in relation to sex-selective abortions, it was started by viewing them through the lens of human dignity. If the very same interpretation is extended to disability-selective abortion, then the legal discourse can create the social reality that persons with disabilities are dignified beings.

---

[88] Dhanda (2014: 9).

The non-discrimination ideal in the convention can be seen as a vision for inclusive society. Thus it is categorical to treat persons with disabilities equally on par with all others. However, this equal treatment requires reasonable accommodation to include persons with disabilities in social and political life along with others. This is a mandate of UNCRPD apart from the responsibility of a just society. In this premise, disability-selective abortion, facilitated by the PNDT Act and the MTP Act is a glaring discrimination, which closes the door to recognize them as equals. The UNCRPD defines persons with disabilities to 'include those who have long-term physical, mental, intellectual, or sensory impairments which in interaction with various barriers may hinder their full and effective participation in society on an equal basis with others'.[89] This is thus a very broad and inclusive definition of disability. At the same time, the PNDT Act covers different disabilities, labelling them as 'abnormal'. The MTP Act permits termination based on disability, as it considers disability to be a substantial risk. Consequently, the legal status of disability-selective abortions declares that persons with disabilities do not have the right to live.

Since disability-selective abortions, as a primary prevention strategy, have been perceived as the correct choice for prevention of disability, the allocation of resources, policies, and programmes does not happen to preserve the lives of persons with disabilities. Consequently, these laws have been rendered questionable in the wake of India's commitment to the UNCRPD. The principles and rights embodied in the convention should reform disability-selective abortion law. However, disability-linked abortions and their legality is still out of the legislative purview, as it is premature to invite such concerns in a society in which disability is perceived as not worthwhile. The existing legal position on disability-selective abortion potentially strengthens the normative conceptualization of disability, which is value-laden. It sets a precedent for elimination of the so-called unfit people. Nivedita Menon warns: 'Once we accept that there can be hierarchy of human beings based on physical characteristics, and that it is legitimate to withhold the right to be born to those at lower levels of this hierarchy,

---

[89] Article 1, UNCRPD 2008.

then this reasoning can be extended to other categories, whether female, inferior races or any other.'[90]

Till the introduction of prenatal diagnostic techniques, the quality of the foetus was not a concern for the parents and medical profession. With the advent of prenatal diagnosis, in clinical practice, the concept of foetus has changed from a generic entity to one with specified properties and the first among such properties were sex of the child.[91] In contemporary India, the technology of prenatal determination of foetal characteristics has disadvantaged both girls and persons with disabilities. In both sex- and disability-selective abortion the mother loses her agency.[92] Because mother's decision is based on the social prejudice subsists against both. Then the legitimate question to be asked is: Where do we draw the line?[93]

***

It can be seen that disability has been considered a legitimate ground to permit abortions as per Indian abortion laws. In contrast, sex-based abortions are prohibited in recognition of equal value to lives of females. The non-problematic disability-selective abortion laws clearly demonstrate absence of a similar equal value perception for persons with disabilities. It implies that they are considered to be 'inferior' and 'undesired'.

Both the PNDT Act and the MTP Act label disability as a medical condition and refer to it as an abnormality. The language used in these laws to refer to disability confirms the legally affirmed negative stereotype that prevails towards life with disability. However, this legal position of disability-selective abortions becomes challenge-able in light of the new human rights paradigm provided by the UNCRPD. The convention is a binding international articulation of disability human rights. It treats the lives of persons with disabilities as equally valuable as that of any other human being. It recognizes inherent human dignity, individual autonomy, and full participation

[90] Menon (2004: 96).
[91] Ghai and Johri (2008: 294).
[92] Ghai and Johri (2008: 295).
[93] Ghai and Johri (2008: 291).

for persons with disabilities. The UNCRPD accords respect to the difference and considers disability as an integral part of human condition. It equally values persons with disabilities because of their inherent self-worth. More significantly, the UNCRPD envisages the right to life for persons with disabilities, combining it with rights of equality and non-discrimination. This stance adopted in the UNCRPD leaves a large scope for interpretation and implementation of all the other rights.

In this context, disability-selective abortion makes persons with disabilities as a means to the ends of others, and not as ends in themselves or holders of rights as envisaged under the UNCRPD. Since the PNDT Act and the MTP Act facilitate selecting out disability, the message is that disability is per se undesirable and life with disability is not worth living. The unproblematic legal sanction for disability-selective abortion means that persons with disabilities do not have the right to live. This legal status is contradictory to the UNCRPD and therefore is unjustifiable. International human rights obligation mandates the state to revisit these laws. India needs to revisit these laws in the context of the convention and consider the legality of prenatal tests and selective abortions on the basis of disability. India has to revisit these adverse laws, which diminish the value of persons with disabilities, as a necessary measure to ensure the enjoyment of rights to equality, non-discrimination, dignity, and life by persons with disabilities on an equal basis with others.

CHAPTER SEVEN

Deliberated Decisions, Not Automated Response

The New Discourse on Disability-selective Abortions

. . . .

In this book so far, we have discussed the implications of interference by science and technology in the natural process of human birth, which is no longer natural. Once women conceive, either naturally or with medical assistance,[1] the pregnancy often comes under the control of medical professionals. This medicalization of a natural process is complex. When human reproduction became medicalized, the supremacy of medical science and quest for utility resulted in scrutinizing the 'qualities' of the foetus. This scrutiny is complex, as it does not check if the foetus is fine or comfortable in the mother's womb, instead it categorizes the foetus in the desired or

---

[1] Through assisted reproductive technology, for instance, in vitro fertilization.

undesired category of humans and confirms if it scores to come into this world. This is to prevent the 'undesirables' from coming into this world. Thus, when the medical professionals mark a foetus out for disability-selective abortion, it implies something more than a mere 'medical decision'.

The prejudiced medical information results in an automatic decision for disability-selective abortion. Systemic permission of such selection is problematic. In the medical world view, disability is an undesired health condition, which should be avoided at any cost. This prejudiced medical thinking on disability influences the social perception of disability. This book has critically appraised the laws that permit disability-selective abortions. This work is an effort to demonstrate why disability-selective abortions are problematic. It has analysed the problem of selectiveness in disability-selective abortions without entering the realm of women's right to choose. Disability-selective abortions are problematic as they are endorsed based on non-analysed perceptions. Conclusions drawn after a study of a specific area have been woven into the chapters themselves. In this chapter, only the conclusions and suggestions that emerge from the study as a whole are being presented.

MAJOR FINDINGS

The major findings of the study in this book can be divided into two parts: the medical perception of disability and the non-medical perception of disability. Let us see the perception of disability through the prism of the medical profession.

Medical Perception of Disability and Disability-selective Abortion

While human reproduction changed into a medicalized process, the major change was in the scrutiny of the 'new being' growing up in the mother's womb. This is where medical professionals decide the standards for a 'perfect' human being. If all the faculties, senses, and organs are fully functional, then it is perfect, otherwise 'defective'. Therefore, it can be said that a decision of disability-selective abortion implies that everyone should fall under this 'medical standard'. Anyone who does not fall under this standard is defective and hence should be prevented from existing in this world along with the 'perfects'.

Prenatal tests are a sophisticated technology to select out such 'defectives'. The medical professionals blankly promote this selective technology, saying that it is better for both the 'perfect' ones and the selected-out 'imperfect' ones. Thus, the medical view of disability is a diminishing perception of disability, and in turn, it produces and feeds the prejudice that life with disability is not worth living and persons who live with disability are incomplete humans. This prejudiced medical thinking of disability significantly influences the perception of disability. This imperialistic view is strengthened by the fact that the medical profession, as a dominant group, has exclusive or primary access to communication in a society.[2] Often, without acknowledging that it does so, the dominant group projects its prejudiced perception as representative of humanity as such.[3] In this manner, each medical decision to abort based on disability implies the diminishing value for the lives of persons with disabilities and it feeds the prejudice against them. But, when the non-medical movement started looking at the lived experience of persons with disabilities, the diminishing medical perception of disability was found not to be true.

Non-medical Perception of Disability

When it was viewed in the non-medical mirror, the image of 'defective' categorization was not found true. The lived experiences of persons with disabilities prove the richness of their lives as they live their lives, just like others. They watch movies, listen to songs, and have opinions. They also create music, movies, literature, and sometimes discover something new, just like others. It affirms the truth that humans are not a homogeneous entity, but rather a variety of groups with divergent ideas as to the meaning and purpose of life. This reality contributes to human diversity and its richness. Yet, this diversity is taken for granted in disability-selective abortions. It is part of the medical effort to wipe out the richness of diversity.

---

[2] Gombos and Dhanda (2009); Fraser (1997).
[3] Young (1990: 58, 59).

The medically oriented understanding of disability contradicts real lives, lived by persons with disabilities. It is evident that realms of activity often thought unimaginable for people with disabilities are now components of many of their lives.[4] People with hearing disability create poetry and theatre in sign language. People with mobility impairment participate in typical or adapted athletics. Persons with autism and Down syndrome are increasingly articulating their views. They live just like others. This contradictory perception of disability points to the need to draw a line for the legal order on disability-selective abortion. Because, non-recognition of the richness of diverse minds and bodies would result in unacceptance or intolerance of any kind of diversity and prevents its existence, categorizing them as 'diminished lives'. Thus, disability-selective abortion that subsists prejudice, result in discrimination for all. The findings in this book about the history of selecting out undesirables point towards this inevitable possibility.

HISTORICAL CONTEXT OF DISCRIMINATION: A JUSTIFICATION FOR DISCRIMINATION AGAINST ALL

The historical incidents of selecting out humans, based on the public policy understanding that one kind of person is less worthy of life, were questioned when they did not stop at persons with disabilities. Such incidents were questioned, when even those in the desired category were started getting included in the strategies of weeding out. It meant that if the permission could be given for disability-selective abortion discriminating against one kind of humans, it would easily become unproblematic to seek practices to get rid of other undesired or desired kind of humans. Thus, disability-selective abortion and its legal permission is a harbinger of legally permitted discrimination against anyone.

The easy demonstration of discrimination would be to justify choosing a child of a valued gender, and thereby permit sex-selective abortions. Similarly, the subsisting unproblematic discrimination can be demonstrated over anyone based on colour, caste, creed, old age, illness, and so on. Since modern technology has sophisticated

---

[4] Asch (2003: 324).

strategies to facilitate this discrimination, it may stay unquestioned, similar to disability-selective abortion. Therefore, the value of technology should first be decided for disability-selective abortion.

But, when technology is used to select out human beings in a more sophisticated manner, can it be justified?

JUSTIFICATION OF TECHNOLOGY

If we have the advanced technology that would easily select out the undesired, imperfect, or burdensome people, why cannot we use it for the benefits of society? From the very beginning of the research in this book, this was the hovering question, from many fronts. But, what is technology? Is it value-neutral?

Obviously, technology is not value-neutral. If it was neutral in value, there was no need to legally prohibit its use for sex selection. Use of the advanced reproductive technology of prenatal tests against one kind of humans was not permitted. This means that the value of technology should be estimated by its usefulness for humans. When medical professionals prescribe prenatal tests and disability-linked selective abortion as useful for humans, it disregards the truth that it is used against a kind of humans, the persons with disabilities. It is detrimental. Even though medical professionals may still hang on to it as a valuable achievement of science, its use for the said purpose contradicts the UNCRPD, the universal law.

DISLOCATION OF MEDICAL PERCEPTION OF DISABILITY
BY UNCRPD DISCOURSE

The UNCRPD has dislocated the medical perception of disability, declaring that human life is valued for itself. It enunciated the inherent value of persons with disabilities. It treats the lives of persons with disabilities as equally valuable as that of any other human being. The convention accords unequivocal rights to life, inherent dignity, equality, and non-discrimination to the lives of persons with disabilities, the very same rights enjoyed by other human beings. The inherent right to life recognized under the UNCRPD mandates the states to ensure it. Consequently, the diminishing utility perception of the medical model has no effect. The UNCRPD's recognition of the inherent value of persons with disabilities prevails over the medical prejudice that diminishes their dignity and value. Whilst this universal law recognizes the value of technology, infrastructure, and its equal availability to everyone, it cannot be a means to the end of others. The affirmation of right to life in itself challenges the medical belief that a life with disability is a less valued life. It endorses the Kantian principle that 'humans are ends in themselves and not the means of others'. What does it mandate for the medical professionals?

UNCRPD's Right to Life, Equality, and Non-discrimination Mandate to Medical Professionals

The medical professionals create a 'single model' of perfect human beings, and demand that one who comes under this single model is the only appreciable one. By endorsing disability-selective abortion, instead of trying to expand the knowledge of how to deal with different kinds of bodies and minds, they are reducing their knowledge to a *square*. Then, they demand that everyone should fall under this model, not allowing any other diversion. This, in fact, narrows the knowledge and the relevance of science. If medical professionals continue with decisions about disability-selective abortion, then the right to life of persons with disabilities is rendered questionable. It means that medical prejudice prevails over the right to life of persons with disabilities. This will be wrong, as life should always prevail over medical prejudice.

This demand has no meaning, when it is certain that not all disability is preventable, and that many disabilities are acquired during the course of one's lifetime. Then, is it not more desirable that medical professionals learn how to deal with diverse human minds and bodies? Is it not more desirable to give to humans the best kind of life with the kinds of minds and bodies they possess, rather than chasing the mirage of the perfect mind and body? That too, to concede the right to life for persons with disabilities, the UNCRPD mandates everyone, including medical professionals, to accept disability as an integral part of the human condition.

The right to life envisaged under the UNCRPD is significant and its application should be informed by the right to equality and non-discrimination. Consequently, parliaments cannot make one-sided legislations that discriminate against persons with disabilities. It imposes a responsibility on medical professionals to view disability from the perspective of persons with disabilities.

Therefore, instead of reducing the medical scope to only one model of humans, medical professionals should explore how to deal with different kinds of competence. For instance, medical profession is willing to apply their skill and knowledge to long-term researches on cancer and AIDS. What justification does the medical profession has to terminate life with disability, an absolute human condition? Thus, instead of eliminating different bodies and minds, medical professionals should explore and expand their knowledge to deal with such diverse human minds and bodies. It would be more desirable for the professionals and in turn the society.

Each time medical professionals prescribe a disability-selective abortion a more rigorous scrutiny should be conducted, because it implies something more about the falseness of the medicalized view of disability. They prescribe disability-selective abortion because they cannot deal with diverse competencies. This inadequacy should be balanced not by completely destroying and avoiding the diverse human competence, but by learning how to accommodate it.

This imperialistic perception held by non-disabled people for themselves and the decision to select out does not affect them, as it is articulated in unproblematic terms. This contradicts the demands of social justice. If mutual advantage is the only basis for social cooperation, it challenges the inherent dependent instinct of human beings. Social justice demands that the concerns of all members of society should find voice, whether or not they participate in the making of the social contract.[5] Persons with disabilities stand excluded from the liberal vision of social justice, because human beings are seen as rational, free, and independent. Such a construction is in denial of the inherent human nature of dependency. It is not because such animal dimension exists in all beings, but because men do not engage with this need and hence can render it invisible.

Thus, when legislations related to disability-selective abortions reinforce disability as a condition that society is unable to accept,

---

[5] Gombos and Dhanda (2009: 75).

they deny social justice to persons with disabilities. This also implies the refusal to recognize them as equal human beings. This unproblematic legal order is under challenge in the wake of equal rights accorded to persons with disabilities under the UNCRPD.

In the wake of the UNCRPD, the whole issue of disability-selective abortion cannot be looked at in the same way as it was earlier. Disability-selective abortion laws reaffirm the stereotypic perception that life with disability is not worth living.

However, disability-selective abortion legislation has strengthened the stereotypes surrounding life with disability with the support of scientific developments. This failure occurs due to the degrading manner in which disability is inducted into our laws. It adorns the imperialistic and supreme view held by selective science. Years ago, we kept them in institutions, calling them 'handicapped'. Today, advanced reproductive technology can destroy them before we need to look at them. Then the need to think of them does not occur. But, we forget the inherent truth that persons with disabilities are still part of our society. If we listen to them, we can know that they enjoy being alive with disability. Do medical professionals acknowledge this? Do they provide the right information about the individual value of a person who is selected out on the sole reason of disability? What do we miss in this selective medical strategy? It certainly denies something valuable to the selected persons and to the society.

Disability-linked selective abortion is not good and unproblematic. It is not an 'unqualified good'. If they are not permitted to be born, for no other reason than their disability, this legal order is clearly problematic.

PROBLEMS OF LEGAL SANCTION OF DISABILITY-SELECTIVE ABORTION

The laws relating to disability-selective abortion, instead of preparing the woman for a child with disability, force her to terminate the pregnancy. The act of offering information about the 'defects' or disabilities in a foetus in a medical setting, where abortion is offered as an alternative, in itself makes abortion more of a 'live option'.[6] Since

---

[6] James (1897).

obstetricians suggest prenatal testing as part of prenatal care, on any suspected foetal disability, women embark upon a course to end in an uninformed decision to terminate pregnancy.[7] The medical professionals and the law facilitate the termination as a *good solution* to avoid the *risk* of bringing persons with disabilities into the world, because disability-selective abortion laws explicitly provide permission to screen out disability, terming those conditions as *abnormalities*. The related law, MTP Act, permits termination on the ground that disability is a substantial risk. Thus, unproblematic disability-selective abortion laws take women on a route to termination, which does not facilitate an informed decision.

When these laws provide a blanket permission to terminate selectively foetuses with disabilities, they do not provide the right information about disability and persons with disabilities. For instance, the first condition permitted to be screened is Down syndrome (chromosomal abnormalities). The law or related health policies do not provide any information to understand what Down syndrome is, and the individual value of persons with Down syndrome.

Down syndrome is a chromosomal condition, where the person has an extra chromosome. Worldwide, it is estimated that over 5.8 million people have Down syndrome.[8] Until very recently, children with Down syndrome were thought to be unable to learn and read. But now it has been discovered that they have a very strong bias towards visual learning.[9] They show their talent in many spheres. They express themselves in as many diverse ways as anyone else in society. Medical advances have discovered that heart problems often accompanying Down syndrome can be easily corrected. Medical research also proves that this extra chromosome protects the individual against certain kinds of cancer.[10] Many persons with Down syndrome acknowledge that having Down syndrome is not painful, and it certainly involves no suffering. Anya Souza, a woman with Down syndrome, says: 'I cannot get rid of my Down's. But you cannot get rid of my happiness. You cannot get rid of the happiness I give

---

[7] Patterson and Satz (2005: 38).
[8] Smith (2011: 1).
[9] Smith (2011: 3).
[10] Smith (2011: 2).

others, either. It's doctors that want to test the pregnant women, and stop people like me being born.'[11]

However, given the 'professional oath', it is understood that the medical professionals are not required to disseminate any knowledge about the attributes of a condition like Down syndrome. Besides, the legally permitted routine screening tests strongly inform the mother that it is a serious condition. Keiron Smith says: 'That's a way to exclude people. It means that, as soon as you have conversation if there is a diagnosis in pregnancy for Down syndrome, you see that metaphor, *you don't see the person*. That's the problem—it's always [a] dehumanising experience when you are perceived as something else.'[12]

When the prenatal tests diagnose chances of foetal disability, medical professionals focus on the condition that is medically undesirable rather than on the person. Once the screening test reveals the possibility of Down syndrome in a foetus, selective abortion laws do not provide an option to the mother to take a decision to continue her pregnancy. Since it is a legally permitted ground for abortion, medical professionals do not feel the need to provide right information to women/parents. It is just deemed that a child with Down syndrome is not a fit person to be born and exist in this world. It just depicts the general manner of medical stand for any disability.

Thus, disability-selective abortion laws provide blanket permission, denying the right to mothers/parents to take informed decisions. At the same time, medical professionals firmly misinform parents about how their new child will never talk, walk, write, or read. This, in turn, denies the women/parents from understanding the individual qualities of the child as a person with disability in general. Consequently, disability-selective abortion laws reinforce the wrong perception that disability is a qualified reason not to protect a life with disability. That is why no need was felt to talk about disability or persons with disabilities.

Thus, in fact, prospective parents are not offered a choice about potential screening options. It is an implicit understanding that

[11] Adeline (2003).

[12] Lewis (2012; emphasis supplied). Kieron Smith talks to Ed Lewis about the ideological and political causes of the stigmatization and exclusion of people with disabilities.

to screen is to screen out or select out but not to carry the baby. In disability-selective abortions, the women are forced to make a non-informed choice and ratify the social prejudices that persist against persons with disabilities.

However, as Ghai and Johri said,

> the medical professionals claim to provide non-directive counselling,[13] enabling parents to make their own choices. Thus, the medical discourse appears to 'empower' couples by 'offering' tests for a growing range of conditions. Yet, the ethical issues and the theoretical and practical possibilities of non-directive counselling have remained largely un-interrogated. Recent research voices serious concerns about the extent to which a genetic counsellor simply reproduces the biases of the larger society.[14]

Annette Patterson and Martha Satz also clearly point out: 'Serving both as purveyors of genetic information and as guides in decision-making, genetic counsellors often preside over prenatal sessions where parents are considering whether to continue or terminate pregnancy. This process has profound implications for society in shaping attitudes about what constitutes a "life ... worth living" and, potentially, the provisions society will make for those with disabilities.'[15]

This non-directive counselling provided by medical professionals remains problematic. Ann Platt Walker suggests in *A Guide to Genetic Counselling*, 'Adherence to a non-prescriptive (often referred to as "nondirective") approach is perhaps the most defining feature of genetic counselling. The philosophy stems from a firm belief that genetic counselling should—insofar as is possible—be devoid of any eugenic motivation.'[16]

The phrase 'insofar as is possible' suggests that the concern that the enterprise of genetic counselling may by its nature be unable to free

---

[13] Psychotherapeutic or counselling technique in which the therapist takes on an unobtrusive role in order to encourage free expression and problem resolution by the client or patient.

[14] Ghai and Johri (2008: 298).

[15] Patterson and Satz (2002: 122).

[16] Walker (2009: 10).

itself totally from a eugenic cast.[17] In *Implications of the Human Right to Life*, Leon Kass explains it as follows:

> Persons afflicted with certain diseases will never be capable of living the full life of a human being.... There is no reason to keep them alive. This standard, I would suggest, is the one which most physicians and genetic counsellors appeal to in their hearts, no matter what they say or do.... Why else would they have developed genetic counselling?[18]

The underlying contention is that though genetic tests are prescribed and performed by doctors and lab technicians, in most cases, it is the genetic counsellor who should present the genetic information and presides over the discussion that proceeds from such testing.[19] This places genetic counsellors in a critical position because they undoubtedly have a strong impact on the perception of genetic conditions and the consequent prenatal decisions to terminate pregnancy.[20]

In India, we do not yet have a body of trained genetic counsellors. Doctors take on that function in the few genetic counselling centres that exist, and doctors are perhaps one of the most biased sections of the population against disability.[21] During the course of counselling, doctors show a systematic bias against persons with disabilities, which replicate the biases of larger society.[22] Thus, the structure of genetic counselling is a biased construction, because it explains the nature of a condition as a medical problem rather than a human condition. Since society has internalized this imperialistic perception of medical profession, disability-selective abortion remains in the shadow of silence. Therefore, non-coercive, unbiased reproductive counselling by a trained genetic counsellor, who integrates the inherent value of persons with disabilities, is necessary to provide parents with the right perspective on disabilities.[23] This necessitates the required change of recognizing the individual value of persons

---

[17] Patterson and Satz (2005: 37).
[18] Kass (1976: 400).
[19] Patterson and Satz (2005: 34).
[20] Patterson and Satz (2005: 34).
[21] Addlakha (2010: 29–30).
[22] Shannon (2005: 35).
[23] Edwards and Ferrante (2009: 4, 6).

with disabilities from the part of medical profession. Information should be disseminated about the individual values of disabilities, which are listed as abnormalities. This will help the parents to take an informed decision, by understanding the potential and not only the limits of all human life. Misinformation inhibited by stereotypes should be removed to enable women to take an informed decision. Science however, cannot remove all the inherent conditions, some of which considered abnormal. If so, is it not better to give up the myth that the *scientific control* through disability-selective abortion will contribute to have only perfect minds and bodies? It would be better to reveal ignorance than to pretend and thereby preclude getting to know each other as people.[24]

A blanket permission of disability-selective abortion is more problematic as it also cost women their health. Disability-selective abortion is provided as a good solution to get rid of disability and a child with disability. The reasons for disability-selective abortion are not the risk to the health of the mother but the possible disability of the child. It can be seen that this complete permission has been granted without taking into consideration the health cost to women. The invasive screening tests, which are necessary to diagnose the listed disabilities ('abnormalities'), carry risk to both the foetus and the mother. The psychological and physiological effects of abortion, though it has been called 'therapeutic', are not in fact therapeutic to either the foetus or the mother. Evidence is mounting that the reaction to the loss of a child from induced abortion is part of the same continuum of grief. One researcher says:

> Grief after induced abortion is often more profound and delayed than grief after other perinatal losses. Grief after elective abortion is uniquely poignant because it is largely hidden. The post-abortion woman's grief is not acknowledged by society because the reality of her child's death is not acknowledged. In order to gain her consent for the abortion she has been told that the procedure will remove a 'blob of tissue' or a 'product of conception' or a 'pre-embryo'.[25]

This prejudicial medical model, which harms many, not the targeted alone, raises the question of the extent to which medical

---

[24] Saxton (2006: 115).
[25] Reardon (2011).

professionals strive to promote its ethics and social justice. The medical professionals' persisting prejudice needs to be changed to acknowledge the value of persons with disabilities.

NEED FOR CHANGE TO ACCEPT INHERENT VALUE OF PERSONS WITH DISABILITIES

Disability-selective abortion is not a simple medical practice. It is problematic as it targets persons with disabilities and their extinction. The non-analytical approach towards the medical conception of 'disability' extends to the legal ordering on disability-related selective abortion. The right to life and equal value of persons with disabilities have not been the focus of judicial concern. Therefore, change should be initiated towards accepting persons with disability as worthy human beings. The change warrants a social recognition of the value and worth of the life of a person with disability. Abortion rights should extend to the choice of becoming a mother or not at a particular time and with a particular partner (pregnancy resulting from rape), but not to choice based on the characteristics of the foetus. Law should enable women to make an informed choice, which is not controlled by the prejudice produced by science and law.

DIAGNOSIS ON REALIZATION OF CHANGE

Suggestions for amendment without assessing the possibility of their implementation may be meaningless in a research work. Therefore, the chances of implementing a complete ban on disability-selective abortion, similar to sex-selective abortion, would be an unwelcome amendment. However, the existing blanket permission for disability-selective abortion should be removed. Law should be amended to enable a woman to take an informed decision about the kind of child she is carrying. This should be done through disseminating unbiased information about the individual value of persons who may be born with disability. The changed law would enable the society to accept disability and persons with disabilities. This would change the persisting negative perception about disability.

MEDICAL ETHICS

Disability-selective abortion is an autonomous strategy prescribed by medical professionals. However, the UNCRPD rights paradigm, which affirms equal status of persons with disabilities, renders this process problematic. What are the ethical parameters that science can bring to cure the wrongness involved in disability-selective abortion?

A medical result, which informs about the possibility of a birth with disability, automatically closes all the choices of parents except selective abortion. Instead, the medical professionals could support parents in appreciating and knowing the qualities of a child with disability. In this way, medical professionals can take part in constructing a society in which all kinds of people have the right to be born.

This is possible if medical professionals would accept the inherent value of persons with disabilities. It is unethical for medical professionals to suggest abortion based on the sole reason of a possible disability. Prenatal tests present the conflict between the genetic counselling ethic that values non-directiveness and a medical ethic that embraces eradication of disease. It is important to understand whether elimination of disability is a legitimate goal. Yet, prenatal testing is not the solution to the elimination of disabilities, when accidents, environmental degradation, old age, and other life contingencies account for a far larger number of disabilities.

Disability is an inevitable and inherent part of human diversity. Though many disabilities, such as sickle-cell anaemia, Down Syndrome, adult onset Huntington's, cystic fibrosis, and haemophilia, are considered grounds for abortion, in reality, many persons with these disabilities do become independent and lead productive lives, if given the opportunities to do so. This does not imply that there would be no persons with disabilities who will require care, but such an expectation is legitimate within a just society. Therefore, information should be provided to the mother or parents with multiple accounts of lives with disabilities and how can they lead a life with a child with disability.

When we realize that an issue is problematic, but are still prepared to accept it, the solution is to start deliberating on the issue. Let us talk to persons with disabilities to understand them. Dissemination of information should be based on an unbiased understanding of life with disabilities. If people with all kinds of disabilities are socially integrated, then there would be no need for prenatal testing. It would mean seeking out and respecting the knowledge and perspective of people with disabilities. The undesirability of disability persists in our society because we do not socialize with persons with disabilities. This exclusion and extreme isolation serve to strengthen the feeling that persons with disabilities are different and they should not be born. Law should enable the society to further human potential, but not to prevent its existence.

REALIZATION OF CHANGE

The said prescription for abortion would also challenge the certainty of medical decisions, when such persons live happily with disability.[26] Such investment in attitudes and the adoption of social justice measures is required to ensure quality of life for persons with disabilities. Quality of life is an important parameter for persons with disabilities. If there is no provision for quality of life, permitting persons with disabilities to born in this world may not make any difference. They may be born, but in the absence of quality of life, they may gradually get killed. Hence, once medical professionals start deliberating on disability in its right perspective, then policymakers will allocate more resources to ensure quality of life to all human beings. Thus, a medical initiative to accept disability as a human condition would contribute to the creation of a society where different competencies flourish.

A WORLD CONDUCIVE FOR ALL HUMANS

Finally, there may be an argument that even the medical professionals may concede, that expanding their knowledge is not enough. This world is not structured to accommodate persons with different kinds

[26] For instance, in 2000, an Indian mother settled in the US was advised to abort, as the prenatal test diagnosed congenital disabilities. However, the mother was so fond of her first baby that she took a decision against the doctor's advice. Now the child, named Philip, is 15 years old and the medical profession has certified his mental capacity as commensurate with his age. He is a public speaker. The mother, Susan Mathews (2012) narrates this in her book.

of minds and bodies or persons with disabilities. Consequently, the argument would be, 'it is better if they never get born in this world'. However, this is cutting off the ethical and legal demand to value and accommodate life with disability at the root. If there are no persons with disabilities, no accommodating facilities or infrastructure would come. If there is no one who requires such kind of facilities, there would be no need to think about it. So, when disability-selective abortion prevents persons with disabilities from coming into this world, it simply closes the channel to such requirements.

Society will start thinking about facilities only when persons who require such facilities are around them. There are educational institutions that have made ramps just to accommodate a single wheelchair user. But later, this was accommodative not only for wheelchair users, but for every person who had a fractured leg or illness. Hence, accommodating facilities are not only for persons with disabilities, but for everyone. Such facilities would simply benefit both persons with disabilities and non-disabilities. Interestingly, many such incidents have occurred not as part of complying with rules or law to enunciate disability rights. Such accommodation had occurred even prior to the rights discourse.

Once persons with disabilities live their life, others may have to think about their needs just like for any other life. If a person with blindness is a student or professor of an educational institution, they should be provided accessibility to Braille. This would accommodate all others, who may join the place with a similar condition. Thus, the presence of persons with disabilities would further enrich the lives of everyone.

The absence of accommodating infrastructure is a bleak justification for disability-selective abortion. Resources and technology should be used to empower the lives of persons with disabilities, not diminish their value by denying them the right to life on an equal basis with others.

BIBLIOGRAPHY

· ·

BOOKS

Addlakha, Renu, Stuart Blume, Patrick Devlieger, Osamu Nagase, and Myriam Winance (eds). 2009. *Disability and Society: A Reader*. New Delhi: Orient Blackswan.

Albrecht, Gary L., Katherine D. Seelman, and Michael Bury (eds). 2001. *Handbook of Disability Studies*. Thousand Oaks: SAGE Publications.

Angel, William D., Jorge Cardona, Giuseppe Porcaro, Jaakko Weuro, and Giorgio Zecca (eds). 2014. *The International Law of Youth Rights*, vol. 2. Leiden: Brill/Nijhoff.

Appleman, Philip. 1979. *Darwin*. New York: W.W. Norton & Co. Inc.

Arras, John D. and Nancy K. Rhoden (eds). 1999. *Ethical Issues in Modern Medicine*. Mountain View, CA: Mayfield Publishing Co.

Asad, Muhammad (trans.). 2003. *The Message of the Quran*. London: The Book Foundation.

Austin, Granville. 1999. *Working a Democratic Constitution: The Indian Experience*. New Delhi: Oxford University Press.

———. 2000. *The Indian Constitution: Cornerstone of a Nation*. New Delhi: Oxford University Press.

Barnes, C. and G. Mercer (eds). 1996. *Exploring the Divide: Illness and Disability*. Leeds: Disability Press.

———. 2003. *Disability*. Cambridge, UK: Polity Press.

Barnes, Colin, Mike Oliver, and Len Barton (eds). 2002. *Disability Studies Today*. Cambridge: Polity Press.

192   *Bibliography*

Barton, Len (ed.). 2001. *Disability, Politics and Struggle for Change.* London: David Fulton Publishers.

Basu, A.M. 1992. *Culture, the Status of Women, and Demographic Behaviour: Illustrated with the Case of India.* Oxford: Clarendon Press.

Bhatnagar, Reshmi Dube, Renu Dube, and Reena Dube. 2005. *Female Infanticide in India: A Feminist Cultural History.* New York: State University of New York Press.

Bob, Clifford (ed.). 2009. *The International Struggle for New Human Rights.* Philadelphia: University of Pennsylvania Press.

Bossuyt, Marc J. 1987. *Guide to the 'Travaux Préparatoires' of the International Covenant on Civil and Political Rights.* Dordrecht and Boston: Martinus Nijhoff Publishers.

Braddock, David. 2002. *Disability at the Dawn of the 21st Century and the State of the States.* Washington, DC: American Association on Mental Retardation.

Brownlie, Ian (ed.). 2003. *Basic Documents in International Law.* New Delhi, Oxford, and New York: Oxford University Press.

Buchanan, Allen, Dan W. Brock, Norman Daniels, and Daniel Wikler (eds). 2001. *From Chance to Choice: Genetics and Justice.* Cambridge: Cambridge University Press.

Burleigh, M. 1994. *Death and Deliverance: 'Euthanasia' in Germany 1900–1945.* Cambridge: Cambridge University Press.

Cachel, Susan. 2006. *Primate and Human Evolution.* New York: Cambridge University Press.

Campbell, Alastair, Max Charlesworth, Grant Gillett, and Gareth Jones (eds). 2002. *Medical Ethics.* New York: Oxford University Press.

Campbell, Tom, David Goldberg, Sheila McLean, and Tom Mullen (eds). 1986. *Human Rights: From Rhetoric to Reality.* New York: Basil Blackwell Ltd.

Carneiro, R.L. (ed.). 1967. *The Evolution of Society: Selections from Herbert Spencer's 'Principles of Sociology'.* Chicago and London: University of Chicago Press.

Cassels, Nancy Gardener. 2010. *Social Legislation of the East India Company: Public Justice versus Public Instruction.* New Delhi: SAGE Publications.

Chester, Robert (ed.). 1977. *Equalities and Inequalities in Family Life.* London: Academic Press.

Corker, Marian and Sally French (eds). 2002. *Disability Discourse.* Buckingham, Philadelphia: Open University Press.

Crary, Alice. 2007. *Wittgenstein and the Moral Life.* London: MIT Press.

Cummins, S. Lyle. 1923. *Goldilocks and the Three Bears.* New York: George H. Doran Company.

Cunningham, Lawrence S. 2009. *An Introduction to Catholicism*. Cambridge: Cambridge University Press.

Dalal, Ajit K. and Subha Rah. 2005. *Social Dimensions of Health*. Delhi: Rawat Publications.

Daniels, Norman. 1985. *Just Health Care: Studies in Philosophy and Health Policy*. US: Cambridge University Press.

Darwin, Charles. 1922. *Descent of Man and Selection in Relation to Sex*. London: John Murray.

———. 1969. *The Autobiography of Charles Darwin 1809–1882*. New York: Norton.

Davar, Bhargavi (ed.). 2001. *Mental Health from a Gender Perspective*. New Delhi: SAGE Publications.

Davies, Margaret. 1994. *Asking the Law Question*. Sydney: The Law Book Company, Sweet & Maxell.

Davis, Lennard J. (ed.). 2006. *The Disability Studies Reader*. New York and London: Routledge.

De Vries, Raymond. 2005. *A Pleasing Birth: Midwives and Maternity Care in the Netherlands*. Philadelphia: Temple University Press.

Dhanda, Amita and Rajive Raturi (eds). 2010. *Harmonizing Laws with the UNCRPD*. New Delhi: Human Rights Law Network.

Dhanda, Amita. 2000. *Legal Order and Mental Disorder*. New Delhi: SAGE Publications.

Douglas, William O. 1956. *From Marshall to Mukherjee: Studies in American and Indian Constitutional Law*. Calcutta: Eastern Law House.

Dworkin, Ronald M. 1993. *Life's Dominion: An Argument about Abortion, Euthanasia and Individual Freedom*. New York: Knopf.

———. 1996. *Freedom's Law: The Moral Reading of the American Constitution*. Oxford: Oxford University Press.

Falk, Richard, Hilal Elver, and Lisa Hajjar (eds). 2008. *Human Rights: Critical Concerns in Political Science*, vol. 2. London and New York: Routledge.

Finger, Ann. 1990. *Past Due: A Story of Pregnancy, Disability and Birth*. London: Seal Press.

Fisher, Louis. 1990. *American Constitutional Law*. New York: McGraw Hill.

Fisher, R.A. 1958. *The General Theory of Natural Selection*. New York: Dover Publication.

Ford, Gary G. 2006. *Ethical Reasoning For Mental Health Professionals*. Thousand Oaks: SAGE Publications.

Foucault, Michel (trans by A. Sheridon). 1977. *Discipline and Punish: Birth of Prison*. New York: Pantheon.

Francis, C.M. 2004. *Medical Ethics*. New Delhi: Jaypee Brothers Medical Publishers Pvt. Ltd.

Fraser, Nancy. 1997. *Justice Interruptus: Critical Reflections on the Postsocialist Condition*. New York and London: Routledge and Kegan Paul.

Gallagher, H. 1995. *By Trust Betrayed: Patients, Physicians and the License to Kill in the Third Reich*. New York: Vandemere Press.

Galton, Francis. 1907. *Inquiries into Human Faculty and Its Development*. London: J.M. Dent & Co.

———. 1908. *Memories of My Life*. London: Dutton.

Gearty, C.A. 1997. *European Civil Liberties and the European Convention on Human Rights: A Comparative Study*. The Hague and Boston: Martinus Nijhoff Publishers.

Ghai, Anita. 2003. *(Dis)embodied Form: Issues of Disabled Women*. New Delhi: Shakti Books, Har-Anand Publications.

Gillespie, Neal C. 1932. *Charles Darwin and the Problem of Creation*. Chicago and London: University of Chicago Press.

Goddard, Henry Herbert. 1914. *Feeble-Mindedness: Its Causes and Consequences*. New York: Macmillan.

Goldstein, Leslie F. 1994. *Contemporary Cases in Women's Rights*. Wisconsin: University of Wisconsin Press.

Gombos, Gabor and Anita Dhanda. 2009. *Catalyzing Self Advocacy: An Experiment in India*. Pune: Bapu Trust.

Good, Ronald. 1981. *The Philosophy of Evolution*. Dorset: The Dovecote Press.

Goodwin, Frederick K. and Kay Field Jamison. 2007. *Manic-Depressive Illness: Bipolar Disorders and Recurrent Depression*. New York: Oxford University Press.

Haller, Mark. 1963. *Eugenics: Hereditarian Attitudes in American Thought*. New Brunswick: Rutgers University Press.

Hans, Asha and Annie Patri. 2003. *Women, Disability and Identity*. New Delhi: SAGE Publications.

Harris, John. (ed.). 2004. *Bioethics*. New York: Oxford University Press.

———. 1985. *The Value of Life: An Introduction to Medical Ethics*. London: Routledge Kegan Paul.

———. 1992. *Wonder Woman and Superman: The Ethics of Human Biotechnology*. Oxford: Oxford University Press.

Herring, Jonathan. 2012. *Medical Law and Ethics*. Oxford: Oxford University Press.

Hilton, Bruce (ed.). 1973. *Ethical Issues in Human Genetics: Genetic Counseling and the Use of Genetic Knowledge*. New York and London: Plenum Press.

Hodge, Jonathan (ed.). 2003. *The Cambridge Companion to Darwin*. Cambridge: Cambridge University Press.

Honderich, Ted. 1989. *Violence for Equality*. London: Routledge Publications.

Ingoldsby, Pat. 1994. *How Was It for You Doctor?* Dublin: Willow Publications.

Irwin, Sarah. 1995. *Rights of Passage: Social Change and the Transition from Youth to Adulthood.* London: UCL Press.

Islamic Fiqh Academy. 2005. *Juristic Decisions on Contemporary Issues.* New Delhi: IFA Publications.

Jain, Mahabir Prashad. 1998. *Indian Constitutional Law.* Agra: Wadhwa & Co.

James, William. 1897. *The Will to Believe and Other Essays in Popular Philosophy.* New York: Longmans, Green, and Co.

Jamison, Kay Redfield. 1994. *Touched with Fire: Manic Depressive Illness and the Artistic Temperament.* New York: Free Press Paperbacks.

Jecker, Nancy S., Albert R. Jonsen, and Robert A. Pearlman (eds). 2010. *Bioethics: An Introduction to the History, Methods, and Practice.* New Delhi: Jones and Bartlett Publishers.

Jonsen, Albert R. 1998. *The Birth of Bioethics.* New York: Oxford University Press.

Karna, G.N. 2001. *Disability Studies in India: Retrospects and Prospects.* New Delhi: Gyan Publishing House.

Keller, Helen A. (ed. by John Albert Macy). 1902. *The Story of My Life.* New York: Doubleday Page & Co.

Kenny, M. 1986. *Abortion: The Whole Story.* London: Quartet Books.

Kevles, Daniel Jo. 1985. *In the Name of Eugenics: Genetics and the Uses of Human Heredity.* London: Pelican Books.

Kuhse, Helga and Peter Singer. 1985. *Should the Baby Live? The Problem of Handicapped Infants.* Oxford: Oxford University Press.

—— (eds). 1998. *A Companion to Bioethics.* Oxford: Blackwell Publishers.

Laughlin, Harry H. 1922. *Eugenical Sterilization in the United States.* Chicago: Psychopathic Laboratory of the Municipal Court of Chicago.

Lifton, Robert J. 1986. *The Nazi Doctors: Medical Killing and the Psychology of Genocide.* London: Macmillan.

Lindemann, Hilde, Marian Verkerk, and Margaret Urban Walker (eds). 2009. *Naturalized Bioethics: Toward Responsible Knowing and Practice.* New York: Cambridge University Press.

Lombardo, Paul A. 2008. *Three Generations, No Imbeciles: Eugenics, the Supreme Court and Buck v. Bell.* Baltimore: The Johns Hopkins University Press.

MacLean, K.S. 2004. *Life and Disability Underwriting.* London: The Chartered Insurance Institute.

Maienschein, Jane. 1988. *Whose View of Life? Embryos, Cloning, and Stem Cells.* London: Weidenfeld & Nicolson.

Marten, J.T. 1924. *Census of India 1921*, vol. I, Part I-Report, Superintendent Government Printing, Kolkata, India, available online at http://dspace. gipe.ac.in/xmlui/handle/10973/18814 (last accessed on 28 February 2016).

Martin, Emily. 1992. *The Woman in the Body: A Cultural Analysis of Reproduction*. Boston: Beacon Press.

Mason, Alpheus Thomas. 1990. *American Constitutional Law: Introductory Essays and Selected Cases*. Eaglewood Cliffs: Prentice Hall.

Mathew, Susan. 2012. *A Mother's Heart*. Chattanooga: Love Without Reason.

Maxwell, Mary. 1984. *Human Evolution: A Philosophical Anthropology*. London and Sydney: Croom Helm.

McMahan, Jeff. 2002. *The Ethics of Killing: Problems at the Margins of Life*. New York: Oxford University Press.

Menon, Nivedita. 2004. *Recovering Subversion: Feminist Politics Beyond the Law*. New Delhi: Permanent Black.

Miller, Franklin G. (ed.). 2000. *Frontiers in Bioethics: Essays Dedicated to John C. Fletcher*. Hagerstown: University Publishing Group.

Mills, Charles W. 1997. *The Racial Contract*. Ithaca: Cornell University Press.

Minow, Martha. 1990. *Making All the Difference: Inclusion, Exclusion, and American Law*. New York: Cornell University Press

Mody, Zia. 2013. *10 Judgments that Changed India*. New Delhi: Penguin Books.

Moeckli, Daniel, Sangeeta Shah, and Sandesh Sivakumaran (eds). 2010. *International Human Rights Law*. New York: Oxford University Press.

Morris, Jenny (ed.). 1996. *Encounters with Strangers: Feminism and Disability*. London: Women's Press.

Muller, Herman J. 1935. *Out of Night: A Biologist's View of the Future*. New York: The Vanguard Press.

Muthulakshmi, R. 1997. *Female Infanticide: Its Causes and Solutions*. New Delhi: Discovery Publishing House.

Nasar, Sylvia. 2001. *A Beautiful Mind: The Life of Mathematical Genius and Nobel Laureate John Nash*. London and New York: Simon & Schuster.

Nettleton, Sarah. 1995. *The Sociology of Health and Illness*. Oxford: Blackwell Publishers.

Nolan, Mary, L. 2011. Home *Birth: The Politics of Difficult Choices*. New York: Routledge.

Nussbaum, Martha C. 2006. *Frontiers of Justice: Disability, Nationality, Species Membership*. New Delhi: Oxford University Press.

Oakley, Ann. 1980. *Women Confined: Towards a Sociology of Childbirth*. Oxford: Martin Robertson & Co. Ltd.

Oliver, Michael. 1996. *Understanding Disability: From Theory to Practice*. New York: Palgrave.

Ospovat, Dov. 1981. *The Development of Darwin's Theory*. New York: Cambridge University Press.

Pandey, Jitendra. 2005. *Civil Liberty under Indian Constitution*. New Delhi: Deep & Deep Pub.

Parens, Erik and Adrienne Asch. (eds). 2000a. *Prenatal Testing and Disability Rights*. Washington, DC: Georgetown University Press.

Patel, Tulsi (ed.). 2007c. *Sex-selective Abortion in India: Gender, Society and New Reproductive Technologies*. New Delhi: SAGE Publications.

Pickett, Kate E. and Richard G. Wilkinson. 2009. *Health and Inequality: Major Themes in Health and Social Welfare*, vol. 4. London and New York: Routledge.

Plato (trans. by Walter Hamilton). 1974. *Phaedrus and the Seventh and Eighth Letters*. London: Penguin.

Priestley, Mark (ed.). 2001. *Disability and the Life Course: Global Perspectives*. Cambridge: Cambridge University Press.

Proctor, Robert N. 1988. *Racial Hygiene: Medicine under the Nazis*. Cambridge, MA: Harvard University Press.

Quinn, Gerard and Lisa Waddington (eds). 2009. *European Year Book of Disability Law*, vol. 1. Oxford and Portland: Intersentia.

Rafter, Nicole H. 1988. *White Trash: The Eugenic Family Studies 1877–1919*. Boston: North Eastern University Press.

Rapley, Mark. 2004. *The Social Construction of Intellectual Disability*. New York: Cambridge University Press.

Ratner, Steven R. 2009. *Accountability for Human Rights Atrocities in Law: Beyond the Nuremberg Legacy*. Oxford: Oxford University Press.

Rawls, John. 1971. *A Theory of Justice*. Cambridge, MA: Harvard University Press.

Reilly, Philip R. 1991. *The Surgical Solution: A History of Involuntary Sterilization in the United States*. Baltimore: Johns Hopkins Press.

Rioux, Maria H. Lee Ann Basser and Melinda Jones. 2011. *Critical Perspectives on Human Rights and Disability Law*. Boston: Martinus Nijhoff Publishers.

Rossum, Ralph A. 1987. *American Constitutional Law: Cases and Interpretations*. New York: St. Martin's Press.

Runco, Mark A. and Steven R. Pritzker (eds). 2011. *Encyclopedia of Creativity*. US: Academic Press.

Ruse, Michael and Robert J. Richard (eds). 2009. *The Origin of Species*. New York: Cambridge University Press.

Sen, Amartya. 2009. *The Idea of Justice*. New York: Penguin.

Shakespeare, Tom. 2006. *Disability Rights and Wrongs*. New York and London: Routledge.

Shannon, Thomas A. 2005. *Genetics: Science, Ethics and Public Policy*. US: Rowman & Littlefield Publishers, Inc.

Sharma, Kusum. 1997. *Ambedkar and Indian Constitution*. New Delhi: Ashish Publishing House.

Shilling, Chris. 1993. *The Body and Social Theory*. London: SAGE Publications.

Silvers, Anita, David Wasserman, and Mary B. Mahowald. 1998. *Disability, Difference, Discrimination: Perspectives on Justice, in Bioethics and Public Policy*. Rowman & Littlefield.

Sims, Nicholas A. 1981. *Exploration in Ethics and International Relations*. London: Croom Helm Ltd.

Singer, Peter. 1993. *Practical Ethics*. New York: Cambridge University Press.

Smart, Carol. 1989. *Feminism and the Power of Law*. London: Routledge.

Smith, Charles H. (ed.). 1991. *Alfred Russel Wallace: An Anthology of His Shorter Writings*. New York: Oxford University Press.

Smith, George P. 2000. *Human Rights and Biomedicine*. Netherlands: Kluwer Law International.

Smith, Kieron. 2011. *The Politics of Down Syndrome*. Alresford: Zero Books.

Solomon, Maynard. 1988. *Beethoven Essays*. Cambridge, MA: Harvard University Press

Spiegelberg, Herbert. 1986. *Stepping Stones Toward an Ethics for Fellow Existers*. Dordrecht: Martinus Nijhoff Publishers.

Stephens, Otis H. and John M. Scheb II. 2003. *American Constitutional Law*. Belmont, CA: Thomson/South-Western West.

Tomuschat, Christian, Evelyne Lagrange, and Stefan Oeter (eds). 2010. *The Right to Life*. Leiden and Boston: Martinus Nijhoff Publishers.

Tribe, Lawrence H. 2000. *American Constitutional Law*. New York: Foundation Press.

Turner, Bryan S. 2005. *Medical Power and Social Knowledge*. London: SAGE Publications.

Turner, Bryan S. 2008. *The Body and Society*. London: SAGE Publications.

Wallace, Alfred Russell. 1905. *My Life: A Record of Events and Opinions*, vol. 2. New York: Dodd, Mead & Co.

Watson, Nick (ed.). 2008. *Disability: Major Themes in Health and Social Welfare*. London and New York: Routledge.

Wendell, Susan. 1996. *The Rejected Body: Feminist Philosophical Reflections on Disability*. London: Routledge.

Westfall, Richard S. 1983. *Never at Rest: A Biography of Isaac Newton*. Cambridge: Cambridge University Press.

White, Edward. 1993. *Justice Oliver Wendell Holmes: Law and the Inner Self*. New York: Oxford University Press.

Williams, Patricia J. 1991. *The Alchemy of Race and Rights: Diary of a Law Professor*. Cambridge, MA: Harvard University Press.

Wright, David. 2011. *Downs: The History of a Disability*. Oxford: Oxford University Press.
Young, Iris Marion. 1990. *Justice and Politics of Difference*. Princeton: Princeton University Press.
———. 2005. *On Female Body Experience: 'Throwing Like a Girl' and Other Essays*. New York: Oxford University Press.

BOOK CHAPTERS

Addlakha, Renu. 2010. 'Disability Selective Abortions in India: Individual Choice, Disabling Environments and the Socio-moral Order', in Ine Gevers, Renu Addlahka, Michel Callon, and Johnson Cheu (eds), *Difference on Display: Diversity in Art, Science and Society*, pp. 176–81. Amsterdam: NAI Ultgevers Publishers.
Asch, Adrienne. 1996. 'Reproductive Technology and Disability', in Sherrill Cohen and Nadine Taub (eds), *Reproductive Laws for the 1990s*, pp. 69–124. Oxford and New York: Oxford University Press.
———. 1999. 'Can Aborting "Imperfect" Children Be Immoral?', in John D. Arras and Nancy K. Rhoden (eds), *Ethical Issues in Modern Medicine*, pp. 317–21. Mountain View, CA: Mayfield Publishing Co.
———. 2000a. 'Reproduction, Ethics, Prenatal Testing, and the Disability Rights Critique', in Thomas H. Murray and Maxwell J. Mehlman (eds), *Encyclopedia of Ethical, Legal, and Policy Issues in Biotechnology*, pp. 957–77. New York: John Wiley & Sons, Inc.
———. 2000b. 'Why I haven't Changed My Mind about Prenatal Diagnosis: Reflections and Refinements', in Erik Parens and Adrienne Asch (eds), *Prenatal Testing and Disability Rights*, pp. 234–60. Washington, DC: Georgetown University Press.
———. 2001. 'Disability, Bioethics, and Human Rights', in Gary L. Albrecht, Katherine D. Seelman, and Michael Bury (eds), *Handbook of Disability Studies*, pp. 297–325. Thousand Oaks: SAGE Publications.
Bailey, Ruth. 1996. 'Prenatal Testing and the Prevention of Impairment: A Woman's Right to Choose?' in Jenny Morris (ed.), *Encounters with Strangers: Feminism and Disability*, pp. 143–67. London: The Women's Press.
Blumberg, Lisa. 1994b. 'Eugenics Experience v Reproductive Choice', in Barret Shaw (ed.), *The Ragged Edge the Disability Experience from the Pages of the first Fifteen years of the Disability Rag*, pp. 218–29. Louisville: Avocado Press.
Bose, Ashish. 2007. 'Female Foeticide: A Civilizational Collapse', in Tulsi Patel (ed.), *Sex-selective Abortion in India: Gender, Society and New Reproductive Technologies*, pp. 80–90. New Delhi: SAGE Publications.

Das, V. 1986. 'Deciding on Moral Issues: The Case of Abortion', in D.L. Eck and D. Jain (eds), *Speaking of Faith: Cross-cultural Perspectives on Women, Religion and Social Change*, pp. 211–20. London: The Women's Press.

Dhanda, Amita. 2010b. 'Status Paper on Rights of Persons Living with Mental Illness in the Light of the UNCRPD', in Amita Dhanda and Rajive Raturi (eds), *Harmonizing Laws with the UNCRPD*, pp. 201–22. New Delhi: Human Rights Law Network.

Eckermann, Liz. 1997. 'Foucault, Embodiment and Gendered Subjectivities: The Case of Voluntary Self-Starvation', in Alan Peterson and Robin Bunton (eds), *Foucault, Health and Medicine*, pp. 151–72. London: Routledge.

Felce, D. and J. Perry. 1996. 'Assessment of Quality of Life', in R.L. Schalock and G.N. Siperstein (eds), *Quality of Life: Volume I, Conceptualization and Measurement*, pp. 63–70. Washington, DC: American Association on Mental Retardation.

Fredman, Sandra. 2005. 'Disability Equality: A Challenge to the Existing Anti-Discrimination Paradigm?', in A. Lawson and C. Gooding (eds), *Disability Rights in Europe: From Theory To Practice*, pp. 199–218. Oxford: Hart Publishing.

Galton, Francis. 1909. 'The Possible Improvement of the Human Breed Under the Existing Conditions of Law and Sentiment', in *Essays on Eugenics*, pp. 1–34. London: The Eugenics Education Society.

Gastaldo, Denise. 1997. 'Is Health Education Good for You? Re-thinking Health Education through the Concept of Bio-Power', in Alan Peterson and Robin Bunton (eds), *Foucault, Health and Medicine*, pp. 113–33. London: Routledge.

Glover, Jonathan. 1992. 'Future People, Disability, and Screening', in Peter Laslett and James S. Fishkin (eds), *Justice between Age Groups and Generations*, pp. 429–44. New Haven: Yale University Press.

Hubbard, Ruth. 2006. 'Abortion and Disability: Who Should and Who Should Not Inhabit This World?', in Lennard J. Davis (ed.), *Disability Studies Reader*, pp. 74–86. New York and London: Routledge.

Kant, Immanuel. 1996. 'Groundwork of the Metaphysics of Morals', in Mary J. Gregor (trans. and ed.), *Immanuel Kant: Practical Philosophy*, pp. 37–108. Cambridge and New York: Cambridge University Press.

Kass, Leon. 1976. 'Implications of the Human Right to Life', in James M. Humber (ed.), *Biomedical Ethics and the Law*, pp. 335–50. New York: Springer.

Lombardo, Paul A. 2000. 'Medicine, Eugenics and the Supreme Court: From Coercive Sterilization to Reproductive Freedom', in Franklin G. Miller (ed.), *Frontiers in Bioethics: Essays Dedicated to John C. Fletcher*, pp. 105–26. Hagerstown: University Publishing Group.

Macklin, Ruth. 2004. 'Which Way Down the Slippery Slope? Nazi Medical Killing and Euthanasia Today', in John Harris (ed.), *Bioethics*, pp. 109–31. New York: Oxford University Press.

Oliver, Michael. 1993. 'Disability and Dependency: A Creation of Industrial Societies?', in J. Swain, V. Finkelstein, S. French, and M. Oliver (eds), *Disabling Barriers: Enabling Environments*, London: SAGE Publications.

Parens, Erik and Adrienne Asch. 2000b. 'The Disability Rights Critique of Prenatal Genetic Testing: Reflections and Recommendations', in Erik Parens and Adrienne Asch (eds), *Prenatal Testing and Disability Rights*, pp. 3–43. Washington, DC: Georgetown University Press.

Parens, Erik and Adrienne Asch. 2012. 'The Disability Rights Critique of Parental Genetic Testing', in Stephan Holland (ed.), *Arguing about Bioethics*, pp. 59–73. New York: Routledge.

Patel, Tulsi. 2007a. 'Introduction: Gender Relations, NRTs and Female Foeticide in India', in Tulsi Patel (ed.), *Sex-selective Abortion in India: Gender, Society and New Reproductive Technologies*, pp. 27–57. New Delhi: SAGE Publications.

———. 2007b. 'The Mindset Behind Eliminating the Female Foetus', Tulsi Patel (ed.), *Sex-selective Abortion in India: Gender, Society and New Reproductive Technologies*, pp. 135–74. New Delhi: SAGE Publications.

Patterson, Annette and Martha Satz. 2005. 'Genetic Counseling and the Disabled: Feminism Examines the Stance of Those Who Stand at the Gate', in Thomas A. Shannon (ed.), *Genetics: Science, Ethics and Public Policy*, pp. 33–58. US: Rowman & Littlefield Publishers.

Ramsey, Paul. 1973. 'Screening: An Ethicist's View', in Bruce Hilton (ed.), *Ethical Issues in Human Genetics: Genetic Counseling and the Use of Genetic Knowledge*, pp. 147–67. New York and London: Plenum Press.

Saxton, Marsha. 1998. 'Disability Rights and Selective Abortion', in R. Solinger (ed.), *Abortion Wars: A Half Century of Struggle, 1950–2000*, pp. 374–93. Berkeley: University of California Press.

———. 2000. 'Why Members of the Disability Community Oppose Prenatal Diagnosis and Selective Abortion', in Eric Parens and Adrienne Asch (eds), *Prenatal Testing and Disability Rights*, pp. 147–64. Washington, DC: Georgetown University Press.

———. 2006. 'Disability Rights and Selective Abortion', in Lennard J. Davis (ed.), *Disability Studies Reader*, pp. 87–99. New York and London: Routledge.

Sen, Amartya. 1980. 'Equality of What?', in Sterling McMurrin (ed.), *Tanner Lectures on Human Values*, pp. 195–220. Cambridge: Cambridge University Press.

Steinbock, Bonnie. 2000. 'Disability, Prenatal Testing, and Selective Abortion', in Eric Parens and Adrienne Asch (eds), *Prenatal Testing and Disability Rights*, pp. 108–23. Washington, DC: Georgetown University Press.

Tromel, Stefan. 2009. 'A Personal Perspective on the Drafting History of the United Nations Convention on the Rights of Persons with Disabilities', in Gerard Quinn and Lisa Waddington (eds), *European Year Book of Disability Law*, vol. 1, pp. 115–137. Oxford and Portland: Intersentia.

Visaria, Leela. 2007. 'Deficit of Girls in India: Can It Be Attributed to Sex Selective Abortions', in Tulsi Patel (ed.), *Sex-selective Abortion in India: Gender, Society and New Reproductive Technologies*, pp. 61–79. New Delhi: SAGE Publications.

Viswanath, L.S. 2007. 'Female Infanticide, Property and the Colonial State', in Tulsi Patel (ed.), *Sex-selective Abortion in India: Gender, Society and New Reproductive Technologies*, pp. 269–85. New Delhi: SAGE Publications.

Walker, Ann Platt. 2009. 'The Practice of Genetic Counseling', in Diane L. Baker, Jane L. Schuette, and Wendy R. Uhlmann (eds), *A Guide to Genetic Counselling*, second edn, pp. 1–36. New York: Wiley-Liss.

Wallace, Alfred R. 1991. 'Human Selection', in Charles H. Smith (ed.), *Alfred Russel Wallace: An Anthology of His Shorter Writings*, pp. 119–216. New York: Oxford University Press.

Wasserman, David. 2001. 'Philosophical Issues in the Definition and Social Response to Disability', in Gary L. Albrecht, Katherine D. Seelman, and Michael Bury (eds), *Handbook of Disability Studies*, pp. 219–49. Thousand Oaks: SAGE Publications.

Weiss, Meira. 2007. 'The Chosen Body and the Rejection of Disability in Israeli Society', in Benedicte Ingstad and Susan Raynolds Whyte (eds), *Disability in Local and Global Worlds*, pp. 114–18. Berkeley: University of California Press.

Wolbring, Gregor. 2001. 'Where Do We Draw the Line? Surviving Eugenics in a Technological World', in Mark Priestley (ed.), *Disability and the Life Course: Global Perspectives*, pp. 38–49. Cambridge: Cambridge University Press.

ARTICLES

Addlakha, Renu. 2010. 'A Legal Precedent: Reproductive Rights of Mentally Retarded Persons in India', *Indian Journal of Medical Ethics*, VII(1): 34–6.

Asch, Adrienne. 1999. 'Prenatal Diagnosis and Selective Abortion: A Challenge to Practice and Policy', *American Journal of Public Health*, 89(11): 1649–57.

———. 2003. 'Disability Equality and Prenatal Testing: Contradictory or Compatible?', *Florida State University Law Review*, 30(2): 315–42.

Bagenstos, Samuel R. 2006. 'Disability, Life, Death, and Choice', *Harvard Journal of Law and Gender*, 29: 425–63.

Beckett, Katherine. 2005. 'Choosing Cesarean: Feminism and the Politics of Childbirth in the United States', *Feminist Theory*, 6(3): 251–75.

Belsky, Alan J. 1993. 'Injury as a Matter of Law: Is This the Answer to the Wrongful Life Dilemma?', *University of Baltimore Law Review*, 22(2): 185–90.

Blumberg, Lisa. 1994a. 'The Politics of Prenatal Testing and Selective Abortion', *Sexuality and Disability*, 12(2): 135–53.

Board of Directors of the American Society of Human Genetics. 1999. 'Eugenics and the Misuse of Genetic Information to Restrict Reproductive Freedom', *American Journal of Human Genetics*, 64(2): 335–8.

Bowler, Peter J. 1976. 'Malthus, Darwin, and the Concept of Struggle', *Journal of the History of Ideas*, 37(4): 631–50.

Burgdorf, Robert L. and Marcia P. Burgdorf. 1977. 'The Wicked Witch Is Almost Dead: Buck v. Bell and the Sterilization of Handicapped Persons', *Temple Law Quarterly*, 50(4): 995–1034.

Chamberlain, J.P. 1923. 'Eugenics and Limitations of Marriage', *Journal of Comparative Legislation and International Law*, 5(4): 253–7.

Cohen, Shelly. 2006. 'De-moralizing Death: A Humanistic Approach to the Sanctity of Life', *Elder Law Journal*, 14(1): 91–125.

Crossley, Michael L. 2007. 'Childbirth, Complications and the Illusion of "Choice": A Case Study', *Feminism & Psychology*, 17(4): 543–63.

Dhanda, Amita. 2008. 'Constructing a New Human Rights Lexicon: Convention on the Rights of Persons with Disabilities', *International Journal on Human Rights*, 5(8): 43–58.

———. 2010a. 'Amartya Sen's Idea of Justice: A Just Idea but an Unjust Application to Persons with Disabilities', *Indian Journal of Constitutional Law*, (4): 132–7.

Fisher, Irving. 1921. 'Impending Problems of Eugenics', *The Scientific Monthly*, 13(3): 214–31.

Franklin, Sarah and Maureen McNeil. 1988. 'Reproductive Futures: Recent Literature and Current Feminist Debates on Reproductive Technologies', *Feminist Studies*, 14(3): 545–60.

Ghai Anita and Rachana Johri. 2008. 'Prenatal Diagnosis: Where Do We Draw the Line?', *Indian Journal of Gender Studies*, 15(2): 291–316.

Goddard, Henry H. 1927. 'Who Is a Moron?' *Scientific Monthly*, 24(1): 41–6.

Green, J.M. 1994. 'Serum Screening for Down's Syndrome: Experiences of Obstetricians in England and Wales', *British Medical Journal*, 309(6957): 769–72.

Haddon, Phoebe. 1985. 'Baby Doe Cases: Compromise and Moral Dilemma', *Emory Law Journal*, 34(3–4): 573–615.

Hahn, Harlan. 1994. 'Feminist Perspectives, Disability and Law: New Issues and Agendas', *Southern California Review of Law and Women's Studies*, 4(1): 97–144.

Hellegers, Andre E. 1970. 'Fetal Development', *Journal of Theological Studies*, 31(1): 3–9.

Hensel, Wendy F. 2005. 'The Disabling Impact of Wrongful Life and Wrongful Birth Actions', *Harvard Civil Rights–Civil Liberties Law Review*, 40(1): 141–95.

Irwin, Sarah and W. Bottero. 2000. 'Market Returns? Gender and Theories of Change in Employment Relations', *British Journal of Sociology*, 51(2): 261–80.

Irwin, Sarah. 1996. 'Age Related Distributive Justice and Claims on Resources', *British Journal of Sociology*, 47(1): 68–92.

———. 1998. 'Age, Generation and Inequality: A Reply to the Reply', *British Journal of Sociology*, 49(2): 305–10.

Kayess, Rosemary and Philip French. 2008. 'Out of Darkness into Light? Introducing the Convention on the Rights of Persons with Disabilities', *Human Rights Law Review*, 8(1): 1–34.

Keown, John. 1997. 'Restoring Moral and Intellectual Shape to the Law after Bland', *Law Quarterly Review*, 113(July): 481–503.

———. 1998. 'The Legal Revolution: From "Sanctity of Life" to "Quality of Life" and "Autonomy"', *Journal of Contemporary Health Law and Policy*, 14(2): 253–85.

Kothari, Jayna. 2010. 'The UN Convention on the Rights of Persons with Disabilities: An Engine for Law Reform in India', *Economic and Political Weekly*, 45(18): 65–72.

Lavi, Shai. 2003. 'Euthanasia and the Changing Ethics of the Deathbed: A Study in Historical Jurisprudence', *Theoretical Inquiries in Law*, 4(2): 729–54.

Lombardo, Paul A. 2008. 'Disability, Eugenics, and the Culture Wars', *Saint Louis University Journal of Health Law & Policy*, 2(1): 57–80.

Manson, Edward. 1912. 'Eugenics and Legislation', *Journal of the Society of Comparative Legislation*, 13(1): 123–9.

Melish, Tara J. 2007. 'The UN Disability Convention: Historic Process, Strong Prospects, and Why the U.S. Should Ratify', *Human Rights Brief*, (2): 37–47.

Miller, B.D. 1989. 'Changing Patterns of Juvenile Sex Ratios in Rural India, 1961–1971', *Economic and Political Weekly*, 24(22): 1229–36.

Mostert, Mark P. 2002. 'Useless Eaters: Disability as Genocidal Marker in Nazi Germany', *Journal of Special Education*, 36(3): 157–70. Available online at https://www.catholicculture.org/culture/library/view.cfm?recnum=7019 (last accessed on 22 May 2015).

Nair, Harish V. 2015. '"Let the Doctors Decide": Supreme Court Says 14-year-old Rape Victim Can Have Late Abortion at 24 Weeks ... if Medics Rule Her Life is at Risk', *Mail Online India*, 30 July, available online at http://www.dailymail.co.uk/indiahome/indianews/article-3178015/Let-doctors-decide-Supreme-Court-says-14-year-old-rape-victim-late-abortion-24-weeks-medics-rule-life-risk.html (last accessed on 29 February 2016).

Nizar, Smitha. 2011. 'Impact of UNCRPD on the Status of Persons with Disabilities', *Indian Journal of Medical Ethics*, 8(4): 223–9.

———. 2015. 'The New Human Rights Paradigm: Convention on the Rights of Persons with Disabilities and Its Implementation in India', *Christ University Law Journal*, 4(1): 49–69.

O'Dwyer, Vicky, Jennifer L. Hogan, Nadine Farah, Mairead Kennelly, Christopher Fitzpatrick, and Michael J. Turner. 2012. 'Maternal Mortality and the Rising Caesarean Rate', *International Journal of Gynecology and Obstetrics*, 116(2): 162–4.

Patchesky, Rosalind Pollack. 1980. 'Reproductive Freedom: Beyond A Woman's Right to Choose', *Women*, 5(4): 661–85.

Patel, Tulsi. 1982. 'Domestic Group, Status of Woman and Fertility', *Social Action*, 32(4): 363–79.

Patterson, Annette, and Martha Satz. 2002. 'Genetic Counseling and the Disabled: Feminism Examines the Stance of Those Who Stand at the Gate', *Hypatia, Feminism and Disability*, 17(3):118–42.

Perry, Ronen. 2008. 'It's a Wonderful Life', *Cornell Law Review*, 93(2): 329–99.

Rabino, Isaac. 2003. 'Genetic Testing and Its Implications: Human Genetics Researchers Grapple with Ethical Issues', *Science, Technology, & Human Values*, 28(3): 365–402.

Rieser, Richard. 2007. 'Lest We Forget: Eradicating the "Useless Eaters" in the Third Reich', *Inclusion Now Magazine*, 17, available online at http://issuu.com/chloeatallfie/docs/inc-now-vol-17 (last accessed on 20 January 2016).

Ronsmans, Carine and Wendy J. Graham. 2006. 'Maternal Mortality: Who, When, Where and Why', *The Lancet*, 368(9542): 1189–200.

Scott, Rosamund. 2005a. 'Prenatal Testing, Reproductive Autonomy, and Disability Interests', *Cambridge Quarterly of Healthcare Ethics*, 14(1): 65–82.

———. 2005b. 'The Uncertain Scope of Reproductive Autonomy in Preimplantation Genetic Diagnosis and Selective Abortion', *Medical Law Review*, 13(3): 291–327.

Shakespeare, Thomas William. 1998. 'Choices and Rights: Eugenics, Genetics and Disability Equality', *Disability and Society*, 13(5): 665–81.

Shakespeare, Thomas William. 2011. 'Choices, Reasons and Feelings: Prenatal Diagnosis as Disability Dilemma', *ALTER: European Journal of Disability Research*, 5: 37–43.

Sharp, Keith and Earle, Sarah. 2002. 'Feminism, Abortion and Disability: Irreconcilable Differences', *Disability & Society*, 17(2): 137–45.

Singer, Peter. 2000. 'Severe Impairment and the Beginning of Life', *The American Philosophical Association Newsletter on Philosophy & Medicine*, 99(2): 246–8.

Stabile, Susan J. 2005. 'Religious Employers and Statutory Prescription Contraceptive Mandates', *Catholic Law*, 43(1): 169–86.

Statham, Helen. 2002. 'Prenatal Diagnosis of Fetal Abnormality: The Decision to Terminate the Pregnancy and the Psychological Consequences', *Fetal and Maternal Medicine Review*, 13(4): 213–47.

Stein, Michael Ashley. 2003. 'The Law and Economics of Disability Accommodations', *Duke Law Journal*, 53(1): 79–191.

———. 2007. 'Disability Human Rights', *California Law Review*, 95(1): 75–121.

Stretton, Dean. 2006. 'Wrongful Life and the Logic of Non-Existence', *Melbourne University Law Review*, 30(3): 972–1001.

Vehmas, Simo. 2002. 'Prenatal Responsibility and the Morality of Selective Abortion', *Ethical Theory and Moral Practice*, 5(4): 463–84.

Verdugo M.A., R.L. Schalock, K.D. Keith, and R.J. Stancliffe. 2005. 'Quality of Life and Its Measurement: Important Principles and Guidelines', *Journal of Intellectual Disability Research*, 49: 707–17.

Visaria, L., V. Ramachandran, B. Ganatra, and S. Kalyanwala. 2004. 'Abortion in India: Emerging Issues from Qualitative Studies', *Economic and Political Weekly*, 39(46–47): 5044–52.

Vitzthum, Virginia. 2008. 'Evolutionary Models of Women's Reproductive Functions', *Annual Review of Anthropology*, 37(1): 53–73.

Ward, Linda. M. 2002. 'Whose Right to Choose? The New Genetics, Prenatal Testing and People with Learning Disabilities', *Critical Public Health*, 12(2): 187–200.

Welsch, Wolfgang. 1996. 'Aestheticization Processes: Phenomena, Distinctions and Prospects', *Theory, Culture and Society*, 13(1): 1–24.

Wendell, Susan. 1989. 'Toward a Feminist Theory of Disability', *Hypatia*, 4(2): 104–24.

Wikler, Daniel and Barondess, J. 1993. 'Bioethics and Anti-Bioethics in Light of Nazi Medicine: What Must We Remember?', *Kennedy Institute of Ethics Journal*, 3(1): 39–55.

Wikler, Daniel. 1999. 'Can We Learn from Eugenics?' *Journal of Medical Ethics*, 25(2): 183–94.

Zola, Irving K. 1972. 'Medicine as an Institution of Social Control', *Sociological Review*, 20(4): 487–504.

ONLINE BOOKS AND MATERIALS

Adeline P. 2003. 'Prenatal Screening: A Personal View', available online at http://www.intellectualdisability.info/diagnosis/prenatal-screening-a-personal-view (last accessed on 7 March 2016).

Alleyne, Richard. 2012. 'Genetically Engineering "Ethical" Babies Is a Moral Obligation, Says Oxford Professor', *The Telegraph*, 16 August, available online at http://www.telegraph.co.uk/news/science/science-news/9480372/Genetically-engineering-ethical-babies-is-a-moral-obligation-says-Oxford-professor.html (last accessed on 15 April 2013).

Bates, Claire. 2011. 'Revealed: The Thousands of pregnancies Aborted for 'abnormalities' Including Cleft Palates and Down Syndrome', *Mail online*, 5 July, available online at http://www.dailymail.co.uk/health/article-2011092/Aborted-cleft-palate-Thousands-pregnancies-aborted-abnormalities-including-500-Downs.html (last accessed on 19 February 2016).

CNN. 1997. 'Pope: Abortion an "Abominable Crime"', *CNN World News*, 4 October, available online at http://edition.cnn.com/WORLD/9710/04/brazil.pope/ (last accessed on 28 June 2011).

Couto, Alexandra. 2007. 'Review–Frontiers of Justice', *Meta Psychology Online Reviews*, 11(30), available online at http://metapsychology.mentalhelp.net/poc/view_doc.php?type=book&id=3749&cn=135 (last accessed on 21 February 2016).

Edwards, Janice G. and Richard R. Ferrante. 2009. 'Toward Concurrence: Understanding Prenatal Screening and Diagnosis of Down Syndrome from the Health Professional and Advocacy Community Perspectives', Consensus Conversation, 17 June, University of South Carolina, available online at https://www.acmg.net/StaticContent/Resources/Consensus%20Conversation%20Statement.pdf (last accessed on 17 March 2016).

Gould, S.J. 1984. 'Carrie Buck's Daughter: A Popular Quasi-Scientific Idea Can Be a Powerful Tool for Injustice (This View of Life)', *Natural History*, available online at http://www.findarticles.com (last accessed on 7 September 2013).

Jackson, Aaron. 2013. 'Oxford Professor Says Genetically Altering Unborn Babies Personalities a Moral Obligation', 22 January, available online at http://www.bibliotecapleyades.net/ciencia/ciencia_geneticfood118.htm (last accessed on 15 April 2013).

John Paul II. 'Homilies 814', available online at http://www.clerus.org (last accessed on 11 April 2011).

Jónsdóttir, Oddný Vala. 2012. 'Medicalisation of Childbirth in Western Society: Can Women Resist the Medicalisation of Childbirth?', available online at http://hdl.handle.net/1946/11156 (last accessed on 7 February 2014).

Kreeft, Peter. 1997. 'Human Personhood Begins at Conception', available online at http://www.catholiceducation.org/en/controversy/abortion/human-personhood-begins-at-conception.html (last accessed on 13 March 2010).

Lewis, Ed. 2012. 'The Politics of Down Syndrome', *New Left Project*, available online at http://www.newleftproject.org/index.php/site/article_comments/the_politics_of_down_syndrome (last accessed on 7 March 2016).

Malthus, Thomas. 1798. 'An Essay on the Principle of Population', available online at http://www.esp.org/books/malthus/population/malthus.pdf (last accessed on 17 March 2016).

Maguire, D. 2006. 'Roman Catholic Position on Contraception and Abortion', available online at http://religiousconsultation.org (last accessed on 10 July 2011).

Masden, Melissa. 1992. 'Pre-Natal Testing and Selective Abortion: The Development of a Feminist Disability Rights Perspective', available online at http://wwda.org.au/issues/eugenic/eugenic1995/masden1/ (last accessed on 14 May 2013).

National Conference of Catholic Bishops. 'Ethical and Religious Directives for Catholic Health Care Services', available online at http://www.usccb.org (last accessed on 15 June 2001).

Paul VI. 1968. 'Encyclical Letter Humanae Vitae of the Supreme Pontiff Paul VI to His Venerable Brothers the Patriarchs, Archbishops, Bishops and Other Local Ordinaries in Peace and Communion with the Apostolic See, to the Clergy and Faithful of the Whole Catholic World, and to All Men of Good Will, on the Regulation of Birth', available online at http://w2.vatican.va/content/paul-vi/en/encyclicals/documents/hf_p-vi_enc_25071968_humanae-vitae.html (last accessed on 27 July 2011).

Pius XI. 1930. 'Asti Connubii: Encyclical of Pope Pius XI on Christian Marriage to the Venerable Brethren, Patriarchs, Primates, Archbishops, Bishops, and Other Local Ordinaries Enjoying Peace and Communion with the Apostolic See', available online at http://w2.vatican.va/content/pius-xi/en/encyclicals/documents/hf_p-xi_enc_31121930_casti-connubii.html (last accessed on 22 April 2016).

Price, David. 1998. 'Of Population and False Hopes: Malthus and His Legacy', *Population and Environment*, 19: 3, available online at http://www.mnforsustain.org/price_d_malthus_false_hopes.htm (last accessed on 22 April 2016).

Reardon, David C. 2011. 'Abortion's Aftermath: The Complexity and Distortions of Post-Abortion Research', available online at http://hopeafterabortion.com/?page_id=221 (last accessed on 8 March 2016).

Quinn, Gerard and Theresia Degener. 2002. *The Current Use and Future Potential of United Nations Human Rights Instruments in the Context of Disability.* New York and Geneva: United Nations. Available online at http://uncrpd.nileshsingit.org/human-rights-and-disability (last accessed on 22 March 2013).

Schulze, Marianne. 2009. 'Understanding the UN Convention on the Rights of Persons with Disabilities', in Handicap International (ed.), *A Handbook on the Human Rights of Persons with Disabilities,* available online at http://iddcconsortium.net/sites/default/files/resources-tools/files/hi_crpd_manual_sept2009_final.pdf (last accessed on 13 March 2016).

Silvers, Anita and Michael Ashley Stein. 2007. 'Disability and the Social Contract', Faculty Publications Paper 664, William & Mary Law School, Chicago, available online at http://scholarship.law.wm.edu/facpubs/664 disability (last accessed on 20 February 2016).

Wood, Allen. 'Hman Dignity, Right and the Realm of Ends', available online at www.web.standford.edu (last accessed on 22 April 2016).

'In the Guise of Human Dignity: A Report on the Mass Hysterectomy Performed on February, 1994, on 25 Women Inmates with Mental Disabilities of Shirur Mad, a Govt. Home, Maharashtra', available online at www.unipune.ac.in. (last accessed on 11 April 2011).

DIRECTIVES, REPORTS, WORKING PAPERS, AND NEWSPAPER REPORTS

Brady, Susan M. and Sonia Grover. 1997. 'The Sterilization of Girls and Young Women in Australia', A Report Commissioned by the Federal Disability Discrimination Commissioner for the Human Rights and Equal Opportunity Commission, Sydney, Australia.

Committee on Government Operations. 1992. 'Designating Genetic Information Policy: The Need for an Independent Policy Review of the Ethical, Legal, and the Social Implications of the Human Genome Project: Sixteenth Report by the Committee on Government Operations'. Washington, DC: United States Government Printing Office.

CRC Committee. 2008. 'Report of the Committee on the Rights of the Child', General Assembly, Official Records, 63rd Session, Supplement No. 41, United Nations, New York, available online at http://www.iom.int/jahia/webdav/shared/shared/mainsite/policy_and_research/un/63/A_63_41.pdf (last accessed on 17 March 2016).

Dhanda, Amita. 2014. 'A Retrograde and Incoherent Law', *The Hindu,* 6 February.

Gonsalves, Colin. 'The Right to Abort versus the Right to Give Birth, Chandigarh Administration v. Nemo' unpublished note.

Indian Express. 1994. 'Wombs of 25 Women to Be Removed', *Indian Express*, Mumbai, 4 February.

Joint Select Committee. 1991. 'Joint Committee Report on Health and Family Welfare, Prenatal Diagnostic Techniques (Regulation and Prevention of Misuse) Bill, 1991'. Parliament Library, Parliament of India.

Langtree, Ian. 2005. 'Famous People Who Are Dyslexic or Had Dyslexia', *Disabled World*, available online at http://www.disabled-world.com/artman/publish/article_2130.shtml (last accessed on 20 February 2016).

Noe, Eileen Cronin. 1987. '"Thalidomide Baby" Grows up', *Houston Chronicle*, 26 July.

Parliament of India. 1994. 'Parliamentary Debate Papers on Pre-Natal Diagnostic Techniques (Regulation and Prevention if Misuse), Bill 1991', Parliament Library, Parliament of India.

Parliament of India. various years. *Parliamentary Papers (East India Company)*, all volumes, Parliament Library, Parliament of India.

Ram, Uma. 2010. 'A Helping Hand for the Foetus', Hindu Sunday Magazine, 4 July.

SAMA-Resource Group for Women and Health. 2006. 'A Report on ART (Assisted Reproductive Technologies) and Women: Assistance in Reproduction or Subjugation?' New Delhi: SAMA.

Suresh, S. 'Understanding the Unborn', *Hindu Sunday Magazine*, 4 July.

World Network of Users and Survivors of Psychiatry. 2001. 'Position Paper on Principles for the Protection of Persons with Mental Illness', available online at http://www.wnusp.net/index.php/position-paper-on-principles-for-the-protection-of-persons-with-mental-illness.html (last accessed on 17 March 2016).

MOVIES

Apatow, Judd. 2007. *Knocked up*. Universal Pictures.

UNPUBLISHED WORKS

Jones, Kathleen Sheppard. 2003. 'Quality of Life Dimensions for Adults with Developmental Disabilities', Unpublished dissertation Paper 335, Kentucky University.

McKinney, Claire. 2009. 'Anti Selective Abortion but Pro-Choice? The Stakes of Reproductive Rights in the Disability Context'. Paper submitted for the Political Theory Workshop, 12 October, University of Chicago.

INDEX

· ·

Index

European Convention for the Protection of Human Rights and Fundamental Freedoms (1950), 43
European Disability Forum, 126

family planning, xlviin58, xlviiin58, 37–8, 149
female child, life of, xxxi–xxxii, xxxv
female deficit, phenomenon of, 64
female foeticide, xxxi–xxxii, xlviin58, xlviiin58, 61, 70, 72, 78, 146–50
female infanticide, xxx–xxxi, 32, 143–4, 147;
Act VIII for the Prevention of the Murder of Female Infants, 146;
among Rajputs, 145;
Bengal Regulation VI of 1802, 143;
colonial efforts to suppress, 145–6;
during colonial rule, xxxi;
convictions for, 144–5;
Female Infanticide Prevention Act (1870), 146;
Law Commission of 1837, 145;
legislation for the suppression of, 146;
Original Law and, 33–5;
Qur'anic references to, 32–3;
societal ramification of, xxxi
Female Infanticide Prevention Act (1870), India, 146
Fisher, Irving, 10
'fitter families for future firesides,' 7–8
foetal deformity, 56
foetal development, stages of, xxix, 40

foeticide, 2, 35, 61, 70, 72, 78, 146–50; *See also* female foeticide; forced abortion
foetus: as human entity, xxviii–xxx; prenatal testing for foetal disability, 52;
'right to life' of, 40
foetus-selection technology, xxxii
forced abortion, 101, 126, 130
formal equality, principle of, 72

gender discrimination, 33, 61, 64, 82
gender equality: as human rights, 78;
social movement for, 64
genetic-based diagnosis and prognosis, 101
genetic engineering, xxxviiin40, 91–2;
bioethics in, xli
genetic identity, 41, 126
genocide, 11, 132
Genome Project, 19
'germ plasm' hypothesis, 8
Goddard, Henry, 7
Gostin, Larry, 101
gross national product, 9

Harris, John, 92
Hawking, Stephen, 105, 107
healthcare system, 117
Hitler, Adolf, xxxviiin41, 9
Hobart, R.T., 146
Holmes, Oliver Wendell, Jr, 16
Holocaust, xxxviii, xln43, 8, 17, 19–20, 88
Hubbard, Ruth, lin65, 19–20
Humanae Vitae of 1968, 36, 39
human birth: medicalization of, xxviii;
mystery of, xxv–xxvi

ABOUT THE AUTHOR

. . . .

Smitha Nizar is an assistant professor of law at Alliance School of Law at Alliance University, Bengaluru, India. She completed her PhD from NALSAR University of Law, Hyderabad. Prior to that, she was a practicing advocate at High Court of Kerala, India.